The Churches and the American Experience

The Churches and the American Experience

IDEALS AND INSTITUTIONS

Thomas A. Askew

and

Peter W. Spellman

Baker Book House
Grand Rapids, Michigan 49506

ISBN: 0-8010-0199-4

Library of Congress Catalog
Card Number: 83-73648

Printed in the United States of America

To
Jean Mary Askew
whose
editorial skills,
insights, and
encouragement
contributed immeasurably
to this book

Contents

Preface

Because the subject of this book far exceeds its size, we wish to clarify some of the principles and priorities that have guided its authors. The book's subtitle, *Ideals and Institutions,* suggests its orientation.

When one is studying the Christian faith in society across the historical epochs, it is crucial to distinguish ideals, those compelling transcultural beliefs and values, from institutions, the organizational and behavioral embodiments of the ideals, in particular human environments.

Ideals interact with institutions and vice versa in a dynamic reciprocal relationship. The lofty goals of the ideals must be translated into concrete objectives and actions in a cultural setting marked by all the positive and negative tendencies of human experience. Institutions, in this case the churches, inevitably become engaged with the social order and reflective of it. At the same time, the Christian faith calls the devout to a higher realm of truth and purity that transcends all boundaries. It is this heavenly vision that so often proves prophetic to the status quo, transforming both men and institutions by revival and reform.

The following narrative overview focuses on the social dimensions of the larger churchly quest in American history. Although some individual denominations receive attention, space limitations preclude any attempt to follow the ecclesiastical fortunes of the very numerous denominations. Neither has the rich and varied course of Judaism or other non-Christian religious traditions in America been explored.

Such an overview necessitates only cursory interpretations; it is the authors' hope that these will stimulate further reading and reflection. Bibliographies for each chapter are included to serve this end, as well as to indicate the major sources consulted in preparing the text. To avoid clutter in the brief narrative, footnotes have been omitted.

The Churches and the American Experience is written not for historical specialists who will find little new material here, but for students and other interested readers. Attention to the Protestant/evangelical tradition is deliberate. The recent resurgence in evangelical religion has generated new visibility for what historian Sydney E. Ahlstrom and others have termed the "great tradition" in American church history. Until 1890 (and in some regions well beyond that date) evangelicalism was *the* mainstream of American religious experience. Although it is no longer dominant, it continues to be a current of considerable and even growing force in most styles of American church life, even in post-Vatican-II Catholicism, albeit in unequal measures and emphases.

Although both authors' heritage and parish membership are within the ranks of historic evangelicalism, we do not believe this precludes self-analysis. History instructs and we have endeavored to be open to its implications, even when they unsettle common assumptions.

The word *evangelical* itself is ambiguous, with many doctrinal and behavioral nuances. In its broadest sense, "evangelical" derives from the New Testament Gospels and emphasizes proclaiming the "good news," a fact highlighted by the word *evangelical* being adopted by a group of Protestant Reformation churches in Germany, both Lutheran and Reformed. More particularly it has been applied in England and America to that strand of the Christian tradition which stresses the Bible as the authority for belief and practice; conversion as the necessary experience for beginning a deliberate Christian life; nurture as an ongoing process of self-aware cultivation of spirituality (in the church and in the home); and mission, in both its evangelistic and social expressions.

The words *conservative* and *liberal* are used throughout this book and merit definition as well. The term *conservative* appears especially in contexts discussing theology and is applied to those who subscribe to historic orthodox doctrines: the divine inspiration and authority of Scripture; the Trinity; Christ's deity and atoning death; the bodily resurrection and a judgment to come; the necessity of grace; the church as the Body of Christ. For stylistic variety the word *conservative* is sometimes employed as near synonymous with *evangelical,* even though we recognize that evangelical priorities reflect a mood or perspective as much as a theology and have sometimes led to actions hardly conservative in nature. The terms *liberal* or *modernist* designate theological formulations that downplay scriptural authority, tilt away from orthodoxy, and emphasize reason and human intuition as the sources for religious truth.

The authors acknowledge a debt to others who contributed to the making of this book. Baker Book House textbook editor Allan Fisher provided encouragement from the outset; project editor Linda Triemstra conscientiously shepherded the manuscript through the publication process. The dedication page cites the substantial assistance of Jean M. Askew. Kathy Lesser prepared the final typescript, which Glyn Jones-Rhodes cheerfully transported many times between Wenham and Salem, Massachusetts. Gordon College professors Russell Bishop, Stanley Gaede, Malcolm Reid, and Marvin Wilson read and criticized various chapters. Research and writing expenses were partially underwritten by a Gordon College Faculty Development Grant.

History, like memory, can be extremely useful to Christian communities. Memory can remind us of possibilities that have been forgotten, and history may suggest alternatives that would otherwise not be considered. As the old adage has it: When we stand on the shoulders of those who preceded us, we can see further. It is our hope that this book contributes to such an enlargement of vision.

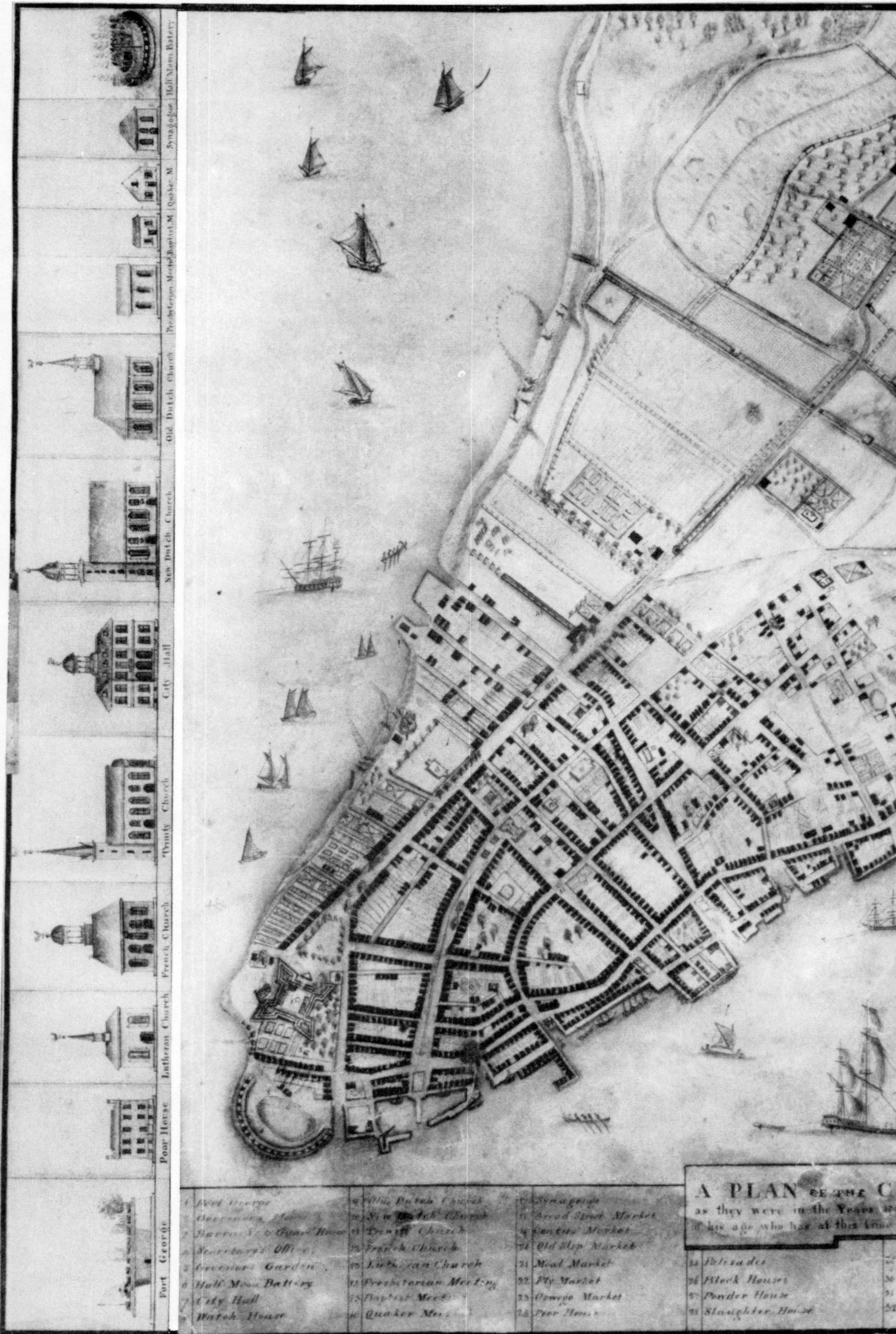
Fort George
Poor House
Lutheran Church
French Church
Trinity Church
City Hall
New Dutch Church
Old Dutch Church
Baptist M
Quaker M
Synagogue
Half Moon Battery
A PLAN
as they were in the Years
Fort George
Governors Garden
Half Moon Battery
City Hall
Watch House
Old Dutch Church
New Dutch Church
Trinity Church
French Church
Lutheran Church
Presbyterian Meeting
Synagogue
Broad Street Market
Old Slip Market
21 Meal Market
22 Fly Market
23 Oswego Market
Palisades
Block House
Powder House
Slaughter House

A plan of New York City and environs (1742–1744). Note the sketches of city churches. Drawn by David Grim, August 1813.

New York Historical Society, New York City

Part 1

The European Legacy

1

The Reforming Impulse

A century and a half has passed since the astute French traveler, Alexis de Tocqueville, observed that "America is still the place where the Christian religion has kept the greatest real power over men's souls." Numerous commentators, before and since de Tocqueville, have sought to unravel the significance of that power in the social and religious development of the nation. Any study of the influence and diverse expressions of Christianity in America, however, must begin with the European churchly legacy, which requires looking first at Europe on the eve of the Protestant Reformation.

The Temper of the Times

By late medieval times western Catholicism was having difficulty maintaining its long-standing dominance over the whole of Europe. The Crusades of the eleventh, twelfth, and thirteenth centuries had unleashed commercial and mercantile impulses throughout the Continent and a spirit of acquisitiveness was displacing religious fervor as the attention of western man turned earthward. Abuses within the church, its simony, luxury, and explicit immorality, invited criticism. Men such as John Wyclif (c. 1320–1384) of England and the Bohemian priest John Hus (c. 1373–1415) found fault with a number of foundational Roman doctrines, including that of the priesthood as a mediatorship between men and God. In contrast, they held to a priesthood of *all* believers and the innate capacity of the common man to read and understand Scripture. To these and other "heretics" the church responded with persecution.

Religious dissent was spurred by the Renaissance emphasis on textual study. Scholars began to question certain documents which the church deemed authentic and which had been used to buttress Rome's economic and political claims to particular regions of Europe. The sharp eye of the textual scholar, however, found many documents (e.g., The Donation of Constantine) to be spurious. With the publishing of these findings the integrity of Rome was further brought into question.

The Magisterial Reformation

Finally, in 1517 the German monk, Martin Luther (1483–1546), compelled by his reading of Scripture, launched a reform of Roman practices. At that time Germany was divided into hundreds of large and small political units over which the central governments of both pope and emperor held little more than nominal sway. Like England and other European countries, Germany was beginning to grope toward national unity. The emergence of a middle class and a regional army fed this embryonic nationalism. Such a political context and the personal support of certain German dukes gave Luther growing influence as he increasingly called for a break with Rome.

The spark ignited by Luther was fanned into flame by others. Ulrich Zwingli (1484–1531) in Zürich and John Calvin (1509–1564) in Geneva both carried on reform campaigns. Calvin, especially through the dissemination of his *Institutes of the Christian Religion* and emphasis on divine sovereignty and representative church government, had far-reaching influence, particularly in England, Scotland, and ultimately, America. With uncontrollable rapidity, through pamphlet, sermon, and conversation, the protest spread into every corner of Europe within twenty years of Luther's initial stand against Rome.

Of the reformers, these three, Luther, Zwingli, and Calvin, are often called the magisterial reformers. This signifies their willingness to link the church in a certain region to the political magistrate of that region. In fact, this cooperation between civic and religious authority seemed desirable for both protection and mutual support. The notion of religious freedom in the modern sense was unthinkable to them. The church and the state were to work together, the one to produce righteousness, the other to bring about external peace and punish evil deeds.

The magisterial reformers taught that Scripture alone is the final authority in a Christian's life. Pulpit replaced altar and sermon replaced Mass as they endeavored to re-emphasize Bible preaching once more in the church. This directly opposed the Roman doctrine that truth is found through a combination of Scripture, tradition, and the interpretation of the pope. A second major difference centered around the doctrine of salvation. How does one become a Christian? The Roman answer is again a combination. A person is saved through faith *and* good works, particularly the partaking of the sacraments rightly administered. The reformers proclaimed that it is by faith *alone* that a person attains salvation; faith in the finished work of Christ. Thus, in his *Commentary on Galatians* Luther writes, "By this means we are delivered from sin and justified, and eternal life is granted to us, not for our own merits and works but for our faith, by which we take hold of Christ."

Other emphases of the magisterial reformers included the careful professional training of ministers, as well as general education for the laity; a view of *all* work—not just the clerical ministry—as divine calling; and a backward-looking orientation. This last feature is often forgotten. These leaders were attempting to get the church back to its roots, and they scanned the early centuries of church history for principles and models to follow. They did not limit their inquiry to only the first-century apostolic church. Luther, in particular, felt that the church had retained its pristine integrity until the tenth century. The spectacles of the Crusades and papal corruption had caused the church to drift. Thus, we can expect to see a respect for church tradition in the Lutheran and Reformed groups that emerged from what has been called the right wing of the Reformation.

The Radical Reformation

The left-wing groups known as the radical Reformation were quite different. Among the early representatives of radical reform two especially stand out: the German, Thomas Müntzer (c. 1490–1525), a former follower of Luther and the author of several vehemently anti-Luther tracts; and the Swiss Anabaptists, who had their beginning among a dissident group of Zwingli's followers led by Conrad Grebel (1498–1526). Dissatisfied with the slow and seemingly compromising reform of their original mentors, these "radicals" set out to delineate the true biblical faith as they understood it.

Among their tenets was an insistence on going back to the New Testament for their patterns. They thus represent a more radical departure from Roman inheritance than the magisterial groups. Whereas Luther and Calvin saw the church as territorial, encompassing all those in a certain region, the radicals viewed the church as a voluntary body called out from society. Entrance into membership came through new birth wrought by the Holy Spirit, registered by the acceptance of God's grace by the individual, and attested to by baptism. The magisterial reformers viewed baptism as a sign of membership in the Christian society which could, therefore, be bestowed on infants. The radicals considered baptism a visible token of that inward regeneration which had taken place. Many of these believers came to be called derisively *Ana*baptists—those who baptize *again.*

Anabaptists constituted a majority of the dissident Protestants. Many rejected war and, preaching nonresistance, suffered martyrdom by the thousands. All stood for strict moral and ethical standards and, in general, excluded from their fellowship any who departed from these ideals. For the most part, they tended to attract the lower economic classes.

Divided into many groups and movements, the Anabaptists had neither a geographical center nor a single formulation of faith. Mennonites, taking their name from the influential Menno Simons (1496–1561) of Holland, were and continue to be the largest of the Anabaptist groups. From homelands mostly in northern Germany and the Low Countries, many eventually found asylum in Pennsylvania. Some Anabaptists founded religious communities in Poland and Moravia. Many others chose the path of individualistic Christian mysticism, gathering about themselves only small groups. The writings of the two Germans, Sebastian Franck (1499–1542) and Jacob Boehme (1575–1624), had wide circulation far beyond their own adherents.

Keeping aloof from rising middle-class civilization, industrialism, imperialism, and nationalism, the Anabaptists sought out the frontiers and fringes of society where social and religious conformity was not required; where the community of saints could live unmolested. During the past four centuries many Anabaptists have succeeded remarkably in maintaining a community lifestyle peculiar to themselves, cut off from the corruptions of the world.

The tendencies and principles planted by both the magisterial and radical reformers found fertile soil in Britain. Unique combinations from both wings would emerge in that corner of the crumbling empire of Christendom, and from there spread throughout the world. Thus, the incipient story of American Christianity is to be found primarily in the struggles surrounding the Reformation in England.

2

English Reformation and Puritan Beginnings

The English Reformation is as colorful a period as any in history. Replete with high intrigue, clashing ideals, dramatic shifts, and human frailties, it has repeatedly been the subject of the novelist's pen and the director's camera.

The Character of the English Reformation

Serious trouble erupted between England and the Roman church in the early 1520s as a result of the marital difficulties of Henry VIII. But distinct rumblings had been heard a century and a half earlier when John Wyclif, the fiery Oxford scholar, had openly challenged the authority of both pope and church by appealing directly to the New Testament. He gave the English their first Scriptures in their native tongue and organized lay preachers, Lollards, to proclaim his ideas across the land. Although their preaching was punishable by death after 1401, the Lollards' reforming ideas were passed from one generation to the next, especially among the lower classes, creating a latent force that readily sprang to action in the religious turbulence of the sixteenth century.

As was the custom among royalty, the youthful Henry dutifully entered into a politically advantageous marriage to Catherine of Aragon, who also happened to be his brother's widow. After sixteen

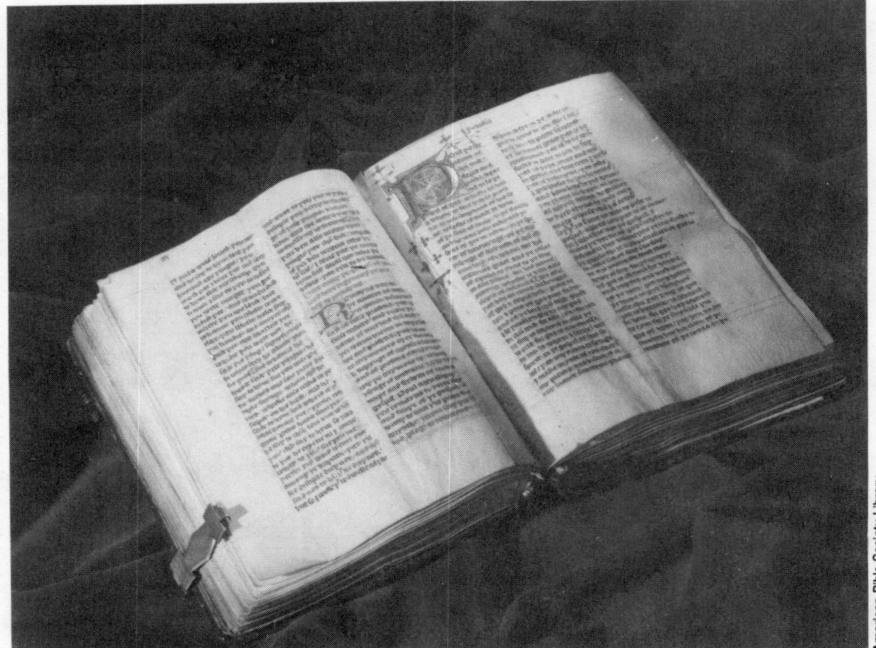

American Bible Society Library

The 1440 Wyclif New Testament.

years, his desperate desire for a male heir frustrated, his heart smitten by Anne Boleyn, Henry appealed to Pope Clement VII for an annulment of his marriage to his brother's widow, an act forbidden by canon law and Leviticus. Clement refused, out of deference to Catherine's influence with her nephew, Charles V, King of Spain and the Holy Roman Emperor. But Henry would have his way. Reducing the English clergy to submission, Henry, in 1534, had a subservient Parliament declare him to be "the Supreme Head of the Church of England," making the break with Rome official. Henry married Anne, was excommunicated by the pope, and had Thomas Cranmer appointed as archbishop in place of Thomas Cardinal Wolsey.

That Henry perceived his reform as political and ecclesiastical rather than theological is demonstrated by his official reaffirmation of Roman dogma, and his entrusting of church matters to the moderate Cranmer throughout his reign. He did, however, make two concessions to the Protestant spirit: the issuing of the Great Bible in 1539, built on the translations of William Tyndale and Miles Coverdale; and the confiscation of more than five hundred monasteries, thereby revitalizing the crown's depleted treasury. By sharing his acquisitions with the gentry he secured their loyalty and gave them an economic interest in the changes he undertook. It would be for other rulers to establish Protestantism in England, but not without mortal struggle and martyrdom.

At his death in 1547 Henry was succeeded by his nine-year-old son, Edward VI, born of his third queen, Jane Seymour. Although he was dead by age sixteen, the deeply religious and anti-Roman Edward, with Cranmer as his mentor, rapidly moved England in this short span in the direction of Protestantism. Images were removed from churches, chantries were abolished, Latin was replaced by English, priestly marriage was legalized, and the communion cup was extended to the laity. Under the direction of Cranmer, a first and then a more radical second Book of Common Prayer was issued, and a moderately Calvinistic creed, the Forty-two Articles, drawn up; all were acted upon by Parliament and officially imposed on the nation, although many Englishmen were still committed to the old ways.

With Edward's early death in 1553, and the accession of Mary Tudor, daughter of Henry and Catherine of Aragon and an ardent Catholic, reaction was inevitable. With relentless zeal, Mary launched a counterreformation by forcing Parliament to repeal all the reform legislation concerning religion enacted during Edward's reign. She and her cousin, Reginald Cardinal Pole (the Archbishop of Canterbury) re-established old statutes against heresy and proceeded to ferret out reluctant clergy for burning. Almost three hundred "heretics" were executed, including five former bishops: Robert Ferrar, John Hooper, Nicholas Ridley, Hugh Latimer, and Cranmer. Many other Protestants left England to settle with their brethren in such places as Leiden, Geneva, and Zürich.

The permanency of Mary's success depended on her producing an heir to replace her half-sister Elizabeth, daughter of Henry and Anne Boleyn, who waited in the wings to rule. But the queen's hopes deteriorated and after a long struggle with cancer Mary died in late 1558, having ruled for only five years, and having earned for herself the inglorious title *Bloody Mary*.

Determined to release England from the religious strife that had divided it for so long, Elizabeth, early in her half-century of rule (1558–1603), firmly established a national state religion—the Anglican church—which all English people were obliged to join. Historians have called this resolve the Elizabethan Settlement. Through it the Church of England was given its Protestant form, which has been largely preserved into the present. The 1559 Act of Supremacy passed by Parliament severed all ties with Rome and made the monarch the "supreme governor" both politically and ecclesiastically. An Act of Uniformity re-established the second Book of Common Prayer, and the

Thirty-nine Articles, an outgrowth of Cranmer's creed, became the formal doctrinal statement which satisfied almost everyone.

To the north, meanwhile, an alliance of Scottish nobles and middle-class burghers was edging Scotland toward a Calvinistic reformed state church, in spite of a Catholic monarch, Mary Stuart (Queen of Scots), who was married to Francis II, King of France. Led by the fearless John Knox, a former priest heavily influenced by John Calvin, the Scottish Parliament in 1560 outlawed the Roman church. A presbyterian form of church government was instituted with ruling elders, local presbyteries, synods, and a national assembly. Mary's tempestuous personal life led to abdication and eventual execution, but her son, James VI of Scotland (James I of England), was able to unify the two Protestant nations under one ruler, although each would ultimately define its own style of established religion—episcopacy in England and presbyterianism in Scotland. Presbyterianism in America is directly descended from the Scottish Reformation, for many Scots migrated to Northern Ireland in the early seventeenth century and from there came two hundred thousand of these Scotch-Irish to America a century later.

The Emergence of a Puritan Faction

From the beginning there had been individuals who wanted to push reform further and faster than their political superiors would allow. Strongly influenced by Calvin's teaching in Geneva, these Protestants were uncomfortable with the retention of practices too Roman for their liking, and so they called for further purification of the English church, thus earning the derisive nickname *Puritan*.

They themselves were divided. Some wanted the state church in England reorganized on the pattern of the Calvinistic churches with a presbyterian representative form of government. Others desired a state church in which each local congregation would regulate its own affairs. A smaller, more radical group of Separatists disdained a state church entirely and, like the Anabaptists, held to the idea of a "gathered" body of believers, autonomous and united in a voluntary church covenant. Each group gained adherents during the long reign of Elizabeth, but all waited anxiously for a chance to gain superiority.

There was hopeful excitement in Puritan circles when James Stuart of Scotland inherited the English throne following the death of Elizabeth in 1603. Rumors spread that he might be warm toward Puritan concerns. Hopes quickly evaporated, however, as James stoutly rejected any church polity but the episcopal model of bishops and king. He did authorize a new translation of the Scriptures, completed in 1611 and known today as the King James Bible. Puritanism, meanwhile, was gaining support in Parliament, and through strong preaching across party and class lines, its influence spread among the populace.

When Charles I (ruled 1625–1649) followed his father James to the English throne, he felt threatened by the diffusion of authority being precipitated by the democratizing influence of Puritanism. He, therefore, strongly asserted his "divine right" to rule, threw all his support to the Church of England, and opposed the Puritans. By 1640 only civil war could settle the conflict between Charles and Parliament. The king's forces (Cavaliers) lost to the Puritans (Roundheads) under Oliver Cromwell's leadership. Charles was beheaded in 1649 and Cromwell became Lord Protector of the English Commonwealth (1653), ruling until 1658.

Meanwhile, Parliament had abolished episcopacy in 1643 and authorized the Westminster Assembly, composed of Puritans and a few Scottish Presbyterians, to draft a new Calvinistic system of worship, theology, and church polity. By 1647 the Westminster Confession of Faith was adopted, making the Anglican church both Calvinistic and presbyterian. It remained so only until the restoration of the monarchy under Charles II in 1660, when episcopacy was again adopted. However, the Westminster Confession remains the cornerstone of both British and American Presbyterianism.

Under Cromwell religious tolerance increased and numerous Protestant Christian sects appeared. One, very relevant to America's history, was the Quakers, founded by George Fox around 1650, as Friends of Truth. Teaching that Christians should be guided by the "Inner Light," he was suspicious of any external forms of religion. In some ways the Quakers resembled the mystical wing of the Anabaptists. By 1670 Fox's Friends had become a formidable sect emphasizing the doctrine of the indwelling light and quietism.

A New World Beckons

Queen Elizabeth's policies did not fully settle the problem of religious differences in England. Yet, in spite of the many dissenters and nonconformists, Elizabeth was satisfied that religious strife was enough abated that the government could concentrate on the more important task of colonizing America. America became a target for English aspirations for two primary reasons: to spread English influence in the wake of Spanish exploration, and to find a western route to Asian markets. In spite of Elizabeth's ambitions, not a single permanent English colony was established in North America before her death in 1603.

With the accession of the young, penniless James I, prospects for successful English colonization of America seemed very dim. Ironically, however, it was precisely the lack of personal fortune that forced James to seek the help of private investors in pushing forward British claims in the New World.

By granting joint-stock companies like the London Company and the Plymouth Company both economic rights and limited political powers through which they became overseas arms of British authority, James accomplished by private enterprise what he could not fund from his royal purse. When the London Company succeeded in establishing a settlement on the banks of the James River of Virginia in May 1607, the stage was set for the gradual development of a British colonial system along the Atlantic seacoast of North America, with the attendant establishment of English-speaking churches.

The Formative Years

(1607–1783)

3

The Protestant Empire Founded

Although Englishmen had been scouting the eastern American coastline for years, and had set up crude fishing stations in places such as Ipswich, Massachusetts, as far back as the 1590s, true and lasting colonization did not begin until 1607. It is commonly thought that the history of the American churches begins with the New England Pilgrims, but it actually commences with the Anglicans of Virginia, when on May 24, 1607, three English ships disembarked 105 men on the low-lying shore of the James River.

Established-Church Beginnings in America: Anglicanism

The instructions of James I in the first charter of Virginia were explicit: "The true word and service of God" was to be "preached, planted and used" in the new colony "according to the doctrine, rights, and religion now professed and established within our realm of England." At Jamestown a permanent English colony in America was born, and born Anglican. However, religious motives were hardly primary for the London merchants who supported this venture. The Virginians, like most early settlers, sought commercial profits; if possible, treasure such as Spain had been extracting from Mexico and South America for more than a century. But, whether nominal or fervent in his beliefs, each of these early Americans was permeated by

Bicentennial Committee, Episcopal Church Center

Colonists landing at Jamestown.

the Christian religion. It was in the air they breathed in their native England, and it formed the ideological basis for law, family, and government in the New World.

The first decades of Virginia's history were fraught with difficulties. When the fearful winter of 1609–1610 was over, only some sixty of the five hundred inhabitants were still alive. Jamestown's palisades were in ruins, the houses burnt for firewood, and the last scraps of food—including cattle and domestic animals—consumed. The colonists came close to abandoning the site but the able leadership of a new governor, Lord De La Warr, restored determination to continue.

Then came the Indian attacks. In 1622 the growing colony was ravaged by a terrifying massacre that brought death to one in seven, reducing the population to eighteen hundred and the number of tobacco plantations from eighty to a bare dozen. In 1644, in a second massacre, more than five hundred people were killed in outlying communities.

Despite the grave troubles a religious colony survived through three successive stages. Between 1607 and 1619 the colony's religious affairs were guided from London by the Virginia Company, which framed church policies and sent out ministers. Following the creation of the Virginia House of Burgesses in 1619, this new local representative body of colonials included ecclesiastical legislation among its responsibilities. Only in the third stage, marked by the appointment of a royal governor in 1624, could Anglicanism be said to be "established" in Virginia. To be an established church at this time meant that it alone was designated as the official tax-supported church which was authorized to hold public worship, which could expel those who dissented from the orthodox position, and whose members alone were eligible to vote and hold public office.

By 1720 there were forty-four unevenly sized parishes in Virginia, each with a church and some with auxiliary chapels, so that the total number of places of worship was about seventy. Unlike New England, Virginia lacked a college for pastoral training, and it became difficult to supply able ministers. Even after the College of William and Mary opened in 1693, young Anglicans who desired ordination to the ministry were still compelled to hazard a journey to England, as only a bishop could ordain. James Blair arrived in Virginia in 1685, deeply concerned about the low tenor of religion in the colony. As resident commissary for Bishop Henry Compton in England, he worked for higher clerical salaries, clerical representation on the Governor's Council, and the general moral improvement of ministers' lives. He was also chiefly responsible for securing a charter for the College of William and Mary.

As the Jamestown settlement expanded and new lands were opened, the colony's economy began to shift from a communal to a more individualistic basis. This geographical expansion meant that a Virginia parish was sometimes sixty miles long; a sparsely populated strip of wilderness in which colonists might easily lose touch with the church.

Church life in early Virginia was also affected by the dramatic rise of tobacco culture, and by increasing dependence on African slave labor. Importation of slaves began in 1619 but reached its zenith in the next century. Slavery became a fundamental feature of Virginian culture, as it would in the other southern colonies wherever agricultural needs made the institution profitable.

The lands south of Virginia, later to be called the Carolinas and Georgia, also maintained a nominal Anglican establishment, although less organized than in Virginia. Most of the inhabitants were runaway slaves from Virginia, Quakers, and later, Scotch-Irish Presbyterians who swept down the Shenandoah Valley into the back country of all three colonies. Anglicanism was officially established in South Carolina in 1706, in North Carolina in 1715, and in Georgia in 1758.

Farther north, New Netherland (later New York) also became an Anglican stronghold. Originally settled by the Dutch West India Company in the 1620s, it was crippled by misgovernment, internal dissension, and extremely slow growth, making it an easy target for expansionist-minded England. In 1664, James, Duke of York and brother of Charles II, sponsored the naval operation that secured New Netherland's peaceful surrender. At this time the new English colony was the most religiously heterogeneous in America. Dutch Reformed, French Calvinists (Huguenots), German Lutherans, New England Congregationalists, Quakers, Mennonites, Baptists, Roman Catholics, and a few Jews encountered each other on Manhattan Island. After repeated rebuffs by the Dutch population, the New York Assembly was finally in 1693 induced by the governor to adopt a vague establishment law under which Anglicanism became the official faith in four of the counties.

The New England Way: Puritanism and Congregationalism

Running parallel to this Anglican history was the New England Calvinist experience. In 1609 a group of Calvinistic English Separatists who had formed an independent, dissenting congregation at Scrooby in Nottinghamshire could no longer tolerate the oppressive conditions in England and sought religious refuge in Holland. After a decade in Leiden, a number of them made arrangements to sail aboard the *Mayflower* bound for Virginia, where they hoped for a new corporate life. In September 1620, thirty-five Separatist "Pilgrims" on their way to a "New Jerusalem" set sail with sixty-six other passengers ("Saints" and "Strangers," as they were classified on the passenger list) on their historic voyage to America.

Strong winds and heavy storms drove the *Mayflower* off course, bringing it to the forbidding shores of Cape Cod. There the company adopted the famous self-governing compact and spent the long winter suffering the effects of inadequate food and contagious disease. Only 44 of the 101 passengers lived until spring, but not a single Pilgrim returned to England. Their view of God's sovereignty and providence gave this small group of dissenters the stability needed to confront the harsh wilderness. In a few weeks a settlement was organized at Plymouth, which maintained a separate identity and status until 1691.

Of greater significance were the successive Puritan migrations to New England which swelled as Charles I insisted that Puritans in England accept all the doctrines of Anglicanism. Between 1630 and 1640 some twenty thousand people left England in search of more peaceful and supportive surroundings. Many of these refugees joined the Puritan colony that had been initiated as a joint-stock company on Massachusetts Bay north of Plymouth, transforming it into a large and influential commonwealth within the decade. The founding vision was to erect a cultural and social order completely under God's sovereignty as revealed in the Bible. These newly arrived Puritans claimed to be members of the Church of England. Once they crossed the Atlantic, however, they became as functionally independent of the Anglican church as the Separatists at Plymouth. They developed in Massachusetts the type of worship they had wanted in England. That is, they set up what became known as the congregational form, without bishops or hierarchical structure; authority resided in the individual congregations with coordination provided by meetings of the ministers sitting in synods.

Stripped of all the outward signs and symbols reminiscent of Catholicism and Anglicanism, the Puritans' places of worship were stark, simple meeting houses, where the congregation gathered both to worship and to transact political business of importance to the entire community. Services consisted of psalms and hymns, prayers, and Communion. There were also lecture days during the week to supplement the Sabbath service. Although there was no central authority to enforce uniformity among the many independent congregations, it was clear that those who lived in the Puritan commonwealth were expected to conform to certain basic moral and religious beliefs.

Next to religion, education was valued by the Puritan settlers of New England. As early as 1636, in the midst of their struggles with poverty, they established a college at Cambridge, later named Harvard. Publicly supported grammar schools soon appeared and in 1642 and 1643 common schools were begun in Massachusetts and Connecticut.

With Governor John Winthrop (1588–1649) overseeing the political welfare of the community and John Cotton (1584–1652), an eminent preacher, presiding over its spiritual destiny, church and state moved hand in hand in Massachusetts Bay Colony. Only Congregationalists were permitted to hold the title *freeman* and only freemen were allowed to participate in the colony's political life. Those who did not practice Congregationalism were permitted to reside in the colony as long as they did not cause disturbances. However, they were excluded from politics and were obliged to contribute to the support of the established church.

Another center of Puritan life was the Connecticut River valley. In 1635, Thomas Hooker (1586?–1647) and his Newtown congregation requested permission to migrate westward from Massachusetts Bay to this region. Granted his request, Hooker set out to found a new colony. As others followed, settlements grew at Windsor, Hartford, and Wethersfield. Hooker had a less restrictive view of church membership. The Fundamental Orders of Connecticut adopted in 1639 did not categorically require freemen to be church members. Property holders of good character were allowed to vote. In 1662 all of the Connecticut settlements were joined into a united colony, including the stricter Bible commonwealth founded by the Reverend John Davenport at New Haven in 1638.

As one might expect, these tight-knit religious commonwealths could hold sway only as long as the numbers of people involved were of manageable size. But people of various national backgrounds and religious persuasions were as interested in what America had to offer as the Anglicans and Puritans. As the seventeenth century progressed, there appeared in the English colonies the first signs of that religious diversity which was to become characteristic in American life. Neither the Puritan saint nor the Anglican divine, however, was intellectually or socially geared to tolerate dissent. It was dissent that first began to weaken the foundations of Puritan society.

One of the first to rebel openly was Roger Williams (1604?–1684), pastor of Salem. He challenged the validity of the royal charter on the grounds that it did not prohibit the taking of lands from the Indians without adequate payment. He publicly assailed the union of church and state, questioned the right of civil authorities to legislate in matters of conscience, and urged the Salem congregation to separate from the rest. The sincerity and eloquence of the young preacher won for him disciples and the majority of the Salem church was ready to follow him.

Obviously such outspoken views were "erroneous and dangerous" as far as Puritan leaders were concerned. They feared that the entire social fabric they had begun to weave would be torn apart by internal dissension. They also feared intervention by England, already suspicious of the young colony. When Williams persisted he was banished by the elected assembly, the General Court, in September 1635. Fearing seizure and deportation to England, Williams fled, journeying through the forests, and founded a settlement, which in gratitude he named Providence. There were no religious requirements concerning political activity, no taxes to support an official church, and no compulsory church attendance. The religious toleration of Providence Plantation quicky drew other dissidents, especially Baptists, oppressed by the exclusive atmosphere in Massachusetts.

Anne Hutchinson (1591–1643), another rebel, was found guilty of sedition at an ecclesiastical trial. Stressing grace rather than works and emphasizing personal revelation (called by her accusers antinomianism), Hutchinson antagonized the orthodox clergy, who ordered her banishment from Massachusetts. Along with exile William Coddington, she and her followers in 1638 founded Pocasset (Portsmouth), only a short distance from Providence.

The arrival in Boston in 1656 of two female Quaker missionaries provoked immediate persecution, including jail, confiscation of books, and swift deportation. The Massachusetts General Court then enacted a law punishing and banishing all Quakers, wherein they are described as the "cursed sect of heretics lately risen up in the world . . . who take upon them to be immediately sent of God." A similar law was passed in Virginia in 1660. Zealous Quakers, however, seeking converts, continued to assail Puritan strongholds. Massachusetts in 1658 resorted to the ultimate repression: condemnation to death for banished Quakers who returned. Three men and one woman were hanged in Boston. It was soon perceived that measures so extreme were as ineffectual as they were cruel, and they were abandoned.

Religious dissent was only one factor in the erosion of Puritan hegemony. While Oliver Cromwell ruled in England (1649–1658) New England Puritanism thrived and the mother country exerted little influence on the political affairs of the young colonies. But after the restoration of the Stuart monarchy in 1660, both New England's independence and Puritanism's control began to disintegrate. In 1662, Charles II ordered that liberty of worship be granted to Anglicans, that they be permitted to partake of the Lord's Supper in Congregational churches, and that baptism be extended to their children. The Puritans refused. Charles sent commissioners to regulate the affair. The Puritans again refused. The king responded by revoking the Massachusetts charter in 1684. The link between church and state now diminished greatly. In 1691, Massachusetts was forced to accept a royal governor and a new charter. Most distasteful to the Puritans, the new charter banned all religious tests for suffrage. From that time the church establishment was seriously weakened and rule by the saints gradually declined, although Congregationalism was not fully disestablished until 1833.

Also reflecting religious tension at this time were the infamous witch trials at Salem in 1692. At least twenty "witches" were put to death before public remorse ended the mass hysteria. The incident embarrassed and reduced respect for the colony's clergy, and dealt a blow to the credibility of Puritanism in general.

Along with religious dissent and political alterations came a number of significant revisions of church policy, the most influential of which was the Halfway Covenant. It was essentially an attempt to come to grips with the new generation of Puritans who were baptized as infants and yet did not profess a conversion experience. The Massachusetts Synod of 1662 asserted that baptized adults who lived uprightly might be accepted as church members, an important agreement because voting rights depended on it. However, their children, baptized as "halfway" members, could not receive the Lord's Supper or participate in church elections. Soon, though, the advisability of admitting halfway members to Communion was being discussed. Solomon Stoddard, grandfather of Jonathan Edwards and pastor at Northampton, began to allow unconverted church members to partake of the sacrament because it might serve as a means by which they would be converted. Spiritual vitality nevertheless waned in New England and the number of members in full communion with the church declined. To many it seemed that the judgment of God was being poured out upon a sinful people.

Preachers responded by publishing jeremiads (named after the Old Testament prophet) calling New England back to its holy "errand in the wilderness." Even poets added their voices to the lamentation. In an epic poem entitled *God's Controversy with New England,* Michael Wigglesworth (1631–1705) has God wondering about his now profligate people:

> What should I do with such a stiff-neckt race?
> How shall I ease me of such Foes as they?
> What shall befall despizers of my Grace?
> I'le surely beare their candlestick away!
> And Lamps put out. Their glorious noon-day light.
> I'le quickly turn into a dark Egyptian night.

The vision of the foundling fathers was fading; the zeal of their times was giving way to the easy peace of self-satisfaction. This was despite the writing and preaching of Boston's Cotton Mather, the last great Puritan divine, who tried to combine piety and intellect in summoning the Bay Colony back to its heritage. Many turned their attention to commerce and New England became less a religious refuge than an economic opportunity. Although Puritan dethronement was complete by 1720, the Puritan tradition would linger long in such American attributes as respect for lawful government, the value of useful work, civic responsibility, and concern for education.

Religious Diversity in the Middle Colonies

It is noteworthy that the first colony in America to embody the principle of religious toleration should have been founded by a Roman Catholic. George Calvert (1580?–1632), the first Lord Baltimore, received a land grant from King Charles I in 1632, but died before he could make use of it. His son, Cecil Calvert (1605–1675), founded Maryland. The Roman Catholics who participated in the colonization of Maryland, however, were in the minority, and soon the Act of

Toleration (1649), granting toleration to all Christians and frequently hailed as a great advance toward religious liberty, was passed by the assembly. Economic and political considerations also motivated passage of the act, which excluded Jews and Unitarians. It was, however, rescinded five years later when Puritans gained control during Cromwell's Commonwealth. Eventually, after several tumultuous decades of religious and political animosities, Anglicans gained the seats of power and the Church of England was established in 1702. There would be no further influx of Roman Catholics to America until the Irish migrations of the nineteenth century.

Although the Dutch Reformed Church was "established" in New Netherland from the beginning of settlement by the Dutch West India Company in the 1620s, the original settlers lacked religious fervor. They had not emigrated to escape religious persecution, for Holland was the chief European sanctuary for the persecuted. Trading, especially in furs, was their supreme interest, and only about seven thousand Dutch ever came to the colony in spite of ingenious incentives to stimulate its growth. The harsh and dictatorial rule of the company softened under Peter Stuyvesant (1592–1672) when he came to govern in 1647. But his regime quickly evolved into religious tyranny as he sought to impose stiff restrictions on personal behavior. Under English rule after 1664, the Dutch Reformed Church, consisting of only a dozen or so struggling congregations, continued to worship in freedom. The most serious obstacle was not the English government but disinterest and complacency. Not until the preaching of one of their ministers, Theodore Frelinghuysen, put into motion the forces of the Great Awakening would the Dutch churches—especially those in New Jersey—be roused out of lethargy. The Dutch Reformed in the seventeenth century were the primary practitioners of Calvinistic presbyterianism in America.

Following George Fox's ministry in England, Quakers emigrated to every British colony during the last half of the seventeenth century. Undaunted by their rejection at the hands of the New England Puritans, they found relative peace in New York, Virginia, Maryland, Rhode Island, and the Carolinas, but the center of Quaker activity in America was New Jersey, Delaware, and especially the Pennsylvania region where religious toleration flourished. By 1681 more than one thousand immigrants, mostly Quakers, had arrived in New Jersey. In this same year, William Penn was granted Pennsylvania in consideration of a debt due his late father from the crown. The next year the Duke of York gave to Penn what is now Delaware. Penn called his colonial enterprise "an Holy Experiment" where all Christians could worship God in peace and love. By 1683 the population was four thousand and six years later Delaware and Pennsylvania contained no fewer than twelve thousand people. By this time, most colonial laws against Quakers had been dropped. As wealth increased and a new generation arose, spiritual life seemed to decline. Traveling Friends (Quakers) in the early eighteenth century speak of "a dry lifeless state" in many of their meetings and "excessive drinking" among a number of their members. On the other hand, the number of Friends continued to increase, and these believers outpaced all others in concern for Indian rights, the plight of slaves, and the peace testimony.

Late in the seventeenth century Germans were also leaving their homeland for America. Religious intolerance, wars, and economic uncertainty drove thousands of Germans to seek a new life abroad. The religious history of the German-speaking regions of Europe following the Reformation is incredibly complex, involving two major church bodies and numerous sects.

The first German settlement in America was in Germantown, near Philadelphia, where a group of Mennonites arrived in 1683 from the Palatinate. Many of these eventually made their way west to Lancaster County. They eschewed outward ritualism and scholasticism in favor of a religion of the heart. Maintaining a sharp division between church and state, they were often pacifistic and opposed to oaths in court as well as to government control of what they felt were private matters. Later German groups included the Dunkers, or Taufers (1719), the Schwenkenfelders (1734), and the Moravians (1735). Most of these also settled in central or western Pennsylvania, which became a haven for all religious minorities.

German Lutherans could be found as early as 1649 in New Amsterdam (New York City). They were part of a very cosmopolitan Lutheran congregation which included Danes, Swedes, and Norwegians. But it was not until after the turn of the century that the Lutheran church in America gained numerical strength.

The German Reformed, emerging out of Switzerland, planted their first church at Germantown in 1719. Marked by a presbyterian polity and a rich devotional tradition, the German Reformed had perhaps fifteen thousand potential adherents in Pennsylvania alone by 1730. In doctrine and worship they were much like the Lutherans and lived and worked harmoniously with them.

Thus, within its first century, America took on that varied character that would distinguish it for its entire history. Some came for commercial adventure and found it. Many more sought a place in which to worship God in their own way. The wide-open frontier, rigorous conditions, remoteness from European restraints, and presence of many Christian groups created a climate in America that could nurture religious toleration and advance social and personal freedom.

4

Awakening

From the turn of the century until the Revolution America continued to draw immigrants from all of western Europe and also continued to experience a cooling of the religious ardor that had marked its early years. Puritan was becoming Yankee and Anglican was evolving into country gentleman as prospects for economic advantage expanded before them. It seemed that as America's interests increasingly turned to earthly prosperity, the spiritual vision gradually paled from neglect. But the Jeremiahs persisted in preaching and their lamentations gained intensity. The second quarter of the eighteenth century witnessed the effects of their faithful proclamation in the new wave of religious devotion known as the Great Awakening.

The Great Awakening in America was but one of many "awakenings" occurring throughout the Protestant world in the eighteenth century. England, Scotland, Wales, and Germany all experienced scattered revivals of religious life. Churches of all denominations joined the surge of fervor and were profoundly affected by its impact.

Besides the waning of spiritual interest in favor of the material, several other conditions worked to make America ripe for revival. Intermittent wars with the French and Indians, such as King William's War (1689–1697), Queen Anne's War (1701–1713), and King George's War (1744–1748), harassed the colonists and created political unrest. British interference in colonial affairs exacerbated fears concerning an uncertain future and made politics a chief topic of conversation as well as a divisive influence in society. These disturbing conditions occupied public attention at the expense of moral and religious affairs. Lastly, winds of the rationalistic Enlightenment drifting across the Atlantic from Europe began to penetrate the minds of church leaders, resulting in marked decline in spiritual zeal.

The Scotch-Irish Presbyterians

The initial signs of awakening in America sprang forth among the Presbyterians and Dutch Reformed of New Jersey. Presbyterianism had emerged out of the Protestant Reformation in the Netherlands, parts of Germany, Switzerland, France, and Scotland, where the prevailing pattern of reformed church government had been presbyterian. The term derives from the Greek word *presbuteros* (elder) and refers primarily to a church that is governed by presbyters, usually elected by the people of a congregation or a group of congregations.

The Scottish Presbyterian church stems directly from the work of John Knox and his mentor in Geneva, John Calvin. When James VI of Scotland became also James I of England in 1603, the importance of Scotland's church for America was immeasurably increased.

The major strength of American Presbyterianism derived from the great migrations of Scots from Northern Ireland in the eighteenth century, although the Dutch Reformed in New York and New Jersey had practiced presbyterianism throughout the seventeenth century. Many Scots had settled in Ireland when James attempted to displace the Roman Catholic Irish population of Northern Ireland by confiscating their property. By 1641, about one hundred thousand Scots, most of them Presbyterians, had settled in Ulster. But trouble plagued the new arrivals. Leases were rearranged to their disadvantage, government restrictions on wool production choked the economy, and in 1704, the Irish Parliament passed legislation that denied Presbyterians

Reformed Church in America

Church at the Fort (First Reformed Church, Albany, New York).

1656 pulpit with stairway.

First Reformed Church, Albany

Stone church built in 1715.

First Reformed Church, Albany

the right to public office. These hardships combined to turn their attention to the New World.

Scotch-Irish immigrants were at first a trickle but rose to full force after 1710. The first large number arrived in Boston in 1718. Failing to receive a welcome there, they moved north to Maine and New Hampshire, and west to the Massachusetts frontier. Still opposed by the entrenched Congregationalism in those outlying regions, the Presbyterians turned to the southern and the middle colonies. By midcentury one-fourth of all Pennsylvanians were Scotch-Irish. Another wave of settlers had poured into the Potomac and Shenandoah valleys and no colony was without its Scotch-Irish element.

The first presbytery in America was organized in 1706 in Philadelphia under the leadership of Francis Makemie (1658–1708), an itinerant Presbyterian preacher and organizer. Such a judicatory ended the necessity of looking to Europe for clergy. It laid a foundation for organizing the great numbers of Scotch-Irish about to arrive and fostered a spirit of interdependence among its member organizations throughout the colonies, thus preparing the way for a national body when ties with Britain would be severed by revolution later in the century. In 1716 a synod was formed with three presbyteries, Philadelphia, New Castle, and Long Island. Two problems in particular were still unsolved: there was no ministerial training available in America outside of New England, and there were inadequate procedures for examining immigrant ministers. The latter was solved in part by the Adopting Act of 1729, which bound all ministers and licentiates to accept the Westminster Confession.

The stability of the denomination was imperiled from another quarter by the emergence of a new group among the Scotch-Irish led by William Tennent, Sr. (1673–1746), a Scottish minister educated at Edinburgh University. Tennent and his sons, Gilbert, John, and William, fostered an experiential form of evangelical Puritanism, teaching that a definite experience of regeneration followed by assurance of salvation was the indispensable mark of a Christian. Many Presbyterian clergy disapproved of the Tennents' flaming, confrontational style of preaching and emphasis on conversion.

The beginning of the Great Awakening is usually associated with the fervent and godly preaching of Theodore Frelinghuysen (1691–1748), a Dutch Reformed minister who had been inspired by Continental pietism before arriving in 1720 to pastor in Raritan, New Jersey. The spiritual revitalization that followed in Raritan was similarly experienced among New Jersey Presbyterians led by the Tennents.

This new revival party was aided by the establishment of a "seminary" at Neshaminy, near Philadelphia, in 1727 by William Tennent, Sr. This "Log College," as its enemies called it, performed a significant service during these critical years by turning out nearly a score of pietistic revivalists for the Presbyterian churches. Inevitable opposition surfaced in 1738 when the Presbyterian synod demanded that ministers without degrees from major universities submit to examination. This struck directly at the Log College men.

In 1739 the young and zealous English preacher, George Whitefield (1714–1770), linked the English and colonial awakenings when he began his second American missionary tour, which resulted in great rejuvenation and numerical increase in the ranks of the revivalists. The antirevival faction, however, became even more incensed and the extreme division is manifest in the designations *Old Side* and *New Side* to describe the quarreling groups of Presbyterians, who formally split in 1741. The New Sides sought to insure their perpetuation by founding the College of New Jersey (later Princeton) in 1746. After some initial setbacks (five presidents died within twenty years, including Jonathan Edwards and Aaron Burr), the new institution emerged as the educational mainstay of the entire region.

The Great Awakening in New England

The same forces that initiated revival in the middle colonies were at work in New England. This northern phase of the Great Awakening was launched by Congregational pastor Jonathan Edwards (1703–1758) at Northampton, Massachusetts, in the fall of 1734.

Edwards was the son and grandson of Congregational ministers, a man of extraordinary intellectual gifts and intense religious piety—that rare combination of scholar and saint. Educated at Yale, he

Presbyterian Historical Society

First Presbyterian Church, Paterson, New Jersey

became assistant pastor to his grandfather, Solomon Stoddard, at Northampton in 1727. Two years later, at Stoddard's death, Edwards assumed full pastoral duties.

It is hard to imagine how Edwards's meticulously logical sermons, hand-held and read by a man of such slight frame, could ever rouse a congregation to anything beyond complacent assent. But the message itself and the sincerity with which it was delivered pierced the heart like a flaming arrow. By 1734, a sense of anxiety and fear of God's wrath gripped Northampton. Within six months three hundred persons were converted and received into the church. The revival spread to other parts of the Connecticut Valley and on to Long Island where it was taken up by other preachers.

In 1740 Whitefield delivered four sermons at Northampton which greatly moved Edwards and his congregation, and a new revival broke out which continued for two years. Whitefield, along with Gilbert Tennent, Eleazer Wheelock, and Joseph Bellamy, toured the region as itinerant "New Light" evangelists, gathering thousands to hear their message wherever they went. By 1742, out of a population of about three hundred thousand, twenty-five to fifty thousand persons had been added to the New England churches.

Edwards was more than the leader of a revival; he was also a theologian and philosopher in his own right, surely one of the several brighter intellects of the colonial era. Amidst his duties as father, husband, and pastor, he managed to write a number of significant books, including *A Faithful Narrative of the Surprising Work of God in the Conversion of Many Hundred Souls in Northampton* (1737); *The Distinguishing Marks of a Work of the Spirit of God* (1741); *Freedom of the Will* (1754); *The Nature of True Virtue* (1755); and *The Great Christian Doctrine of Original Sin Defended* (1758). The first, *A*

Faithful Narrative, had a profound effect on both John Wesley and Whitefield. Most of Edwards's theological labor was in defense of traditional Calvinistic orthodoxy against the relentless inroads of Arminianism. In short, he attempted to reconcile the revival with Calvinism. Although he was fighting for a declining cause, Edwards's work enhanced religious thought and continued to influence American theology for generations to come.

Revival in the South

In the first half of the eighteenth century the Baptists were a relatively weak and scattered denomination, especially in the South. The picture began to change, however, with the coming of the Great Awakening, which had largely run its course in the middle colonies and New England by 1740.

Stemming from the revival in New England were the Separate Baptists led by New Light Congregationalist Shubal Stearns. They arrived in North Carolina in 1755, settling in the Sandy Creek section of Guilford County. From the mother church at Sandy Creek sprang a number of Baptist churches. By 1760, the North Carolina congregations had organized into the first Separate Baptist Association, and their missionaries had made inroads in Virginia. Preachers such as Dutton Lane, James Reed, and John Waller traveled through the back country and conducted successful revivals. Waller, in particular, was active in founding eighteen churches and baptizing more than two thousand persons into the Baptist faith.

Baptist success on the frontier must be attributed to the fact that the movement went to the people and spoke their language. Denominations of more traditional stance, which insisted upon an educated clergy and dignified worship, could scarcely impress rude frontiersmen who were barely literate. Baptist preachers, on the other hand, developed rapport with these rural folk, coming themselves, more often than not, from the less privileged classes. Although their tendency was toward anti-intellectualism, emphasizing emotions over reason, Baptists eventually founded schools and accorded the life of the mind a more valued place in their parish life.

The Baptists, with their views of the sharp separation between church and state, and their disregard for laws requiring a licensed clergy, came into conflict with the established denominations. Not only state governments but also irresponsible mobs harassed Baptist groups, often resorting to illegal methods of brutality. Persecution did not retard Baptist growth, for by 1776 this group claimed ten thousand adherents.

Methodism acquired its name from the disciplined and methodical Christian life that Anglicans John (1703–1791) and Charles (1707–1788) Wesley modeled for their followers. The Wesleys' teachings were a combination of Anglicanism, Puritanism, and German pietism. They believed in salvation not merely as a gift received through the power of the Holy Spirit at conversion, but as the Christian life itself, a present reality reflected in the expression of perfect love and pure motive. Once converted, a person should be vividly conscious of the Spirit's work within, and that awareness should express itself in joy, enthusiasm, and devotion. One of the best ways one could give evidence of conversion would be to renounce the usual pleasures and pursuits of society, such as card playing, dancing, gambling, and theater going. These proscriptions came to profoundly influence evangelical Protestant conceptions of morality in both England and America.

Although John Wesley had served as an Anglican missionary to Georgia (1736–1738), Methodism as such was brought to America in the 1760s by unofficial lay preachers; thus, Methodist expansion occurred after the Great Awakening had subsided. The quick dissemination of the Methodist faith in the colonies was due to the itinerant ministry its preachers practiced. With nothing but a horse and a Bible, the circuit riders carried on extensive ministries in Maryland, Virginia,

United Methodist Church, General Commission on Archives and History

"The Vision of the Circuit Rider," a painting by Charles Lennox Wright.

United Methodist Church, General Commission on Archives and History

An engraving of the John Street Church, the first Methodist church in America.

and North Carolina, preaching in the open air to any who would hear. By 1770, there were Methodist societies in these three colonies as well as New York, Delaware, and Pennsylvania.

By the opening of the Revolution in 1775, the Methodist revival in the South was approaching its peak. The total membership of colonial Methodism was 6,968; of these only 764 lived north of the Mason-Dixon line. At the Methodist Conference of 1777, a meeting of Methodist preachers first organized in 1773, there were 4,449 persons listed as members of the societies in Virginia as opposed to only 100 four years earlier. During this time John Wesley had been sending to America his ablest associates to supervise the work. Of these, the most important was Francis Asbury (1745–1816), who would emerge as the guiding genius of the denomination.

During all of this time Methodism was officially linked to the Anglican church, and during the Revolution (which John Wesley opposed) Methodists were thought of as Tories and loyalists, especially in the North. Not until they became an independent denomination would Methodist numbers increase further as the denomination became a primary participant in the Second Awakening in the 1790s.

The Impact of the Awakening

One of the most noteworthy outcomes of the Great Awakening is that it provided Americans with their first truly national experience. There had been nothing in their previous history to unite all Americans.

Travel and communications were as yet undeveloped, and most people kept to themselves within their ethnic communities. Nourished by itinerant revivalists, however, the Awakening cut across regional, ethnic, and religious boundaries. Historians agree that this national revival prepared Americans for the national revolution that was to follow in just thirty years. Religious cooperation thus prepared the way for political and military cooperation. On the community level, the Awakening often challenged traditional religious authorities and unleashed a type of individualistic, democratic impulse.

The Awakening figured just as prominently in the upsurge of new humanitarian expression. In every section of the colonies there were evidences of a deeper concern for man and a wider commitment to ameliorating his suffering.

In New England, where missionary work among the Indians had lain dormant since the death of John Eliot in 1690, a new effort to reach native Americans surfaced. Through the labor of Edwards, John Sargeant, and especially the tireless David Brainerd (1718–1747), Indian missions were established in western Massachusetts, New York, Pennsylvania, Delaware, and New Jersey. Outstanding among Congregational missionaries to the Indians was Eleazer Wheelock (1711–1799), who secured a charter to found a college for Indians in New Hampshire; in 1770, Dartmouth College opened its doors. In the middle and southern colonies the Presbyterians, Anglicans, and Moravians each took up ministry to the Indians. Out of the Moravian labors came numerous Christian Indian settlements, reaching into New England and as far west as the Ohio country.

Between 1714 and 1760, the number of black slaves in America jumped from 58,850 to 310,000, largely because of the diminishing supply of indentured servants. Although slavery was not extensive in most of the North, due to economic impracticality, New England

Billy Graham Center Museum

John Eliot, the "apostle of the Indians."

Drawing of an Indian meetingplace.

merchants were heavily involved in the slave trade in hopes of becoming wealthy. Because several British courts had decided that baptized slaves must be freed, many American slave owners approached the question of evangelizing slaves with extreme caution. Even when several colonies passed legislation to the effect that baptism did not confer the right to freedom, little work was carried on among slaves prior to the Great Awakening. The Anglican church, through its Society for the Propagation of the Gospel in Foreign Parts (SPG), was first in the colonies to devote much attention to the blacks. Few Anglicans within the colonies took up the task, however; it was the many missionaries, catechists, and schoolmasters sent from England who felt called to convert the blacks.

The first public protest of the slave trade originated among the Society of Friends (Quakers) and the Mennonites of Germantown, Pennsylvania. Proponents of reform were the Quaker mystic and humanitarian, John Woolman (1720–1772), and others. Due largely to their influence, the Philadelphia Yearly Meeting of Friends in 1758 repudiated slavery and by 1775 terminated fellowship with Friends who refused to emancipate their slaves.

The clash between the Christian faith and slavery would recur again and again over the next century, finally erupting in a civil war that would decide the matter, at least legally. The conflict of viewpoints

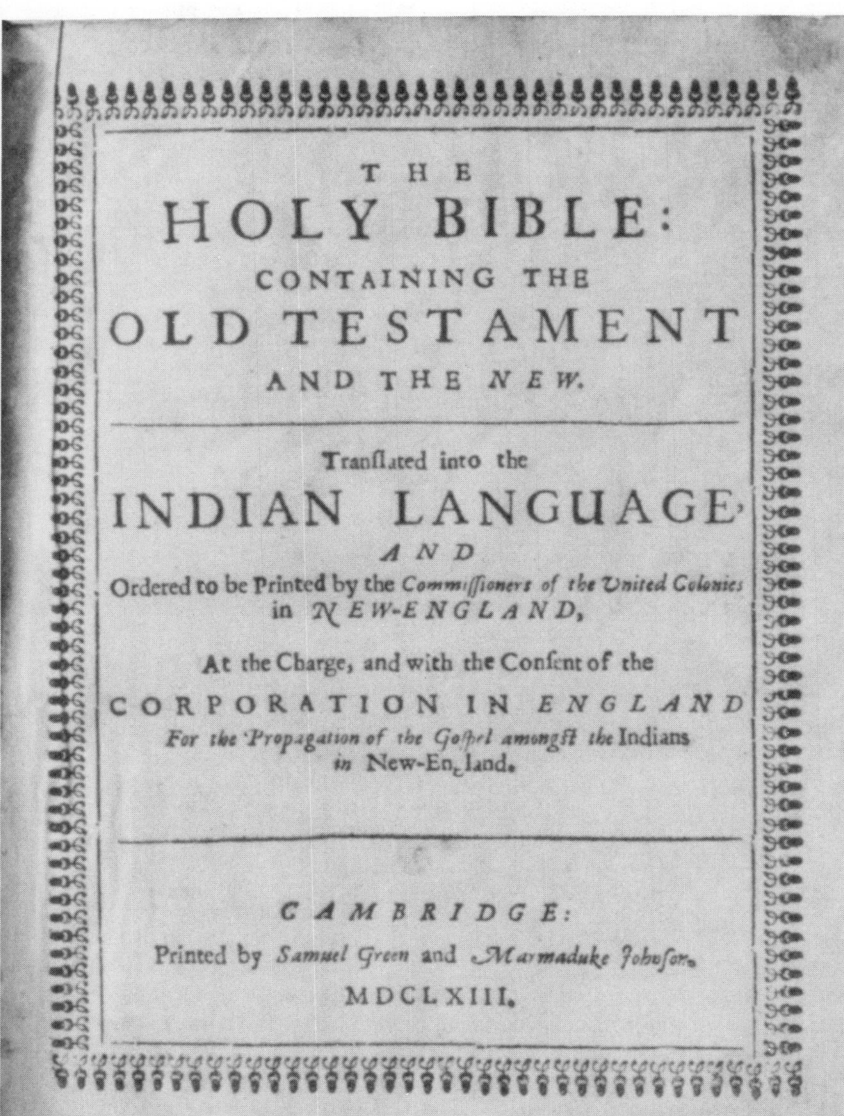

THE
HOLY BIBLE:
CONTAINING THE
OLD TESTAMENT
AND THE *NEW.*

Tranſlated into the
INDIAN LANGUAGE,
AND
Ordered to be Printed by the *Commiſſioners of the United Colonies* in *NEW-ENGLAND,*

At the Charge, and with the Conſent of the
CORPORATION IN *ENGLAND*
For the Propagation of the Goſpel amongſt the Indians *in* New-England.

CAMBRIDGE:
Printed by *Samuel Green* and *Marmaduke Johnſon.*
MDCLXIII.

American Bible Society Library

The Bible, translated into Algonquin by John Eliot, was printed in 1663. This was the first Bible printed in the New World.

John Woolman. This watercolor portrait was drawn from memory by Robert Smith III, of Burlington, New Jersey.

raises the larger question of the relationship between Christianity and its social expression. How could individuals who professed the same faith come to such disparate conclusions? This will be explored in more detail in chapters 8 and 10.

Apart from the rapid multiplication of churches, the major institutional survivals of the Awakening are the facilities for higher education necessitated by the swelling numbers of ministerial recruits. The Presbyterians were especially active, establishing the College of New Jersey (later Princeton) in 1746 and Hampden-Sydney College in 1775. The Baptists organized several academies and, in 1764, founded Rhode Island College (later Brown University). Dartmouth has already been mentioned. In 1766, the revivalists among the Dutch Reformed obtained a charter for Queens College (later Rutgers University) in New Jersey.

But, as we noted in tracing early Presbyterian experience in America, the Awakening also contributed to the divisive character of American denominationalism. Not everyone could go along with the new religious tides, and especially the excesses, of which there were many. Besides the Presbyterian split into Old and New Sides, schism also occurred in New England Congregationalism. The Old Light group, led by Charles Chauncy (1705–1787), pastor of the First Church of Boston, opposed itinerant preachers of revivalism and the "antinomian" doctrines they preached. The New Lights, headed by Edwards, favored revival, lay exhorters, and a looser church structure. It must be admitted that some of the Old Lights' accusations were grounded in fact. Certain evangelists, such as the Reverend James Davenport, did resort to sensational and offensive practices that cast reproach upon the movement.

From the Awakening a distinctly American revivalist tradition emerged; it was marked by emotional evangelism with emphasis on sin, salvation, and dramatic conversion experience. This relatively new phenomenon in western Christianity resurfaces and subsides a number of times throughout the history of American Protestantism.

5

The Church and Revolution

The European Enlightenment, characterized by a firm belief that reason would lead man to knowledge, help him to understand nature, and aid him in reforming society, began to infiltrate the American colonies early in the eighteenth century. Although the seeds of Enlightenment thought appeared earlier, most historians date its beginning in Europe from the publication of Isaac Newton's *Principia Mathematica* (1687) and John Locke's *Essay Concerning Human Understanding* (1690). There followed a self-conscious effort by English and Continental thinkers to cast off the constraints of tradition.

Enlightenment and Changing Patterns in Theology

Enlightenment ideas began to appear in the writings of certain American clergymen, even those who participated in the Great Awakening. Jonathan Edwards, for example, appropriated much of Locke's theory of knowledge after carefully reading his book at Yale. A few years later Edwards indicated equal enthusiasm for the works of the "incomparable Mr. Newton." He, however, remained a champion of scriptural authority against the more secular implications of Enlightenment humanist thought.

Later exponents of Edwards's theology adjusted it further. Joseph

Bellamy (1719–1790) and Samuel Hopkins (1721–1803), two of Edwards's students, began to modify the Calvinistic emphasis upon the inherited nature of original sin and opened the way for more human volition in directing the human experience that results from the divine act of regeneration. Both Bellamy and Hopkins thus sought to make intellectualism and revivalism acceptable to the eighteenth-century mind.

Meanwhile, a decidedly more liberal position was developing in sharp contrast to the theology of Edwards and his followers. Its roots are traceable to the teachings of the English Presbyterian theologian and archfoe of covenant theology, John Taylor (1694–1761). Taylor rejected the doctrine of original sin altogether, maintaining that sinfulness came by choice rather than by inheritance. His views caught hold in the Boston area where a sharp reaction to revivalism and its Calvinistic concepts took root. Taylor's chief representatives in New England were Charles Chauncy and Samuel Webster (1718–1796).

While the churches engaged in theological debate, a more general, yet powerful, philosophical force was steadily gaining strength. Deism, a religious expression of Enlightenment rationalism, was making considerable impact upon English intellectual life. Deists recognized divine creatorship of the universe and emphasized universal moral law, natural religion, man's innate ethical potentials, and revelation tested by reason. Gradually these views spread to the colonies, where they first surfaced in the colleges.

Deism appealed strongly to a nation desiring to demonstrate its reasonableness and inherent virtues to Britain and the world. Many Deists maintained nominal connection with a church without fully adhering to its doctrines, as in the case of George Washington (1732–1799). Others, such as Benjamin Franklin (1706–1790) and Thomas Jefferson (1743–1826), displayed friendliness toward organized religion without becoming church members. None, however, would have affirmed what Protestant evangelicals today hold to be biblical orthodoxy. A certain antisupernaturalism marked their views and Jefferson went so far as to publish his own version of the New Testament shorn of all references to miracles.

These early Deists envisioned an ideal society, ruled by reason, ennobled by benevolence, and blessed by freedom. The Deist mood, which characterized many Revolutionary leaders, was moderate and ethical, shaped by Protestant Christianity; this was in contrast to Voltaire's in France, so strongly anticlerical. Without directly attacking the churches, American Deism advanced man's autonomy through downplaying God's *present* activity and authority in the world.

The new philosophical and theological ideas took form in a new

Historical Committee of the Mennonite Church, J. F. Funk Collection

Mennonite meetinghouse in Germantown, Pennsylvania, built in 1770. This picture was taken about 1870.

American denomination—Unitarianism. Denying both the Trinity and the deity of Christ, Unitarianism preached the unity of the Godhead and tailored its liturgy accordingly. It also sought to demonstrate that genuine religious community could exist without doctrinal conformity.

Historical Committee of the Mennonite Church, J. F. Funk Collection

Interior of the first Mennonite church in America, as it was in 1915.

First table in Mennonite church in America, 1683.

Ironically, the first Episcopal church in America (King's Chapel, Boston) became in 1785 the first American church to declare itself Unitarian. Soon a number of Congregational churches in eastern Massachusetts followed suit. By the early nineteenth century Harvard College emerged as the bastion of American Unitarian thought. A separate Unitarian denomination was established in 1825.

The Churches in Revolution

While the Unitarians were revolutionizing theology, social and political upheaval was also brewing. From 1760 to 1775 relations between the American colonies and England steadily deteriorated. British economic intrusions such as the Sugar Act (1764), the Stamp Act (1765), and the numerous stifling navigation acts aggravated the colonists and sentiment favoring resistance grew. Also contributing to American hostility was the Anglican cry for an American bishop. John Adams states that this agitation contributed "as much as any other cause, to arouse the attention, not only for the inquiring mind, but of the common people, and urge them to close thinking on the constitutional authority of Parliament over the colonies." On April 19, 1775, at Lexington Green, the War for Independence formally began. What role did the churches play in this violent revolution?

Both English and American Protestants had long been provoked into political theorizing. Although sensitive to Paul's admonition that Christians be subject to the powers that be, they were not inclined to accept oppression if a plausible religious reason could be found for

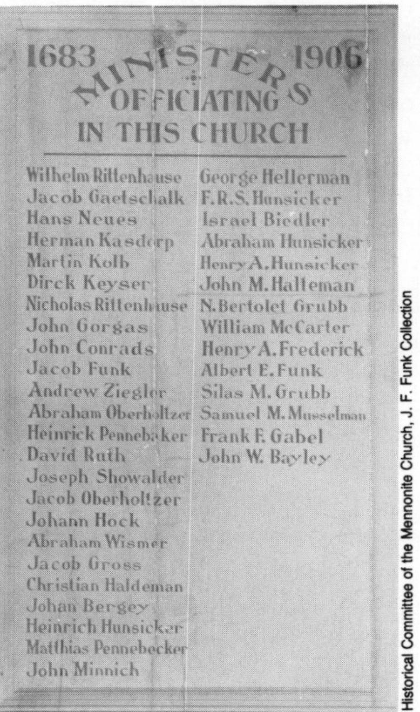

Historical Committee of the Mennonite Church, J. F. Funk Collection

Roster of ministers of the Germantown church.

resisting. Colonists of British origin easily recalled the Puritan Revolution of the 1640s and the Glorious Revolution of 1688, both popular reforms of the power of the British crown. Such precedents encouraged contemplation of revolt. By combining ideas from natural law and from the Calvinistic concept of government as a compact under God between ruler and ruled, they formulated a doctrine of active resistance.

But not all Christians were of the same mind on the issue of rebellion. Some, especially among the Quakers and Mennonites, were unable to justify revolt on any grounds. Others felt that a certain measure of reform was necessary but wished to see it accomplished through redress of grievances rather than through use of arms. Still others, clergy included, wholeheartedly supported war when it erupted.

The Established Churches

No religious body surpassed the New England Congregationalists in contribution to the Revolutionary cause, and the clergy were the primary catalysts. Besides acting as recruiters, most New England clergy supported the war with their pens and meager salaries. For generations ministers had educated their parishes in the principles of civil government on election days, days for "fasting and humiliation," and thanksgiving days. Jonathan Mayhew (1720–1766) of Boston, for example, warned his people against the insidious growth of tyranny: "Civil tyranny is usually small in its beginnings . . . till at length, like a mighty torrent, or the raging waves of the sea, it bears down all before it, and deluges whole countries and empires."

At each point of crisis in the decade from 1765 to 1775, the New England pulpiteers thundered and dwelt increasingly on the rights of the provincial populace. Enriching their vocabularies from the Bible, the clergy made colonial rights and resistance a holy cause. Earnest laymen like Samuel Adams (1722–1803) furthered the democratic ideals of the Revolutionary cause through eloquent written and oral persuasion.

The Anglican church, although it produced some of the Revolution's most ardent proponents, was, of all denominational organizations, the most thoroughly loyal to Britain. Nevertheless, most of its laity supported the rebellion in spite of clergy who were largely loyalist. In fact, it was so dangerous for some ministers to preach loyalist convictions from the pulpit that Jonathan Boucher of Virginia deemed it necessary to preach with loaded pistols before him on a cushion!

In the northern colonies, especially Connecticut and New York, the Anglican clergy were even more inclined toward loyalty than those farther south. Many were forced to flee or risk being tried for high treason by the new provincial governments. It was through laymen such as Washington, James Madison, Patrick Henry, John Marshall, and Alexander Hamilton that Anglicanism made its deep and lasting contribution to the American patriotic cause.

The Voluntary Bodies

The role of the nonestablished churches during the Revolution is complex. Each has its own unique history during these years and none was entirely loyalist or patriot.

Presbyterians, mostly of Scotch-Irish derivation, still burned with resentment toward England for the wrongs that had precipitated their migrations. Most, therefore, welcomed the chance to unify behind the Revolutionary banner. Outstanding among Presbyterian patriots was John Witherspoon (1723–1794), who had come to America in 1768 to assume the presidency of the College of New Jersey (later Princeton). As one of five delegates representing New Jersey in the Continental Congress, Witherspoon was the only clergyman to sign the Declaration of Independence.

Concordia Historical Institute, Saint Louis, Missouri

Henry Melchior Mühlenberg, the patriarch of Lutheranism in America.

Concordia Historical Institute, Saint Louis, Missouri

The Honorable Frederick Augustus Mühlenberg, the statesman.

Concordia Historical Institute, Saint Louis, Missouri

General John Peter Gabriel Mühlenberg, the patriot.

Concordia Historical Institute, Saint Louis, Missouri

Gotthilf Henry Ernest Mühlenberg, the pastor and scientist.

The Baptist churches, steeped in a long tradition of a compact theory of government and zealous for religious liberty, wholeheartedly supported the patriot cause. Their solidarity against British intrusions commended the Baptists to their former ecclesiastical oppressors in New England and Virginia, and gained for Baptists the legitimacy they had been seeking for generations.

The Methodists, however, were not as united. Their eminent leader, John Wesley, held staunchly to Tory convictions and loyalty to King George. Wesley engaged his adversaries with his pen and became highly influential in molding British opinion on the American issue. He advised his American ministers to remain neutral, but pressures drove them all, except Francis Asbury, back to England by 1778.

Colonial Methodists suffered great harassment for their supposed Toryism. Some were jailed, others beaten, and many more fined. Such episodes underline the reality that Christians who believe the same creed and the same Bible will often come to different conclusions concerning the social expression of their faith. Despite persecution, Methodist numbers increased throughout the Revolutionary period, tripling by 1780 to thirteen thousand members.

Like the Baptists, the Dutch Reformed were intensely patriotic. But because their churches were located mainly in the Hudson Valley, lower New York, and New Jersey, where the British were most active, they became prime targets. Churches were scattered, ministers imprisoned, and property destroyed. Lay people gathered where they could and sustained their church life in small groups, setting aside certain days for fasting, prayer, and thanksgiving.

The Lutherans and German Reformed were largely of patriot sentiment with a small loyalist minority. By all standards, the Mühlenberg family was the most influential among Lutherans during this period. Henry, the father, had been exercising an informal governorship over all the churches from New York to Georgia. Although he himself claimed neutrality, his sons were ardent patriots. A colorful incident relates to one of his sons, John Peter Gabriel, a pastor in Woodstock, Virginia. In a farewell sermon, after describing the colonial situation, he concluded: "In the language of Holy Writ, there is a time for all things. There is a time to preach and a time to fight; and now is the time to fight." With that, he stripped off his pulpit robe and stood before his congregation in a colonel's uniform! He then, with drum roll as background, began enlisting his parishioners.

Some church groups, who sought to honor Jesus' words about turning the other cheek, were unable to offer any direct military aid to the Revolutionary cause. Many "conscientious objectors," especially among the Quakers, were persecuted for their convictions. The

Moravians also suffered, although many rendered indirect service to the cause of independence. It was through Indian missions, however, that their fortitude is best remembered. Moravian Indian leaders persuaded their tribes to be sowers of peace and to resist taking sides. This, of course, was misinterpreted by both the British and the Americans, who were already biased against the Indians. Moravian Indians underwent cruel treatment, and in one infamous case in Ohio, were herded together and butchered in cold blood by American militiamen.

Colonial Catholics generally affirmed the patriot cause. Several Roman Catholic regiments were organized throughout the colonies. Among signers of the Declaration of Independence and the Constitution were Catholics Thomas Fitzsimmons, Daniel Carroll, and Charles Carroll. Although Catholics were few, they emerged from the Revolution in a favorable light and thereby advanced their own cause of religious freedom.

The Revolutionary experience had a profound effect on the way in which American Christians came to view their newly independent country. Some believers worked for the Revolution with measured understanding. They realized that their highest loyalty belonged to a God who stands above all and judges all earthly societies, each of which reflects the frailties of mankind. Other Revolutionaries, however, totally sanctified the admirable aspects of the American effort with biblical imagery, and ascribed to the struggle with England a sacredness and purity of purpose borrowed from Christianity. Some historians have termed this tendency to idolize the state, especially during America's wars, the American civil religion.

Religion and Politics in the Framing of the Republic

It is perhaps evidence of man's need to legitimize his social structures and actions with divine sanction that these early Americans constructed a national framework with materials drawn from both the Christian religion and the English political heritage. Although a legal separation between church and state was written into the federal Constitution and subsequent Amendments, Christianity played a crucial role in supplying values, vocabulary, and symbols to undergird the national purpose.

The wedding of religion to politics has deep American roots. The Puritans drew heavily on biblical imagery in order to make sense of their lives and circumstances; through repeated practice this custom was dyed deeply into the American fabric. It recurred with renewed force during the Great Awakening. In fact, in his "Thoughts on the

Revival of Religion in New England," Edwards related that he was seeing the descent of the millennium on American soil.

A salient feature of this tradition is the idea that America has been singled out from among nations for a special mission and destiny. Throughout most of the colonial period England too was included in this purpose, but after the Revolution a shift occurred and Americans began to view themselves as God's "New Israel." Laymen Jefferson, Franklin, and John Adams were as vigorous as any clergymen in affirming that the United States had come into being as a grand design of Providence for "the illumination of the ignorant and the emancipation of the slavish part of mankind over all the Earth." These sentiments were preserved for posterity in the national motto: E pluribus unum—Annuit coeptis—MDCCLXXVI—Novus ordo seclorum (One Out of Many—He [God] Has Smiled upon Our Undertakings—1776—A New Order for the Ages). Reflecting the spirit of the eighteenth century, the new age did not include Indians, blacks, or women on its agenda, at least not yet.

When the war's outcome was in America's favor it was read as a sign of God's special affection for America. In 1783, Ezra Stiles, president of Yale, reviewed how "the wonder-working providence of God" had been displayed in the events of the war, and looked ahead to the coming freedom, prosperity, and splendor of the United States. Thus, the perspective of American Christians shifted from that of a chosen people challenged to a special task to that of a chosen nation treated to divine favor. In the words of H. Richard Niebuhr, "The Kingdom of God in America became the American Kingdom of God," with the emphasis on *American.*

The tension inherent in this mixing of religion and nationalism would hold potent implications for a society claiming such high ideals and special providential mission.

Part 3

The Nationalization of the American Churches

(1784–1860)

6

New Churches for a New Society

Uncertainty, experimentation, and adjustment marked every aspect of the early American republic. Americans had cut the mooring lines of colonial submission, but faced the responsibilities of independence with few precedents to follow. Both churches and nation had to establish their own bounds within the new freedoms.

Grappling with the New Religious Freedoms

Religious freedom had been in the making for generations, receiving impetus from several sources. Foremost was the English example. As early as 1660 Englishmen realized that ongoing political health was likely only if the destructive energies of religious conflict were tamed by toleration. Also important was the leavening influence of religious minorities, for whom freedom was a basic tenet of their convictions. America, of course, became a haven for radical Reformation groups such as the Separatists, Baptists, and Quakers, and they refused to muffle their cries for religious liberty. As minorities flourished, diversity of theological opinion increased. For example, early on the New England Puritans fashioned concessions such as the Halfway Covenant. Too, the Great Awakening tempered the strict Calvinism of the early colonial fathers and encouraged a more experience-oriented Christian life. Religious rigidity further withered through the secular-

Quaker meetinghouse in Burlington, New Jersey. The hexagonal meetinghouse (c. 1685–1785) was used as the site of the Philadelphia Yearly Meetings every other year until 1760. This is an eighteenth-century drawing by an unknown artist.

izing force of rationalism. Deism and Unitarianism rejected the miraculous and other traditional dogmas, substituting a vague least-common-denominator religion.

All of these influences culminated in the formal declarations of religious freedom enshrined in the federal Constitution. Its Sixth Article states that "no religious test shall ever be required as a qualification to any office or public trust under the United States." Its First Amendment promises that "Congress shall make no law respecting an establishment of religion, or prohibiting the free exercise thereof."

The Constitution emphatically states that the American government is, indeed, prohibited from sponsoring any one religious body; however, the state is not separated from religion in general, as some have suggested. The American relationship between religion and politics is complex but can be clarified by comparison with other judicial definitions of separation. France since 1905 offers a classic one. The French view separation of church and state not only in our sense of a religious antitrust act, but also in the sense of the state being entirely separated from religion in any form. This difference springs from the divergent histories of the two countries: the anticlerical tradition of French revolutionary republicanism on the one hand, and the Puritan origins of American democracy on the other.

The consequences and implications of the new religious freedoms shaped the future course of all the churches. The Constitution assured the rightful participation of any minority sect in the democratic process of the government, thereby protecting the liberty of sects under the law. The provision extended theoretically to non-Christians and even to the nonreligious. It followed that churches ultimately became wholly voluntary institutions, dependent exclusively on their ability to reach and persuade free people to join and support them. The state took on the role of an impartial guardian of order between independent and uncoerced denominational competitors.

In *The Sacred Canopy*, sociologist Peter L. Berger discusses at length the consequences of religious liberty and pluralism for the American churches. The key characteristic of all pluralistic situations, he says, is that the religious ex-monopolies can no longer take for granted the allegiance of their client populations. Membership is strictly voluntary. As a result, the religious tradition, which previously could be authoritatively imposed, now has to be marketed. It must be "sold" to a clientele that is no longer constrained to "buy." It is Berger's contention that the pluralistic phenomenon becomes, through sheer press of circumstances, a competitive situation in which religious institutions are marketing agencies and religious traditions are consumer commodities. In practical terms, this has often led to an emphasis in American churches on "results," bureaucratic structuring, a susceptibility to "fashion," and a demand for a more entrepreneurial than pastoral style of leadership. Berger's economic parallel is helpful in understanding how the American churches adapted to the new social environment of the nineteenth century.

The new religious pluralism was applauded by most Americans, but at the state conventions for ratifying the Constitution, some resisted the elimination of religious tests. In Massachusetts, for example, one critic complained that "Roman Catholics, Baptists, and Pagans" would connive their way into office, and expressed the fear that without proper religious safeguards "Popery and the Inquisition may be established in America." In this protest we can detect what historian Richard Hofstadter calls the "paranoid style" in American political discussion, where an attempt is made to preserve established power by evoking provincial fears. The protest also reveals a tension that characterizes American social life even into our own century: the gradual erosion of the "Protestant establishment" by other religions and races. Freedom increased opportunity. Nonwhite and non-Protestant Americans gradually gained access to arenas of influence from which they had formerly been barred.

The removal of government financial support of churches forced the rediscovery of personal responsibility and financial commitment. People made up their own minds about Christianity without the legislative arm dictating their ecclesiastical choice. Although many still attended church out of habit or for the sake of respectability, many did not. After the Revolution spiritual life waned and some clergymen began looking to heaven for another awakening.

Movements Toward Church Disestablishment

Disestablishment followed naturally the formal declaration of religious freedom. In a broad sense disestablishment may be viewed as an acceleration of the general democratization process in American culture. Voluntarism in religion was essential to the process. Nevertheless, one way or another a number of states held tenaciously to their traditional religious establishments.

In Anglican Virginia, where more than half the population was non-Anglican, a movement of protest against the official church had been seething for half a century and now came into its own. Baptists and Presbyterians were the most determined of all dissenting groups to bring about Anglican disestablishment. Political leaders such as James Madison and George Mason were equally insistent on the issue. Decisive in initiating this process was Thomas Jefferson's Bill for Establishing Religious Freedom, first presented in 1779. Jefferson regarded it as one of the most significant achievements of his life and requested that after his death it be recorded on his tombstone. It stated

> that no man shall be compelled to frequent or support any religious worship, place, or ministry whatsoever, nor shall be enforced, restrained, molested, or burthened in his body or goods, nor shall otherwise suffer, on account of his religious opinions or belief; but that all men shall be free to profess, and by argument to maintain, their opinions in matters of religion, and that the same shall in no wise diminish, enlarge, or effect their civil capacities.

But it took another fifty years and numerous other legislative measures to bring about functionally a complete separation of church and state in Virginia.

Other states also moved to terminate formal connections with Anglicanism. Maryland's Declaration of Rights of 1776 guaranteed full religious freedom to all Christians, but that state did not grant full political rights to Jews until 1826. The Halifax Congress of North Carolina in 1776 adopted a constitution stating that there should be no establishment of any particular church in the state. It did, however, restrict the holding of public office to persons who affirmed "the truth of the Protestant religion." After approving two initial constitutions which left the subject of religion virtually untouched, South Carolina passed a third in 1790 which recognized no establishment of any kind. Georgia abolished its Anglican relationship in its first constitution of 1777 and guaranteed freedom of conscience to all. In New York, the only state north of the Mason-Dixon line in which Anglicanism prevailed, the tenuous bond between church and state dissolved in 1777.

The situation in New England was quite different. Because the Congregational establishment had been overwhelmingly on the patriot side, the severance of ties with England had little bearing on the state-church situation. To most clergy and influential laymen, political independence did not necessarily mean religious independence, especially where their own interests were at stake. Even though official ties between state and church would eventually end through legislative fiat, a less visible influence structure would linger on in New England for many decades.

Connecticut was perhaps the most resistant to disestablishment initially. It stubbornly retained the old royal charter and refused to draft a state constitution for more than forty years after independence. Protest mounted. Baptists and Methodists especially pressed for the complete separation of church and state. Joined by Unitarians, Universalists, Quakers, and Episcopalians, they together worked with the Republican Party to oppose the conservative Federalists and to exert a more liberalizing influence in the state government. Finally, in 1818, a constitutional convention at Hartford drew up a document stipulating that "no preference shall be given by law to any Christian sect or mode of worship."

Policies were slightly more flexible in New Hampshire. Although it was the first state to draft a constitution (January 5, 1776), it made no provision concerning religion. A second constitution, in 1783, allowed citizens to support the denomination of their choice, although functionally Congregationalism was still favored. Spurred on by the

Baptists, however, the state legislature, in 1817, placed all churches on the same basis, bringing to an end the Congregationalist hegemony.

Despite innovative impulses in Massachusetts, Congregationalism prevailed the longest there. The state's first constitution, drafted in the midst of the Revolution (1779), asserted the government's right to make provision "for the institution of the public worship of God, and for the support and maintenance of public Protestant teachers of piety, religion and morality." Dissenters, however, were given the privilege of directing their religious tax to their own denomination. The Congregationalists continued to exert official influence, and it was only after years of heated debate that the state finally approved a bill of disestablishment, ending the oldest religious establishment in New England in 1833.

Denominational Readjustments

The divestment of government sponsorship demanded that the churches rethink their resources and goals. Disestablishment was only one element of the changing religious climate, for theological liberalism continued to flourish, especially along the northeastern seaboard. It should be remembered that the European Enlightenment reached America relatively late, postponed while pressing political concerns were settled. Enlightenment ideas, however, for years had been attracting some of the best minds in the youthful nation. Now such ideas began to penetrate the popular mind as well. Books like Ethan Allen's *Reason the Only Oracle of Man* (1784) and Thomas Paine's *Age of Reason* (1794) were eagerly read by lay persons.

Consequently, religious zeal progressively deteriorated. Attendance at worship meetings noticeably dwindled and most congregations added a mere four or five new members a year. In 1798 the Presbyterian General Assembly noted with alarm "a general dereliction of religious principles and practice among our fellow citizens . . . and an abounding infidelity, which in many instances tends to atheism itself." Conditions were even more depressing on the frontier. Cut off from the stabilizing social life of the East, and forced to be concerned chiefly with bare material sustenance, the pioneer found little time for things of the spirit or the life of the mind.

All religious bodies therefore reassessed their relationships to this rapid social change. The Anglican church scouted its American congregations rather than England for prospective bishops. Its name became the Protestant Episcopal Church in 1783. The next year, Conneticut loyalist Samuel Seabury was consecrated an Episcopal bishop in Scotland. In 1787 Samuel Provost and William White were

The archives of the Episcopal Church

Samuel Provost.

The archives of the Episcopal Church

William White.

The United Methodist Church, Commission on Archives and History

Francis Asbury, the first Methodist bishop in America.

consecrated Episcopal bishops as well. Although many Americans remained suspicious of bishops, the Episcopalians displayed enough moderation to palliate these fears.

Methodism, still considered a religious society within the Anglican church, began to form independent congregations as early as 1799. When John Wesley returned from England to reclaim his authority after the war, Francis Asbury called a General Conference to pass judgment on the founder's proposals, an act symbolizing the emerging autonomy of American Methodism. The Methodists designated themselves the Methodist Episcopal Church and henceforth Wesley's authority was merely nominal. Methodism continued to gain new adherents throughout the closing years of the eighteenth century and would experience great growth during the Second Awakening in the next century.

Unlike expansive Methodism, New England Congregationalism, secure in its regional prosperity and heritage, tended to look inward and assumed a provincial attitude toward the rest of the nation. Mounting doctrinal disputes created numerous factions. Jonathan Edwards the Younger (1745–1801) and Timothy Dwight (1752–1817) championed trinitarian orthodoxy against the inroads of Unitarian thought. Lack of unity made it difficult if not impossible for Congregationalism to forge any undertaking on the national level.

The unprecedented growth of Presbyterianism in the postwar years demanded efficient organization. Under the able leadership of John Witherspoon and others, a General Assembly was called and rules for discipline and doctrine adopted in 1789. Although marked by a vigorous theological conservatism during these years, Presbyterianism reflected a highly rationalistic style of theology, a trend manifest, for example, in the substitution of Scottish Common Sense Realism for the traditional Edwardsean theology at Princeton. Common Sense empiricism assumed one can assuredly and intuitively know the first principles of morality and reality with no discontinuity between inner thought and outer reality.

The Baptists, with many hard-fought battles over religious freedom behind them, made rapid gains throughout the new nation. Although their church polity was ardently voluntaristic, they nevertheless saw value in cooperation. Accordingly, by 1800 about fifty Baptist associations existed.

Other American churches adjusted in similar ways to their new national environment. Lutherans created synods in New York (1786), North Carolina (1803), Ohio (1818), Virginia (1820), and Maryland (1820) in response to a need for regional assemblies to recruit, train, and ordain ministers. In addition, the General Synod, formed in 1820,

Protokol

der

General Synode,

der

Evangelisch Lutherischen Kirche

in den Vereinigten Staaten.

gehalten zu Friederichstadt Maryland,

October 21, 22, 23, 1821.

Lancaster,

Gedruckt bey J. Schnee.

Protokol ꝛc.

Da dieses der, zur Zusammenkunft der Evangelisch Lutherischen General Synode, bestimmte Tag war, so versammelten sich die Prediger und Gemein-Deputirten, in der Lutherischen Kirche um 10 Uhr Vormittags.

Der Ehrw. Dr. Lochman predigte Vormittags, in deutscher Sprache.— Der Ehrw. Pastor J. G. Schmucker Nachmittags, in deutscher Sprache, und der Ehrw. Dr. Endreß Abends, in englischer Sprache— Der Ehrw. Pastor Schober predigte Vormittags deutsch in der Reformirten Kirche.

October 22, 9 Uhr Vormittags.

Die Prediger und Gemein-Deputirten versammelten sich. Pastor Schober wurde zum Vorsitzer ernannt, welcher die Sitzung mit einem herzlichen Gebet eröffnete. Folgende Herren legitimirten sich als Abgeordnete.

Von der Synode in Pennsylvanien.

Pastor G. Schmucker.
" " Dr. Lochman.
" " Dr. Endreß.
Carl A. Barnitz, Esq.
F. Scherrets. Esq.
P. Brua, Esq.

Von der Synade in N. Carolina.

Pastor G. Schober.
" " D. Scherer.

Von der Synode in Maryland u. Virginien.

Pastor D. F. Schäffer. *A. M.*
Joh. Ebert. Esq.

Concordia Historical Institute, Saint Louis, Missouri

Cover and first page of Protokol, (Lutheran) General Synod of Maryland, 1821.

became a melder of the heterogeneous elements of American Lutheranism. The Dutch Reformed Church broke formal ties with Holland in 1792, organized into an independent American body, and renamed itself the Reformed Church in America in 1867.

Although Roman Catholicism was in a stronger position after the war, it too had its share of serious problems, particularly its low ratio of priests to communicants (thirty to twenty-four thousand). Roman Catholicism gained a surer footing in America after the consecration of John Carroll (1735–1815) as Bishop of Baltimore. His many achievements included the founding of Georgetown College (1789; later Georgetown University) for the training of priests. By 1808 there were suffragan sees in Boston, New York, Philadelphia, and Bardstown (now Louisville), Kentucky, and a metropolitan see in Baltimore.

America's new democracy not only permitted the continuance of all the old divisions of the Christian church, but also allowed, and perhaps encouraged, the growth of new groups. As we previously noted, the Great Awakening (a leveling and therefore democratic

Drawing of the first church building, First Reformed Church, Grand Rapids, Michigan, 1842.

movement) had the effect of splintering many of the established churches. Most of its proponents preached in English to English-speaking audiences. There remained a large German-speaking population set apart because of the language barrier. By the late eighteenth century these also received the biblical message in their own tongue.

John Carroll, first Roman Catholic bishop of Baltimore.

Philip Otterbein (1726–1813), a minister of the German Reformed Church, arrived in America in 1752, and adopted the techniques of his friend Asbury in organizing class meetings and lay leadership among his German-speaking converts. With Martin Boehm, a Mennonite, he founded the United Brethren in Christ in 1800 with Methodist polity and doctrine.

Jacob Albright (1759–1808), a Pennsylvania tilemaker and farmer, converted in midlife, felt a similar burden for his German-speaking compatriots. Although reared a Lutheran, he gained a license as a Methodist lay preacher. Again, because of the language problem, another new denomination was formed in 1807: The Newly Formed Methodist Conference, known simply as the Evangelical Association and later as the Evangelical Church. These two German groups would combine in the twentieth century into the Evangelical United Brethren Church.

By 1850 a United States citizen could establish residency in any of thirty-one states as far west as California. The same person could join any of three times as many religious denominations. Such a phenomenon raises questions as to why there is such an array of American denominations, all calling themselves Christian and all professing adherence to the same Bible. Why have these emerged and what is their significance for Christianity in America?

In his provocative book, *The Social Sources of Denominationalism* (1929), H. Richard Niebuhr tackled these searching questions. While conceding that theological, ethnic, and national sentiments have played important roles in the growth of denominations, he suggests that they are frequently also the products of social and economic factors as much as religious. Niebuhr interprets American denominationalism as "the accommodation of Christianity to the caste-system of human society"; this is in contrast to Jesus, who revolted against the Jewish class distinctions of his day. Thus, for example, the European magisterial Reformation is seen by Niebuhr as reform mainly for the middle and upper classes. It was only a matter of time before its inherent inequalities were challenged by the less powerful groups of the radical Reformation. In a relatively short time, Europe and later America were dotted not only with Lutheran, Dutch Reformed, and Presbyterian churches, but also with Anabaptist, Mennonite, and Quaker groups; the first cluster representing initially the more secure classes and the second the lower rungs of society.

The same can be said of the Methodist and Baptist revivals, which appealed largely to those groups that felt alienated from the more privileged communions. Later the American Civil War, a fiercely political and social upheaval, further divided churches and created additional American denominations. It is not Niebuhr's intention to reduce all ecclesiastical distinctions to merely social causes, but his study does illuminate the way human concerns and cultural bearings condition our definitions and preferences for church life and, in particular, how denominationalism has come to flourish on American soil where individual freedom of choice and association has been maximized.

7

The Second Awakening:
Eastern and Western

It was generally a wintry season for the churches of the post-Revolutionary period. A historian of the Episcopal church characterized the era as one of suspended animation and as "the lowest ebb-tide of vitality in the history of American Christianity." Lyman Beecher (1775–1863), who was a student at Yale in 1795, described the religious conditions there in his *Reminiscences:* the college "was in a most ungodly state. The college church was almost extinct. Most of the students were skeptical, and rowdies were plenty . . . intemperance, profanity, gambling, and licentiousness were common." Presbyterians decried "the profligacy and corruption of the public morals" and the Baptists, evoking biblical imagery, lamented that "the love of many waxed cold; some of the watchmen fell, others stumbled, and many slumbered at their posts."

The western frontier was populated by "experimenters," unmoored from social restraints so that they could freely migrate and search for appropriate homesteads. Predictably, it was a life more conducive to reliance on primitive instincts than on the circumspect boundaries of religious piety. Ministers were few, churches even fewer. David Rice, the first settled minister in Kentucky, states that when he came to the region in 1783 he "found scarcely one man and but few women who supported a creditable profession of religion. Some were grossly ignorant of the first principles of religion." The times were ripening for a renewed emphasis upon vital religion throughout the society.

Perry Miller has suggested that the revivalist preachers of the nineteenth century were natural successors to the patriotic creators of the Revolution and the religious exhorters of the Great Awakening before them. The Revolution had been preached with religious zeal and had, of course, succeeded. Now, due to the slackening of fervor, new spokesmen picked up at the close of the 1790s where the patriotic orators had disengaged. They were thus sustained by a strong sense of continuity with their religious and political predecessors.

The new generation of clergy could not pretend, however, to speak for the collective conscience of American Christians. The America of 1800 had grown too large, too sprawling and diverse to support utopian ideas of national religious uniformity. Church leaders saw that the centrifugal forces of a burgeoning society had to be balanced by the centripetal power of a widespread faith commitment; they refashioned the technique of revivalism to serve this function. In again calling Americans to repentance preachers sought to bring souls to God and assert the unity of a culture in danger of fragmentation.

The Eastern Phase of the Awakening

Signs of revival were first evidenced in the coastal East. Almost imperceptibly people began taking new interest in religion; churches were strengthened by the addition of fresh converts and new congregations, especially in New York, Long Island, and New Jersey, were again being established.

Interestingly, it was among college students that the revival fires were first kindled. As early as 1787, Hampden-Sydney College and Washington College, both Presbyterian institutions in Virginia, experienced awakening among their students; a number made decisions to enter the ministry. These thirty or forty men who sought ordination eventually served Presbyterianism in the frontier West.

The spiritual advance in New England was, no doubt, partly due to the introduction of Methodism, with its strong evangelistic emphasis. By 1796 the New England Methodist Conference organized with three thousand members; a network of circuits soon covered all the New England states. In central and western New York there were revivals of sufficient scope and number for local analysts to refer to that region as the "burned-over district" (burned by the flame of the Holy Spirit).

The changing religious current is well illustrated by events at Yale College. Timothy Dwight (1752–1817), grandson of Jonathan Edwards, was elected president of Yale in 1795 and immediately set about upgrading the educational and religious climate of the distinguished institution. He met the students on their own ground and offered a series of frank discussions on timely issues. His chief crusade was against infidelity, which led him to commence his four-year cycle of discourses on the Christian religion, expounding salient doctrines and pointing out their moral implications. After six years of perserverance spiritual renewal finally took hold at Yale. More than one-third of the student body (mostly in ministerial training) professed conversion and multiple awakenings followed at Yale and also at Dartmouth, Williams, and Amherst colleges.

Yale's revival was significant for several reasons. First, because of Dwight's friendship with the old, antirevivalist Calvinists, his influence and leadership helped bring many of them over to the revival party and healed a long-term breach. The revival also produced future evangelical leaders. For instance, Beecher was to become the organizer and promoter of the Second Awakening in New England, and Nathaniel Taylor (1786–1858) its theologian. Finally, events at Yale served as catalyst for the involvement of other eastern colleges, which sent their graduates forth to found new colleges and churches in the West.

The Western Phase of the Awakening

The frontier phase of the Second Awakening was patently different from that in the East. The seaboard revivals were quiet, orderly, and restrained; those in the West exploded with religious excitement, emotional outbursts, and physical aberrations. Revivalist preachers on the frontier were dealing with people on the move. Conditions did not allow for the long-term Christian training practiced in the East and instead prompted a greater urgency in proclaiming the gospel message and a heightened appeal to the emotions.

The men who sparked the frontier revival were mostly Presbyterians in the Appalachians. James McGready, Barton W. Stone, and William McGee worked in cooperation with their Baptist and Methodist colleagues in a genuine ecumenical effort to reach the unchurched. They were all intensely concerned with salvation and presented it to all who would accept it in faith. More people were attracted than the churches could hold, necessitating outdoor meetings. Participants came prepared to spend several days on the site, bringing provisions with them. Thus was born the frontier camp meeting.

The summer of 1800 marked the high point of the southern revival. Multiple meetings were held at Red River with the emotional pitch steadily rising with each service through the week. By Sunday people were falling to the floor in tears crying, "What shall I do to be saved?" More than a hundred conversions were reported.

The revival flames spread rapidly through Kentucky and Tennessee into North and South Carolina, western Virginia and Pennsylvania, and into the settled regions north of the Ohio River. The Cane Ridge camp meeting of August 1801 proved to be the apex of the Kentucky meetings. Nearly twenty thousand people were present, some from as far away as Ohio. Among the dusty travelers and crude makeshift tents, evangelists mounted their stands and pleaded with their hearers to be "washed in the blood of the Lamb." The loneliness of the farmer's normal life contrasted sharply with the exhilaration of fellowship with thousands like himself.

The meeting was accompanied by extraordinary outbursts of feeling. One Methodist preacher reported that as he preached, hundreds fell prostrate, writhing in spiritual agony before him. Others, newly converted, rose and proclaimed the message that had saved them. Some jerked their heads furiously; still others unabashedly leaped as they experienced the smiting power of the Holy Spirit. These accounts were probably exaggerated by both friendly and hostile witnesses, but they were sufficiently numerous to arouse misgivings in the minds of many.

The Presbyterian General Assembly of 1805, while giving faint praise to the revival, observed that "God is a God of order and not of confusion; and whatever tends to destroy the comely order of his worship is not from him, for he is consistent with himself." The assembly was also alarmed by the tendency of Presbyterian revivalists to accept a Methodist doctrine of grace, and by undue laxity regarding ordination requirements.

All of these issues led to schisms among the Presbyterians between 1803 and 1805, the most notable of which were the departures of the prorevivalist Cumberland Presbyterians from the Kentucky Synod, and the Christian Church or New Light schism led by Cane Ridge minister Stone. The Baptists and Methodists experienced no such division. For them the camp meetings were harvest times; the theologies of both groups melded more naturally with revivalism than did the Presbyterians' Calvinism.

Sporadic revivals continued to erupt throughout the 1820s and '30s. As the camp meetings became more routine much of the early excitement disappeared. By 1840 the frontier camp meetings had metamorphosed into summer Bible conferences where the faithful could gather to hear inspirational addresses. The final great thrust of the Second Awakening, however, was yet evolving in the North.

Charles Finney and the "New Measures"

Charles Grandison Finney (1792–1875) united within his person both the scholarly qualities of the East and the emotional emphases of

Engraving of American Methodists proceeding to a camp meeting, March 1, 1819. The artist was J. Milbert and the engraver, M. Doubourg.

the frontier. Born in Connecticut and reared in western New York, Finney early rebelled against the strict Calvinism of his youth. Soon after a quiet conversion in 1820, he resolved to preach the gospel of "free and full salvation." Because of his antagonism toward formal

Charles Grandison Finney.

theological training, Finney was almost denied ordination but was finally licensed to preach by the St. Lawrence Presbytery in 1824; this was despite some reservations about his theology, for he rejected the doctrine of election, believing instead that the atonement was for all rather than for a chosen few, and he tended toward accepting the idea of Christian perfectionism.

Beginning his ministry in Jefferson County, New York, the six-foot two-inch Finney preached a type of gospel that aroused the whole community and soon brought censure from his clerical brethren. He felt increasingly restrained by a settled ministry and began to travel, holding meetings in Pennsylvania, Ohio, and throughout New England. His most successful revivals were those in Rochester, New York; during the 1830s, '40s, and '50s great campaigns secured nearly three thousand conversions.

Until Finney appeared, the northern phase of the Second Awakening had been firmly in the hands of settled ministers, who had discouraged emotionalism and disorder. The controversial features of Finney's revivalism were his "new measures." These included singling out sinners by name while preaching, using "you" instead of "they" when speaking of the wicked, encouraging the "convicted" to come forward to the "anxious bench" where attention could be centered upon them, holding prayer meetings at "unseasonable hours," and allowing women to testify and pray at public meetings. Finney was frank about his use of human measures to bring about conversions. In his *Lectures on Revivalism* (1835), he declared that "a revival is not a miracle, or dependent on a miracle in any sense. It is a purely philosophical [i.e., scientific] result of the right use of the constituted means."

Some historians, such as J. Edwin Orr, have hesitated to use the term *revival* to describe Finney's work, seeing true revivals as works of God and Finney's as overt human manipulation. That his "new measures" were accepted was due in part to the character of American evangelical Protestantism. In America, revivalism seldom led to ascetic withdrawal or spiritualistic contemplation. Evangelical Christianity was, above all, activist, pragmatic, and oriented toward measurable results. The fame of Finney and the other great revivalists depended on the numbers of converts. This was its main and enduring appeal.

Finney was credited with bringing the camp-meeting revival to the city. Wherever he traveled, congregations were held spellbound by his piercing eyes and stentorian voice, which he used with theatrical effect. His activity in urban centers also brought him into conflict with the more restrained evangelical ministers, especially Beecher, who attacked his methods and perfectionistic theology. Finney's revivals were a significant force in the rising antislavery impulse and in the broadening of opportunity for women in education and ministry.

The last bright flames of the northern revival coincided with the financial crash of 1857, which brought severe depression and unprecedented unemployment among factory workers. The distinctive feature of the revival during 1857 and 1858 was its absence of evangelists. Instead of preachers imploring the hearers to repent, thousands of clerks and businessmen united spontaneously for midday prayer and Bible study. The first such gathering occurred at the Old Dutch North Church on Fulton Street in New York City on September 23, 1857. Urban newspapers devoted large sections to accounts of the revival, and soon the businessmen's prayer meeting was a regular activity in small towns and large cities from Indiana to Quebec. "It would seem," wrote one enthusiast, "that the mighty crash was just what was wanted . . . to startle men from their golden dreams."

The Significance and Consequences of the Second Awakening

The Second Awakening had numerous consequences for American religion in both the short and long run. First, it resulted in a swelling of church membership, especially in the South. In Kentucky alone, between 1800 and 1803, the Baptists gained more than ten thousand new members and the Methodists an equal number. The Second Awakening also represented a subtle shift away from traditional Calvinism as the dominant theological mode in American religious life.

United Methodist Church, General Commission on Archives and History

First Methodist church in Kentucky, at Masterson Station, near Lexington, 1790.

Many moderates accused the revivalists of allowing emotion to run away with logic. But it went beyond this, for much greater emphasis came to be placed on man's efforts to stimulate revival as opposed to God's sovereign prerogative to pour out his Spirit when he wills. Finney's "new measures" illustrated that the promotion of revival had become a matter of calculation and technique.

This Awakening also had the unintended effect of splintering churches. This should not be surprising in view of the schisms that had resulted from the Great Awakening a century earlier. The Lutheran, Congregational, Unitarian, and Reformed churches, as well as the Presbyterian church, experienced divisive controversy over the Awakening. Directly or indirectly, the revivals were instrumental in the emergence of more than a dozen hybrid denominations.

But the most outstanding consequence of this Awakening was the enormous increase in humanitarian and reform efforts. Missions, social and educational reform, and abolitionist societies received dynamic impetus from those touched by the revival spirit. This fresh Christian social vision is the subject of chapter 8.

8

The Christian Social Vision

The diverse nature of the Second Awakening does not negate that it was instrumental in forging a mainstream tradition for American evangelical Protestantism. Essentially orthodox in theology, experiential in faith, and Puritan in outlook, this mainstream tradition played a formative role in the social and religious life of nineteenth-century America.

The effects of American religious fragmentation were offset by a conscious blurring of doctrinal distinctions among the competing denominations in this mainstream. Confidently evangelical, they proclaimed a life-transforming faith based on an authoritative Bible, a personal Savior, and a moral universe having its origin in the Triune God. The various religious groups also espoused a common creed of identity with the nation that worked to unify the culture more than any legal establishment of religion ever could have. Throughout the first half of the nineteenth century most churches resisted the secularizing effects of the Enlightenment and the First Amendment and urged the republic to recognize its basis in Christianity. Political, as well as religious, leaders repeatedly warned that the success of the American experiment depended on the moral and intellectual character of its people. To this end educators, missionaries, revivalists, popular orators, and essayists combined their talents to shape and direct the developing American character. The result of their labors was the birth of a sprawling array of "interlocking directorates" and reform societies that became known as the Benevolent Empire.

Lyman Beecher called these proliferating reform societies "the disciplined moral militia." And, in truth, terms like "battle," "campaign," and "crusade" were quickly seized and enlisted into the rhetoric of reform.

The voluntary societies through which these legions of reform efforts organized were interdenominational in character and national in scope, allowing divergent churches to pool their collective means to meet particular needs. Also, by concentrating on a single objective, they were able to enjoin the broadest possible support and avoid peripheral and potentially divisive theological issues. Chartered as nonprofit corporations, they harnessed lay energies and were ideal instruments for quick, concerted action. There was no need to wait for decisions from an official ecclesiastical body. These societies set the pattern for all future American philanthropy. They multiplied so rapidly that Orestes Brownson, a Roman Catholic convert, complained that "a peaceable man can hardly venture to eat or drink, to go to bed or get up, to correct his children or kiss his wife" without the guidance and sanction of some society.

Many Christians believed that it was through benevolence that God intended "the glorious things foretold in the Bible" to be accomplished. Most did not anticipate the immediate dawning of millennial glory, but they did believe that humanitarian efforts would ultimately bring about the kingdom of God on earth. Such a millennium could not simply be prayed for; it would be introduced, said President Eliphalet Nott of Union College in 1806, "by human exertions." In giving the millennium such a temporal and material character, and by identifying the kingdom of God with the prospects of the republic both at home and abroad, Protestant spokesmen directly encouraged the American concept of progress and mission.

Missions

The tens of thousands who poured over the Appalachians into the opening western lands caused alarm among the eastern clergy. Who would feed and care for these wandering sheep? Denominations were challenged to develop strong missionary programs if frontier society was to be won to Christian ideals and practices. The burgeoning home-missionary movement became a means whereby the West, the nation, and ultimately the world might be redeemed from the effects of immorality and undisciplined greed.

Protestants had been tardy in developing a missionary conscious-

Mennonite Brethren Church

Each year special revival services were conducted at Oak Post Mission (Mennonite) in Oklahoma. This picture shows how the Indians moved to the mission and camped in tents for the duration of the meeting.

ness. While the Reformation churches displayed little interest in the heathen during the sixteenth and seventeenth centuries, the Roman Catholic Church spearheaded missions in Africa, Latin America, Japan, China, India, and the Philippines. It was the evangelical revivals of the eighteenth and nineteenth centuries, combined with European imperialist expansion, that opened up vast new populations to the Protestant impulse. European Protestants formed voluntary mission societies, beginning with the Baptist Missionary Society

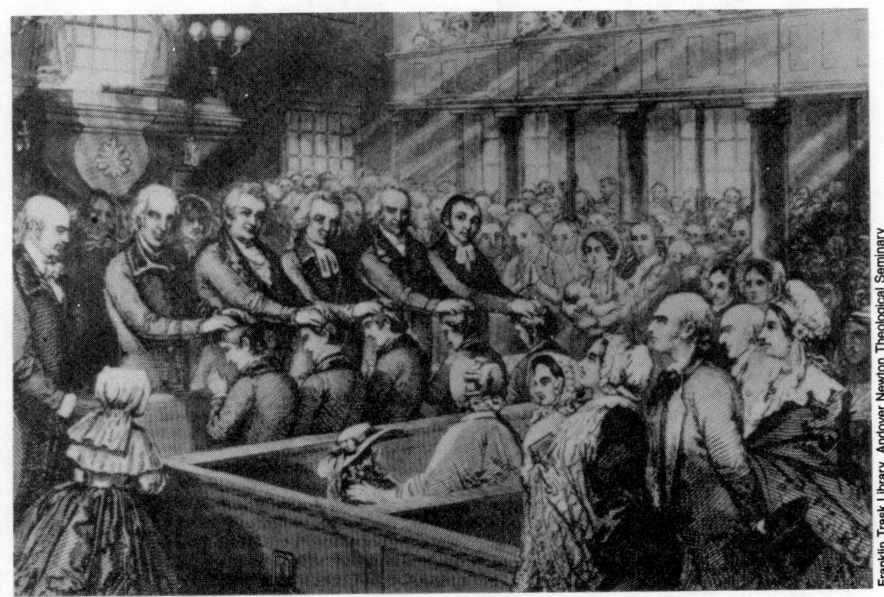
Franklin Trask Library, Andover Newton Theological Seminary

Ordination of the first foreign missionaries sent from America.

(1792), the London Missionary Society (1795), the Netherlands Mission Society (1797), and the Basel Mission Society (1815). The American churches soon followed their lead.

At first American missions concentrated on converting the American Indian. Thus, for example, the New York Missionary Society was formed in 1796 of Presbyterians, Dutch Reformed, and Baptists to carry the gospel to the southern Indians. In New England a number of Congregational mission societies emerged, the earliest being the Connecticut Missionary Society in 1798. It purposed to "Christianize the heathen in North America, and to support and promote Christian knowledge in the new settlements within the United States." During the next few years at least eight such societies originated in New England, all of them with numerous local auxiliaries. From 1820 onward, missionary work among the Indians received impetus from the annual subsidies distributed by the federal government to agencies engaged in tribal missions.

Labor among the Indians inevitably brought missionaries into contact with white settlers in frontier regions. The roving missionary evangelists preached the gospel, planted and pastored churches, and tried to bring Christian civilization to the disorder of the West. Outstanding among domestic mission agencies was the American

Hawaiian Mission Children's Society

The Reverend William Patterson Alexander preaching in a grove of tutui trees at Kauai in the 1830s. This engraving was first published in an account of the U.S. exploring expedition.

Billy Graham Center Museum

Building of the American Bible Society.

Home Missionary Society, formed in 1826 in New York by 126 delegates from four denominations. A large portion of the missionaries were young men sent forth from colleges and seminaries to spread Christian morality and institutions on the frontier. By 1850 the society sponsored 1,065 missionary workers in the field.

As American ships traded in far-off lands and British Christians opened new foreign ministries, Americans received a challenge to overseas missions. The growing concern was activated by the dedication of a group of students at Andover Theological Seminary in 1810. Led by Samuel J. Mills, Jr., the group, which included Adoniram Judson, Samuel Newell, and Samuel Nott, petitioned the Congregational General Association of Massachusetts to inaugurate a foreign mission and offered themselves as candidates. The association thrilled to the prospects and soon generous donations flowed in. With support seemingly providentially provided, the young missionaries were ordained and sent to India in February 1812. Some were Williams College alumni who had pledged themselves to foreign service several years earlier during a prayer meeting beside a haystack in the midst of a thunderstorm.

Other foreign-mission societies followed. Baptists from eleven states gathered at Philadelphia in May 1814, and launched the General Missionary Convention of the Baptist Denomination of the United States of America for Foreign Missions. This effort was the first broadly based organization of American Baptists. Congregationalists and others coalesced into the American Board of Commissioners for Foreign Missions (1810), which dispatched nearly seven hundred missionaries in its first thirty years. Among its most notable achievements was the Christianization of the Hawaiian Islands begun in 1820; five years later the Ten Commandments were made the basis for law in the islands. Although the Episcopalians were somewhat late in entering the missions movement, in 1821 they organized the Domestic and Foreign Missionary Society of the Protestant Episcopal Church, concentrating efforts in the Northwest. By 1860 American missionaries could be found on every continent and in every major nation of the world.

Mission agencies received crucial support from the many new Bible and tract societies that sprang forth during these years. Distribution of Bibles and Christian literature went hand in hand with missionary outreach. To this end the American Bible Society was organized in New York in 1816, and its sister organization, the American Tract Society, in 1825. Agents from these two societies canvassed the North American continent, supplying the poor with books and tracts. The growth of denominational publishing houses, such as the Methodist Book Concern (1789) and the American Baptist Publication Society (1840), complemented the work of the Bible and tract societies. By 1840 more than 850 religious periodicals were printed in America, 250 of which originated on the frontier. These represented a primary means of bringing Christian knowledge into homes and of influencing the lives of many thousands in a positive way. It is impossible to overestimate the importance of this cascade of religious literature for the nurturing of faith in an increasingly literate society.

Education

One of the most important by-products of the era of benevolence was a passion for learning. All over America church leaders recognized that without rigorous education in Christian principles America would not achieve its destiny. The West, once again, was the primary focus. Beecher, aroused by the supposed threat of Catholic immigrants whom he pictured as subverters of republican institutions, urged a campaign to educate the West: "For population will not wait, and commerce will not cast anchor, and manufacturers will not shut down the gate, and agriculture, pushed by millions of freemen on their fertile soil, will not withhold her corrupting abundance. We must educate! We must educate! Or we must perish by our own prosperity."

The years from 1780 to 1860 have been called the "denominational era in American higher education." During these eighty years the

Concordia Seminary, Saint Louis, Missouri, founded 1839.

number of colleges in the United States increased from 9 to 173 which survived, and perhaps four times that number which became defunct by the end of the century. Congregational, Presbyterian, and Episcopal church leaders led the way. The Congregationalists, who had traditionally emphasized education, controlled 21 colleges located mainly in New England and the Midwest. The Presbyterians, similarly motivated, operated 49 colleges extending from Princeton in the East to Pacific University in the West. During that same period the Episcopalians founded 11 institutions, the Lutherans 6, the German Reformed and Universalists 4 each, the Friends and Unitarians 2 each, and the Dutch Reformed and United Brethren 1 each. The Baptists, who had only 4 colleges in 1830, increased that total to 25 by 1860. In the same thirty-year interval, the Methodists founded 34 institutions of higher learning.* Staffed primarily by ministers and with clergy for presidents, these denominational colleges were the backbone of American higher education prior to the Civil War.

*Among the early Presbyterian colleges were Transylvania (1780), University of Tennessee (1794), Washington (1806) and Jefferson (1802; merged 1865), Centre (1823), Lafayette (1826), Wabash (1832), Hanover (1833), and Davidson (1837).

Congregationalists founded Williams (1793), Middlebury (1800), Amherst (1821), and Oberlin (1833); also Illinois College (1829), and Knox (1837).

Baptist colleges that survived the century included Colby (1818), Colgate (1819), George Washington (1821), Furman (1826), Georgetown (1829), Denison (1832), Kalamazoo (1833), and Franklin (1837).

Episcopalian colleges included Hobart (1822), Trinity (1823), and Kenyon (1824).

Methodist participation was somewhat delayed with Randolph-Macon (1830), McKendree (1830), Wesleyan (1831), Emory (1836), and DePauw (1837).

Gettysburg (1832) was the first Lutheran college, and Franklin (1787) and Marshall (1836; merged 1853) the earliest German Reformed.

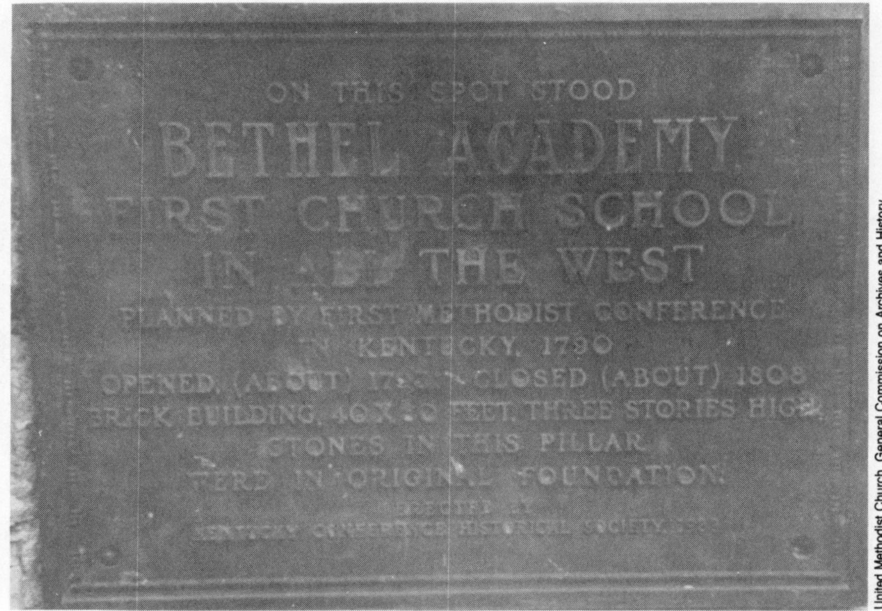

United Methodist Church, General Commission on Archives and History

Plaque marking the site of Bethel Academy.

Franklin Trask Library, Andover Newton Theological Seminary

The first three buildings of Andover Theological Seminary.

The founding of theological seminaries was another innovation of ante-bellum Protestant educational activity. Traditionally, aspiring young ministers had attended one of the colleges such as Yale or Princeton, and then had joined themselves to clergymen with whom they lived and worked, gaining practical experience. By 1800, however, the expansion of American society and the proliferation of churches forced the development of graduate professional schools to credential the needed clergy.

The first permanently located theological seminary was founded by orthodox Congregationalists at Andover, Massachusetts, in 1807, in reaction to Harvard's drift toward Unitarianism. In 1816 the Congregationalists opened their second seminary, Bangor Theological Seminary, in Maine. A conservative wing of Congregationalism established Hartford Theological Seminary in 1834. The Presbyterians opened their first seminary at Princeton in 1812, their second at Auburn, New York, in 1819, and their third, Union Theological Seminary, at Richmond, in 1824. "New School" Presbyterians were responsible for launching Union Theological Seminary in New York City in 1836 and the Episcopal church founded General Theological Seminary in New York City and another at Alexandria, Virginia, in 1824. Divinity schools at Harvard and Yale universities were established in 1816 and 1822 respectively. On the frontier, schools such as Chicago's McCormick Theological Seminary (1830) and Cincinnati's Lane Theological Seminary (1832) were founded through combined Congregational and Presbyterian efforts.

The early nineteenth century also witnessed the rise of public education. Where tax-supported schools existed a strong sectarian influence usually prevailed, as in the case of Congregationalism in the New England schools. By 1825 the trend was clearly toward secularization. The primary catalyst in this movement was Horace Mann (1796–1859), under whose leadership Massachusetts in 1837 developed a system of secular schools under state control. Mann desired a Christian-infused education without sectarian intrusions. Some churchmen, especially Presbyterians, Lutherans, and Catholics, felt this was theologically superficial, and instead developed parochial schools where youth could be shielded from corrupt values. Although the Presbyterian program withered by 1870, the Catholic and Lutheran schools thrived.

These years also saw the birth and progress of the Sunday school. From its inception in 1769 in England by Methodist Hannah Ball and its popularization by Robert Raikes, the goal was to provide religious instruction to children whose parents could not afford to send them to school. Early American Sunday schools were organized and operated

Billy Graham Center Museum

Cover drawing of *Harper's Weekly*, showing members of the National Sunday-school Convention, 1869.

mainly by societies formed especially for that purpose. In 1804 the Union Society began to provide education for the poor female children of Philadelphia. Other large cities such as Pittsburgh, Boston, New York, Albany, Baltimore, and Charleston followed suit, and in 1824, the American Sunday School Union was founded to provide lesson materials for the classes.

The Sunday schools afforded opportunity for women to serve the churches by teaching the young; this encouraged the emerging women's movement as the century progressed. In fact, the churches were the real seedbeds for women's rising consciousness. Although viewed before the law as a nonentity and in the professions as an intruder, in church a woman was all that a man was: a sinner saved by grace.

Cover of the 1835 *Temperance Family Almanac.*

Billy Graham Center Museum

Women's influence was so great in nineteenth-century Protestant parishes that some historians have spoken of the "feminization of American religion" during these years; this was suggested by practices such as earlier baptism of children, the quiet disappearance of the doctrine of infant damnation, and a new emphasis on themes of submission, love, mercy, and meekness in both hymnody and the doctrine of Christ. Above all, evangelical women stood in the forefront of the women's-rights movement and helped organize the great Seneca Falls (N.Y.) Convention on women's rights in 1848.

Social Reform

The aim of the whole Benevolent Empire was not only to evangelize individuals and plant new churches, but also to remake society. Hence, its supporters not only encouraged revivals and promoted missions, but also championed moral and social reform and showed compassion to the disinherited.

The benevolent societies launched numerous great crusades. Among the most compelling were those for prison reform, education, peace, and the abolition of slavery. For example, a sweeping drive for reform in drinking practices was spearheaded by the American Temperance Society (1826). Methods perfected in the winning of Christian converts were employed in battling "ardent spirits" and "demon rum." The drinking habits of the bulk of American Christians changed and considerable public opinion developed in favor of prohibition. In 1846 Maine became the first state to legislate prohibition.

Britain had generally provided the model for American Christian benevolence efforts, but in forming peace societies, Americans themselves took the initiative. Through a combination of factors such as disillusionment over the outcome of the War of 1812, currents of Enlightenment optimism, and the pacifistic tradition of Quaker and Mennonite groups, several state peace societies organized; a national body, the American Peace Society, followed in 1828. For more than a decade the society stimulated discussion on the evils of war and the possibilities of a "Congress of Nations" to avoid it. During the Mexican War crisis (1848), the Quakers sent the government a petition (bearing nine thousand signatures) asking that peace be made with Mexico at once. Internal tensions between extremists and moderates weakened the crusade and the Civil War submerged it completely. It did not resurface until the Spanish-American War of 1898.

Other targets for Christian reform included the practice of dueling, which was outlawed in Connecticut in 1818 and in Virginia a year

Sketch depicting the dedication ceremony of the Young Men's Christian Assocation, Boston, 1851. From *Harper's Weekly*.

later. Although numerous southern states followed with prohibitory legislation, duels continued to plague the nation for the rest of the century.

Christian compassion also led to the organization of associations for young men and women. The Young Men's Christian Association (YMCA), originating in London in 1844, opened its first American branch in Boston in 1851. Within a decade more than two hundred such organizations served young American adults.

The problem of female drunkenness and prostitution led to the establishment in 1830 of Magdalen Asylum in New York by a Presbyterian minister; and in 1834 to the founding of the American Female Moral Reform Society.

The restoration of the criminal to responsible citizenship was the aim of the Philadelphia Society for Alleviating the Miseries of Public Prisons, originating in 1787. After the War of 1812, renewed interest in prison reform led to the establishment of new penal institutions such as that at Auburn, New York, based on the philosophy that inmates could best rehabilitate themselves through communal labor. Christians were often in the vanguard of these efforts.

The reform of economic structures generally was of low priority in the social thought of evangelicals. They were confident of the potential prosperity of any individual freed from the grips of sin, liquor, indolence, or even secret societies. After the devastating effects of the panic of 1837, however, certain Christian activists realized that the problem of urban poverty demanded attention. For instance, Joseph Tuckerman (1778–1840), a Unitarian, formed the Benevolent Fraternity of Churches in Boston to bring ministry and charitable aid to the city's poor. After absorbing the socialist sentiments of Robert Dale Owen, Orestes Brownson helped form the Workingman's Party in New York City, and by 1836 was ministering in Boston through his own Society for Christian Union and Progress.

But, for the most part, a predominantly rural and highly individualistic Protestantism did not seriously address itself to the emerging industrial and urban issues of the mid-nineteenth century. Reformers' thinking on economic questions was often simplistic. Moral exhortation substituted for informed analysis of structural societal problems. When reformers spoke of the relationships between religion and worldly business, their concern chiefly centered on the ethical conduct of individuals rather than on entities such as government or corporations.

Abolition

Slavery was an ugly and perplexing blot upon the record of a nation conceived in liberty. Although it was one of the oldest institutions of American society, slavery had always been under attack by humanitarians, both within and without the camp of organized Christianity. The attackers now intensified their offensive.

In the northern states, where there was but a fraction of the number of slaves in the South, antislavery legislation was enacted soon after the Revolution. By 1787 Rhode Island, Massachusetts, New York, Connecticut, Vermont, New Hampshire, New Jersey, and Pennsylvania had either abolished slavery or provided for its gradual demise. The Northwest Ordinance of 1787 excluded slavery forever from the Northwest Territory. Although the Constitution was silent on slaveholding, the Congress provided for the abolition of the slave trade in 1808.

Slavery was deeply entrenched in the South. Whereas the North moved increasingly in the direction of industrialism, the South, because of expanded cotton production resulting from invention of the cotton gin in 1793, tended more toward agrarianism and, consequently, dependence on slave labor. By 1860 the cotton industry accounted for 75 percent of the slaves in the South. Although several southern states had, before 1800, either prohibited the further importation of slaves or placed restrictions upon their importation, they now began to

Billy Graham Center Museum

A number of prominent Americans supported abolition.

manifest a defensive posture regarding the "peculiar institution." Thus the antislavery agitation in the North appeared concurrently with an equally aggressive proslavery movement in the South. An ominous cloud was forming over the American future.

Abolition societies, composed of both blacks and whites and humanitarians of many stripes, launched a vigorous campaign against human bondage. Early organizations appeared in Philadelphia (1775), New York (1785), Maryland (1790), Connecticut (1791), New Jersey (1792), and Delaware (1794); a fresh effort took shape in 1833 under the auspices of the American Antislavery Society. Outstanding clergymen, including Beecher, Charles Finney, Theodore Dwight Weld, and numerous New England Unitarians, lent their influence to the crusade. Sarah and Angelina Grimké, Harriet Beecher Stowe, and Julia Ward Howe enlisted financial support and devoted themselves to organizational tasks for abolition. Soon antislavery chapters sprang up within churches too; Baptist associations and Methodist conferences, particularly in New England, began to pass strong antislavery resolutions. The Maine Baptist Association, for example, declared in 1836: "Of all the systems of iniquity that ever cursed the world, the slave system is the most abominable."

The southern response to these northern attacks must be understood in the context of how deeply embedded slavery was in that region. It is important to remember that most slaveowners, Christian and otherwise, inherited slavery just as one inherits one's culture. By 1800, slavery was so stubbornly lodged in southern economic and social life that to entertain thoughts of abolition threatened not only southern culture, but also security for the slaves themselves.

A historical profile may help to illustrate this. In his autobiography, Jeremiah Jeter, a Virginia Baptist clergyman, recorded his anguish over the slavery question. Jeter grew up determining never to own a slave. Then he married a woman who held slaves, and he thereby became an owner. During their engagement they had agreed that after they married Jeter could dispose of the slaves in whatever way he thought proper. When the time came, however, he was overwhelmed with the difficulty of finding a solution. To free them was to break the laws of the state. Even if freed, could the slaves support themselves? What about mothers with dependent children? Should he send them all to Liberia? None wanted to go there. If he did send them there, they would be forced to leave spouses and children belonging to other masters. What was he to do? Jeter's dilemma boldly underlines the tragic fact that slavery had become a systemic problem for the Southerner. To tamper with one part of the system was to inevitably incur undesirable consequences in another part. The burden of an inherited past was heavy for Southerners troubled by the "peculiar institution."

On the other hand, to many Southerners slavery could be defended as a positive good, an arrangement that was in the best interests of the blacks themselves. Often the proslavery arguments were based on premises of paternalism and racial superiority; above all, slavery was defended from the Bible by ministers and lay persons alike. Although not a Southerner, even the renowned Princeton theologian, Charles Hodge, found no direct biblical quarrel with slavery. Also, many northern churchgoers, although not supporters of slavery, viewed as unwelcome agitators the abolitionists who sought freedom and civil rights for blacks. The abolitionists themselves found difficult ethical dilemmas as they appealed to a higher moral law but violated civil laws by aiding runaway slaves and circulating antislavery literature in the southern states.

By 1840 internal conflicts had shattered all hope of a united national front among Christian reformers. Growing divisions, especially over slavery, intensified suspicions and grievances that were festering on every level. While reformers fought to reshape the outward characteristics of American society, other forces were penetrating the ideas and values undergirding American Christianity.

9

New Departures in American Religious Thought and Practice

American society in the nineteenth century experienced rapid change. Factories replaced cottage industries; dawdling barges yielded to steamships; new states expanded the Union; immigrants arrived; innovative ideas promoted development from sea to sea. It was a country in ferment and the churches were profoundly affected by developments in the industrial, commercial, political, and particularly the intellectual realm.

During the age of benevolence denominations muted their differences and cooperated for the improvement of the social order. But it was only a matter of time until differences resurfaced as geographical expansion heightened sectional and sectarian interests. The liberalization of theology in the traditional denominations promoted this trend.

Liberal Trends in the Traditional Denominations

Unitarianism had emerged among the New England clergy and prosperous businessmen of the Boston area in the second third of the eighteenth century. Its popularity grew following the mass publication of William Ellery Channing's (1780–1842) famous sermon, "Unitarian Christianity." By 1825 the American Unitarian Association included

King's Chapel, originally an Episcopal church, was the first church in America to become Unitarian.

125 churches. A movement yet more liberal developed within Unitarianism by the 1830s which was too humanistic for Channing, but included such luminaries as Congregational minister Ralph Waldo Emerson (1803–1882) and the more radical Theodore Parker (1810–1860). Both reformulated their theology by drawing on German romanticism. These Transcendentalists, as they were termed, viewed each person as an incarnation of God, reason as the guiding principle of life, and religion as simple ethics.

Closely associated with Unitarianism was Universalism, imported from England and first organized into an American congregation in 1779 in Gloucester, Massachusetts. Although it early affirmed most of the traditional theological doctrines, Universalism quickly abandoned these touchstones. In its Winchester Platform of 1803, specific affirmations were made on the perfectibility of man, the ultimate (universal) salvation of all people, and the humanness of Jesus Christ. Its chief early spokesman, former Baptist Hosea Ballou (1771–1852), brought Universalist doctrine into essential agreement with the Unitarian creed through his *Treatise on the Atonement* (1805). The two groups would merge in 1961 to form the Unitarian-Universalist Association.

Although Unitarians and Universalists departed from Congregationalism, there remained within the denomination ample theological flexibility. New Haven's Nathaniel Taylor, an avowed follower of Jonathan Edwards, separated from his master, particularly in viewing moral depravity as a choice made after birth rather than as an inherited condition (as taught in traditional Calvinism). In 1834, conservative opponents of Taylor organized the institution that became Hartford Theological Seminary "for the defense of truth and the suppression of heresy."

Theodore Parker.

Ralph Waldo Emerson.

It was a student of Taylor's, Horace Bushnell (1802–1876), who expanded his teacher's views by publishing *Christian Nurture* (1847). He developed a new theory of Christian education which viewed the child not as morally depraved until experiencing conversion, but as needing only a Christian rearing in which the child would grow into grace. Predictably, Bushnell was attacked for discounting the special agency of the Holy Spirit in man's conversion, and for reducing Christianity to a vague form of religious naturalism. His humanized view of Christ as merely a revealer of mercy, patience, and compassionate love was widely criticized at the time but quite accepted in liberal Protestant thought by 1900.

During the early decades of the nineteenth century an increasing demand for greater freedom in theology, church polity, and social life led to a number of other denominational ruptures which were felt most acutely in the eastern churches. Baptists split over the question of free will versus predestination; the normally placid Quakers divided over whether the Bible or their own "Inner Light" should be the final authority in religious life; Methodists splintered over the call for greater lay participation in the General Conferences (1830); and five ministers of the Dutch Reformed Church seceded from their communion over looseness of doctrine and discipline; they formed the True Reformed Church (1822), later part of the Christian Reformed Church.

Calvinistic rigidity had proved somewhat incompatible with the revivalism of the Second Awakening on the frontier. Those expressing Arminian tendencies had been forced to leave Presbyterianism. In Pennsylvania, Alexander Campbell (1788–1866) and his followers modified their Presbyterianism to a more Baptistic core of what they considered essential biblical Christianity. Ironically, by preaching a simple message transcending denominational distinctions, Campbell was forced to form his own denomination—Campbellites, also called the Disciples. In 1832 these joined with Barton W. Stone's Christian Church to become the Disciples of Christ.

Orthodox Calvinism was dealt another blow on the frontier when

Unitarian-Universalist Association

The First Parish Church (Unitarian), in Hingham, Massachusetts, known as "the old ship church."

Charles Finney accepted a theology chair at Oberlin Seminary, Oberlin, Ohio, in 1835. Although his views were distinct from New England humanism, Finney taught a theology of Christian perfectionism or entire sanctification, a doctrine with deep roots in Methodism. No major splits resulted from the Oberlin theology but tensions continued as Finney's graduates were denied admission to Presbyterian and Congregational associations because of their "unscriptural" views.

Sectarian Heyday

In the search for an American religious consensus the historian is frustrated at every turn. By 1830 any stalwart orthodoxy that had once stood to judge deviant doctrines had vanished. Americans were free; free to worship how, where, and when they willed. Such freedom encouraged nonconformity and dissent.

Religion in preindustrial America reflected the strains of the society. Resentment by the poor toward elite rule found religious expression in revolt against the authority structures of such denominations as the Presbyterian, Methodist, and Baptist. The desire was not to control the existing denominations but to form independent assemblies directly controlled by the body of believers. The men and women who led such movements combined belief in the Bible with vigorous assertion of the worth of the individual, however poor in worldly goods. This appeal was often heightened by denouncing the sins of the urban rich and contrasting their evil ways with the superior morality of the converted poor.

Sweeping rejection of current social values was obvious in various millenarian doctrines, which taught that the end of the world, the millennium as promised in the New Testament, was at hand. People were exhorted to forsake sin, be saved, and await Christ's imminent return. Among the many millenarian groups the most significant was founded by William Miller (1782–1849), a farmer in upstate New York. After some thirteen years of painstaking Bible study and numerological speculation, Miller became convinced that mankind would come before the bar of final judgment on April 23, 1843, when the second advent of Christ would consummate history.

At first Miller's message was confined to a constituency in New York State, but the work of skillful publicists such as Joshua Himes gave millenarian ideas widespread circulation throughout New England and the whole Northeast. As the appointed day approached, converts sold or gave away their property. Farmers deserted their plows and artisans their benches. When the date passed without drama Miller revised his calculations to October 22, 1844. Expectations again climaxed but nothing happened.

Aurora College Library

Plaque from the William Miller Memorial Chapel.

As is necessarily the fate of all millenarian movements, great disappointment followed and Millerism as such came to an end. Its founder died a few years later. Some of Miller's followers, however, were not easily deterred. They found a new leader in Ellen Gould White (1827–1915) of Maine. She persuaded them that Christ's failure to appear was due to neglect of proper Sabbath observance, and in 1845 they formed the nucleus of what became the Seventh-Day Adventist Church.

Perhaps the most extreme in its expression of social alienation was the Church of Jesus Christ of Latter-day Saints, also known as the Mormons, founded in 1830 by Joseph Smith (1805–1844). Smith's imagination was of the highly concrete, literalistic sort that manifested itself in a fascination with the esoteric implications of the dimensions of the Great Pyramid, the literal fulfillment of the prophetic books of Daniel and Revelation, and the prospect that American Indians were the ten lost tribes of Israel. In 1830 Smith's translation of The Book of Mormon, allegedly interpreted off golden tablets by way of angelic informants and special looking glasses, was published in Palmyra, New York, and a small group of believers set up a community in Fayette, New York.

However, local hostility to the Mormons erupted and the first of multiple migrations began in 1831. From Fayette to Kirtland, Ohio;

Church Archives, Church of Jesus Christ of Latter-day Saints

This sketch depicts Mormons being driven from Missouri.

from Kirtland to Jackson County, Missouri; from Missouri to Nauvoo, Illinois. In Nauvoo the Mormons set about creating a cohesive community and perchance a perfect society; they built a temple, organized a defense force, and established a government. Four years later, in 1844, a mob killed Smith. In an effort to avoid more

Church Archives, Church of Jesus Christ of Latter-day Saints

Mormons also suffered persecution in Nauvoo, Illinois.

bloodshed, Brigham Young (1801–1877), Smith's successor, determined that the next exile would be voluntary. Beginning in February 1846, nearly sixteen thousand Mormons trekked across the prairies to found a new Zion.

Eventually, in July 1847, the right place was located—the Great Salt Lake valley in Utah. It was arid, wild, remote from the "gentiles," and at the time was still part of Mexico. Here the Mormons created their own state of Deseret. It was a society in which self-interest was subordinated to the needs of the community. Indeed, Mormons found individual expression and fulfillment in contributing to the well-being of the whole. Their society had neither unemployment nor poverty and skilled workers could find full scope for their talents. In 1850 Deseret was incorporated into the American political system as the Utah Territory. Mormon distinctiveness gradually eroded except in faith and morals; even there concession to federal law necessitated renunciation of polygamy.

The Utopian Vision

Outright in rejecting the American social and economic order were various utopian colonies, which attracted thousands of seekers. These groups attempted to restore a sense of community based on shared labor and shared wealth. Some reflected daring acceptance of a new role for women by proclaiming sexual equality. Some were inspired by religious ideals; others were purely secular. The depression of 1837 stimulated interest in such experiments, but communitarian ideas were in the air both before and after the economic collapse. Even in times of prosperity some Americans questioned the moral validity of individualistic capitalism. Of the religious utopian colonies, two are noteworthy: the Shakers and the Oneida Community.

The Millennial Church, called the Shakers because of their bodily shaking and ritual dancing to shake out sin, was one of the most radical and successful of the utopian communities. Their English originator, "Mother" Ann Lee (c. 1736–1784), turned to a radical Quaker group, probably as a result of her unhappy marriage and the loss in infancy of her children. She claimed visions and spoke in tongues; she also repudiated sexuality, considering it the source of all sin. This teaching eventually gained institutional embodiment in the Shaker practice of celibacy and segregation of the sexes.

Because of considerable persecution in England, Lee and a handful of followers emigrated to New York State in 1774, where they began to evangelize widely and found communities. The newly opened lands of Ohio and Kentucky were advantageous for their endeavors and a

The Shaker almanac of 1885 shows Sisters at work.

Shaker Museum at Old Chatham, New York

number of colonies were settled in the frontier areas as well as in New England. After Lee's death in 1784, Joseph Meacham assumed leadership, gathered the members into several families for communal living, drafted the constitution of the society, and systematized Shaker doctrine.

The Shakers were in many ways a Protestant expression of the institutionalized *communitas* that monasticism had represented in Roman Catholicism. Shaker celibacy, communal ownership of goods, simplicity in lifestyle, subordination of the individual to the authority of ruling elders, and segregation were all parallels to the traditional Christian commitment to the collective cultivation of godliness and withdrawal from the world. The two dozen or so Shakers alive today reside at the communities of Canterbury, New Hampshire, and Sabbathday Lake, Maine.

A novel attempt to adjust sexuality to perfectionistic ideals was conceived by John Humphrey Noyes (1811–1886), founder of a communal group in Putney, Vermont. Enough opposition arose that he moved with his followers to Oneida, New York, and there founded the Oneida Community in 1848. Noyes advocated "complex marriage," a plan whereby every woman in the community was the wife of every man and vice versa. All sex relations, however, were regulated and quotas set for the number of offspring to be produced in a given year.

Noyes himself was a product of the Finney revivals and ardently embraced regeneration, perfection, and millennialism. But he passed beyond the individualism of most revivalists and promoted the inescapably social nature of religion. His theology was a potpourri of ideas relating to the possibility of human sinlessness, the superiority of Spirit-filled love over static moral law, and the progressive realization of the kindness of God in this world. Coupled with his religious zeal was a Yankee shrewdness in mundane affairs, reflected in the economic productivity of the Oneida Community, which prospered from manufacturing superior-quality animal traps and later, silverware.

No nineteenth-century American community would react kindly to such an unusual view of marriage or the notoriety surrounding it. In the face of increasingly hostile opposition from neighbors, Noyes, who had already withdrawn from active leadership of Oneida, felt compelled by 1879 to abandon the system of complex marriage. A year later the principle of economic communism was similarly repudiated, and the colony became a joint-stock company. This decline was part of the general abatement of revivalist and millennial enthusiasm in post-Civil-War America, a development discussed in succeeding chapters.

The communitarians fundamentally sought to attain the realization of the church as fellowship or *koinonia.* They tried to perpetuate permanently this fellowship of love and sanctification by expanding their church life to include the world and by restricting their world to the church. The very fact that the utopian experiments were tolerated at all indicates the increasing openness of American society in the nineteenth century, and a willingness to engage in social experimentation. But the tolerance was selective rather than general. Nineteenth-century America also witnessed the growth of the Roman Catholic Church as a countervailing movement, and with its rise intense outbreaks of nativistic, anti-Catholic hostility.

The Progress of Roman Catholicism

Two currents developed in American Catholicism during the nineteenth century. On the one hand, the Irish replaced the French and English in leadership positions, because the former numerically overwhelmed the latter during the enormous migrations resulting from the Irish potato famine (1845–1848). On the other hand, much of the Irish and Irish-American hierarchy that emerged remained faithful to the earlier tradition of the rapid Americanization of the church. Commonality of language aided the process. Catholics participated in political life, supported numerous Protestant reform movements, and at least flirted with the possibility of educating their children in public schools with released-time provisions for religious education. As a result of the unsuccessful revolutions of 1830 and 1848, thousands of immigrants from southern Germany also came to America, settling mainly in the country north of the Ohio River. Perhaps one-third of these Germans were Roman Catholic.

Of considerable import to American Catholicism was the re-

Elizabeth Seton, founder of the Sisters of Charity and the first native-born American to be named a saint.

emergence of the Jesuits (1814), who had been suppressed by the pope in 1773. Also noteworthy was the founding of the Order of Sisters of Charity at about the same time, and the organization of other female orders, such as the Order of Ursulines, the Order of Our Lady of Mount Carmel, and the Ladies of the Sacred Heart of Jesus, with their numerous urban schools, convents, and religious houses. By 1835 every large city in the United States contained houses of these orders.

Cathedral of the Assumption, Baltimore, where the first Plenary Council was held.

Meanwhile, year by year new dioceses were established: Charleston (1820); Richmond (1821); Cincinnati (1823); Mobile (1824); Saint Louis (1826); Detroit (1832); and between 1834 and 1847, Dubuque, Little Rock, Nashville, Pittsburgh, Milwaukee, Chicago, Hartford, Oregon City, Albany, Buffalo, and Cleveland, among others. The Roman Catholic Church claimed 3.1 million adherents in 1860, making it the largest denomination in the United States.

Some Catholic beliefs and customs in predominantly and dogmatically Protestant surroundings aroused fears in native groups. Anti-Catholicism in America was never purely religious, for social and economic factors aggravated suspicion of the stranger. Some of the recent arrivals could be less than orderly neighbors and also crowded the labor market. Yet this hardly justified the extreme reaction. Salacious stories, which followed a formula that has never completely died in Protestant American folklore, led to the burning of the Charlestown, Massachusetts, convent in 1836. The chartering of Saint Louis University by the State of Missouri aroused hysterical fears of Roman domination in the West. Catholic churches were burned in Philadelphia in 1844; in New York a show of armed defense by Catholic congregations frightened off would-be torchers. Opposition to Roman Catholicism gave rise to the Native American Party in 1837, an organization that sought to curtail immigration and require aliens to live in the country twenty-one years before becoming eligible for citizenship.

Despite efforts to thwart Roman Catholic gains, the church flourished. Indicative of stunning advance was the first Plenary Council of the hierarchy held at Baltimore in May 1852. Of the thirty-two bishops present, only nine were native-born. The council issued twenty-five decrees which dealt with such themes as parochial schools, administration of church property, and the standardization of discipline, but it ignored divisive issues such as slavery. The chief significance of the council was its recognition that Catholic problems were no longer purely provincial but national in scope.

Part 4

Years of Midpassage

(1861–1916)

10

War and Expiation

Two earnest publications distributed in 1851 highlight the hiatus that the slavery debate had wrought in American Christianity. In that year Harriet Beecher Stowe, daughter of Lyman Beecher and wife of theologian Calvin E. Stowe, added to the popular denunciation of slavery with her best seller, *Uncle Tom's Cabin*, a thoroughgoing indictment of the nation for harboring such an evil. Her character, Uncle Tom (who during the 1960s received undeserved fire as the symbol of toadyism toward whites), served as a thinly disguised Christ figure, whose greatest triumph came through his unmerited suffering and death. The South resented characterization as crucifiers.

In contrast to *Uncle Tom's Cabin,* a thorough biblical defense of slavery was penned by the Reverend James Henley Thornwell, a prominent Presbyterian theologian. Following a typical line of reasoning, Thornwell observed that the church's "only argument is *thus it is written.*" Then, appealing to Holy Writ, he declared,

> The Scriptures not only fail to condemn slavery, they as distinctly sanction it as any other condition of man. The Church was formally organized in the family of a slaveholder [Abraham]; the relation was divinely regulated among the chosen people of God [Israel]; and the peculiar duties of the parties are inculcated under the Christian economy [Philemon].

Consequently, to call slavery sinful was in effect to reject the Bible in favor of a rationalistic mode of thought. "Opposition to slavery," concluded Thornwell, "has never been the offspring of the Bible."

Slavery and the Conflicts of Faith

In retrospect it is evident that much of the antagonism between North and South stemmed from differing definitions of slavery. Northerners presented an abstract definition based on the moral philosophies of William Ellery Channing, William Whewell, and Francis Wayland. They viewed slavery as ownership of one man by another and consequently, the absorption of the humanity of one individual into the will and power of another. The southern perspective, based on the thought of the Scottish philosopher William Paley, saw slavery as "the obligation to labour for another man . . . independently of the provisions of a contract." Under the terms of this definition, the master had a right "not to the *man* but to his labour." Moreover, the master's right to the slave's labor did not deny to him the possibility of moral, intellectual, and religious cultivation and, therefore, did not deprive him of his humanity. The purpose of the southern argument was to show that slaveholding in that region was not immoral. Defenders of the practice attempted to stop abolitionists from talking about slavery in the abstract and to focus attention on slavery as it was perceived to exist in the South.

The churches obviously faced an extremely difficult dilemma. Honorable, ethical, God-fearing people as well as self-seeking, egotistical types were on both sides of the question. With the full politicizing of the issue by 1840, denominations felt compelled to take a stand. Some church bodies, such as the Congregationalists and Unitarians, maintained their unity because of being located largely in the antislavery North. Quakers too, both North and South, opposed slavery and therefore escaped schism. Other denominations, such as the Episcopalians and Lutherans, took no political stance, determined to remain disentangled from political matters. The Roman Catholic hierarchy was unfavorably disposed toward slavery, but wished for the passage of time and due process of law to bring about its termination. Thus, these churches did not separate until forced to by war itself in 1861. When the conflict ended their reunion was natural and spontaneous.

The Presbyterians, Methodists, and Baptists, however, became embroiled in the slavery question, which strained ecclesiastical unity. Initially they held to the doctrine of noninterference. The compromise announced at the South Carolina Methodist Conference in 1838 was repeated in most other church synods:

Aurora College Library

This Adventist church, built in 1867, typifies the churches of the Civil War period.

> Whereas we hold that the subject of slavery in these United States is not one proper for the action of the church, but is exclusively appropriate to the civil authorities—Therefore, *Resolved* that this conference will not intermeddle with it in any way, farther than to express our regret that it has ever been introduced in any form into any one of the judicatories of the church.

This uneasy position lasted for only a few anxious decades. As tensions deepened the largest Protestant denominations were torn by schism.

The Methodist Episcopal Church was among the first to be rent. By 1843 the 1,200 Methodist clergy owned 1,500 slaves, and 25,000 church members owned 208,000 more. Although northern abolitionists had tried unsuccessfully throughout the thirties to gain a majority in the General Conference, it was 1844 before they succeeded. The symbolic vote on slavery actually centered on Bishop James Andrew of Georgia, who had inherited some slaves through bequest and by marriage. The antislavery delegates insisted that he manumit his slaves or resign from office; the southern delegates replied that the bishop had broken no regulation of the church. After eleven days of heated debate the northern interests won two to one, and the southern delegates drafted a proposal for two General Conferences which was approved. Although relations between the two new denominations were amicable at first, strife over the allegiance of the border states and lawsuits concerning property rights heightened the strain and assured a prolonged separation. Methodists of the North and South did not reunite until 1939. The smaller antislavery Wesleyan Methodist Church, founded in 1843, never did return to the larger denominational fold.

Fear that radical abolitionists might gain control of the missionary societies precipitated the rift among Baptists. Despite the persistent antislavery agitation of Baptist abolitionists, it was apparent at the 1844 Triennial Convention that the moderates still controlled the floor. Resolutions were passed which, in effect, left the slavery question up to the individual conscience; nevertheless, rumors circulated that the northern delegates were planning a dissolution of the organization. The crucial vote again involved an individual. Southern churchmen were incensed by the rejection of a slaveholding missionary by the board of the Home Mission Society. In response the board set forth its conviction clearly: "One thing is certain, we can never be a party to any arrangement which would imply approbation of slavery." Without further ado the southern state conventions and auxiliary foreign-missions societies formally seceded from the national body, forming themselves into the Southern Baptist Convention in 1845. Within a century this new group was to become the largest American Protestant church body.

The Old School and the New School Presbyterian churches, having divided in 1837 over theological issues, sought to muffle the slavery controversy so as to prevent further cleavage. The New School group, located mainly in the North, succeeded in doing so for a time, but it finally split in 1857 when its assembly repudiated the doctrine that slavery is "an ordinance of God" and is "Scriptural and right." Through astute diplomacy the Old School Presbyterians forestalled any break until the onset of war.

The significance of these schisms for the nation's immediate political future should not be underestimated. One by one the institutional links between North and South were dissolving. Most historians agree that the ecclesiastical divisions of the forties and fifties paved the way for the political disintegration of the sixties; some even suggest that they were the chief cause of the final break. Attempts at compromise proved to be vain and ephemeral strategies for escaping the hard responsibility of decision. By 1860 the crisis was at hand. Even the venerable Democratic Party had split, opening the way for a northern Republican to become president. As soon as the presidential election returns assured Abraham Lincoln's victory, southern legislatures summoned state conventions to formally declare the dissolution of the nation. On April 12, 1861, Fort Sumter was shelled and the Civil War commenced.

The Churches amid Civil War and Reconstruction

The long agitation carried on in the churches over slavery had prepared them to take definite stands when hostilities ignited. And no American war aroused more unanimous support from the churches. In both North and South, preachers marched with the troops—some to bear arms, others as chaplains. To the common soldier and his family the war was not an abstract debate over constitutional interpretation, but a personal matter of survival. From the confused and incomplete war records it appears that about 2.5 million men served in the two armies. Of these, 622,000 perished—a death toll of nearly 25 percent. Disease was rampant, payment miserable, supplies poor. In North and South the churches gave their full spiritual support for the waging of a conflict both sides believed to be under divine control. The North fought initially to preserve the Union and later to free the slaves; the South to defend local institutions against the encroachment of federal power.

Chaplains served in the field and in the hospitals on both sides. They counseled homesick and frightened soldiers, wrote to families, comforted the sick and wounded, buried the dead, and tried to add some spiritual order to the chaos that gripped so many individual lives. Some even organized regimental churches and conducted protracted revival meetings during long periods in camp.

Ministers from all denominations were always welcomed into the military camps. In the South, Episcopalian Robert E. Lee and Presbyterian Thomas J. (Stonewall) Jackson believed fervently that their victories were the Lord's doing and encouraged ministers to hold prayer meetings among their troops. One of Lincoln's informants expressed concern to the president that the southern soldiers were "praying with a great deal more earnestness" than the Union troops. In the winter of 1863–1864 a great revival broke out among the Confederate soldiers at Orange Courthouse, Virginia. Estimates suggest that perhaps one hundred thousand to two hundred thousand military men in both armies were converted during the war and many more strongly affected by religion in some way.

A number of northern clergymen used their influence to solicit foreign support for the Union cause, which dramatically gained in moral purpose following the Emancipation Proclamation of January 1, 1863. Roman Catholic Archbishop John Hughes went to Europe at Lincoln's request to win good will for the Union, and Henry Ward Beecher of Plymouth Church in Brooklyn visited England in 1863 for the same purpose. In the face of irritating heckling he addressed mass meetings at Liverpool and Manchester.

The northern churches also responded with organized charitable institutions during the war. In 1861 the United States Sanitary Commission was formed under the leadership of Unitarian minister Henry Bellows. Commission workers cared for the sick and wounded, provided food for soldiers, and drove ambulance wagons. The United States Christian Commission, organized in the same year, grew out of the YMCA with the purpose of distributing both religious and secular books to word-hungry soldiers. Voluntary workers also opened libraries and reading rooms in hospitals and army camps throughout the North. The American Bible Society determined that each Confederate as well as each Union soldier should be supplied with either a Bible or New Testament. By 1864 the society had distributed close to one million Bibles among both armies.

As the war progressed and Union troops pushed farther into the South, the numbers of blacks dependent upon the care and protection of military commanders increased. This urgent need led to the founding of numerous freedmen's relief societies and departments of Negro affairs to provide food, clothing, and shelter; search out employment possibilities for newly freed blacks; and organize schools for their improvement. In 1865 Congress finally established the Freedmen's Bureau to discharge this enormous national responsibility.

All of these efforts were either spearheaded or supported by church people, both ministerial and lay. Ecclesiastical endorsement of the war was overwhelming but not entire. Some abolitionists felt that Lincoln acted too slowly in freeing the slaves of the Confederacy. There were also pockets of dissent in the pacifist denominations of Quakers and Mennonites. When the federal government resorted to conscription in 1863, most northern Quakers declared themselves conscientious objectors, refusing to fight or pay war taxes. After considerable debate provision was made for them to do alternative service. The South was less understanding of the objector, probably because the need for men was more acute in the Confederacy. Nevertheless pacifists were finally exempted from military service if they paid five hundred dollars or provided a substitute.

During the years of war and the reconstruction to follow, Americans reflected on what terrible events had overcome their great nation. In consequence of the fratricidal rupture America could no longer so confidently promote herself as a shining example to the nations. Evasion of responsibility for the tragedy was impossible; no other country was involved and the instruments of peace were cast aside to allow the war machine to settle differences between brothers. The self-righteous prayers offered up by both sides reduced God to their own sectional interests. Some, like Lincoln, however, were self-critical and reluctant to make this reduction. Several weeks before his assassination, in his second inaugural address, the tormented leader shared his insights:

> Both [sides] read the same Bible, and pray to the same God; and each invokes his aid against the other. It may seem strange that any men should dare to ask a just God's assistance in wringing their bread from the sweat of other men's faces; but let us judge not, that we be not judged. The prayers of both could not be answered. That of neither has been answered fully.

Theologian Horace Bushnell and church historian Philip Schaff echoed these sentiments and developed them further. The war, they said, was a divine act of judgment for the collective guilt of the American people. Believing that without the shedding of blood there is no remission of sins, they viewed the conflict as a sacrificial and cleansing tragedy with the potential of not only preserving the nation but regenerating it as well. This idea, along with Lincoln's martyrdom (a microcosm of the larger war), and the rise of Memorial Day, Robert E. Lee Day, and Lincoln's Birthday as national and quasinational holidays, found its way into the rhetoric of civil and religious celebrations and provided unifying symbolism for a fractured nation, calling it back to its proper vocation and ideals.

The Churches, the South, and the Black Church

Given the intensity of moral and religious struggle that marked the Civil War, sectional hostility persisted after the end of military conflict. Dominant southern churchmen and the ex-Confederate leadership in general sought to restore pre-1860 conditions; except, of course, for the institution of slavery. The conduct of the northern armies in the South all but eliminated the likelihood of the Presbyterians, Methodists, and Baptists reuniting with their northern counterparts. The result was the consolidation of the southern churches into a separate and sectional pattern that came to be characterized by revivalism, orthodoxy, vigorous foreign missions, and an identifiable alliance with southern culture and mores.

There was no full agreement among northern churchmen as to the punishment deserved by the South. A few, like Henry Ward Beecher, encouraged unconditional conciliation; most, like Theodore Tilton, Beecher's successor as editor of the *Independent*, chose a more vengeful way, referring to Richmond, for instance, as "Babylon the Great." Republican pastors regularly used their pulpits to advocate black suffrage, aid for the freedmen, and strict measures for the "apostates" of the Confederacy. Some northern Christians felt called by God to purge the southern churches of their depravity, sending missionaries to those bereft of leadership. Such an approach did little to heal a fractured relationship and Southerners greeted these missionaries with scorn and bitterness.

Northern Protestant denominations provided much of the idealistic zeal and political support for the radical Reconstruction program enacted by Congress in 1867 for the South, a reform effort undergirded by the presence of an occupation army. Despite the charges of corruption and mismanagement that can be leveled against some of the state regimes during Reconstruction, the period from 1867 to 1877 was one of significant achievement. On the governmental level, enactment of the Thirteenth, Fourteenth and Fifteenth Amendments to the Constitution, as well as numerous laws aiding the freedmen and promoting civil rights, laid the foundation for the civil-rights breakthroughs of the mid-twentieth century. Also, a generous outpouring of northern philanthropy flowed to the former slaves. Hundreds of home missionaries and teachers, many of them women, dispatched by the American Missionary Association (founded in Albany, 1846), labored amidst ridicule and privation to bring education and opportunity to the blacks. Indeed, all the black colleges founded before 1900, and most of their faculties, derived from missionary efforts mounted in the North.

Gradually interest in the plight of the freedmen subsided, both in the sanctuary and the Congress, with the result that other political and economic priorities usurped attention and weakened federal commitment to justice for the former slaves. In general, American society did not rise to the moral challenge presented by emancipation. After 1877 the South regained complete home rule, and by party organization, legislation, and coercion, gradually disenfranchised the blacks. On the other hand, the ex-slaves were able to construct a totally self-determining institutional structure within the black churches.

During the colonial period, Christianization of slaves was often opposed by masters fearing that the New Testament promises of

The Quaker Collection, Haverford College Library

Freedmen's School, founded by Friends at Southland, Arkansas, 1864–1924.

liberation might be interpreted in a literal, political sense. Members of the Anglican Society for the Propagation of the Gospel in Foreign Parts (SPG) led most of the evangelism among blacks. Their efforts were largely unsuccessful; many workers were inept and the rigid, liturgical style of Anglicanism failed to appeal to most blacks. Although the Great Awakening and the Second Awakening unleashed democratizing religious forces, reaching both whites and blacks, the Baptists and Methodists who harvested the fruits of revival soon yielded to accommodation with local and regional mores.

Some slaves, under close supervision by their masters, attended church services during the ante-bellum period, but were usually assigned to separate galleries. At the same time an "invisible institution" was arising among the slaves, a genuine folk religion composed of Christian elements adapted in texture and tone to the new practitioners: the slaves' counterchurch. Its theology was expressed through spirituals, songs of longing and hope for both heaven and present liberation. Preaching was more exhortation than discourse, and the call-response pattern characteristic of African ceremonies found new expression in the active participation of slave congregations while being exhorted by their own preachers. With a few exceptions, black churches did not emerge as independent institutions before the Civil War. The emotional and demonstrative character of Baptist and Methodist worship had early captured black allegiance, but racial tensions prevented blacks from being assimilated into these parent churches.

The first known black church in America was a Baptist congregation at Silver Bluff, South Carolina, in 1775. Other black Baptist churches followed in Savannah (1788), Boston (1805), New York (1807), Philadelphia (1809), and many smaller cities. When white Methodists in Philadelphia tried to restrict their black worshipers, the blacks separated and eventually formed the African Methodist Episcopal Zion Church in 1821. Both of these groups grew rapidly following the Civil War. Some urban blacks did prefer to join white middle-class denominations such as Presbyterian; but most found that their own denominations offered both a more appropriate form of worship and an autonomy denied them on the basis of numbers, if not because of overt discrimination, in the predominantly white churches. What had necessarily been extraecclesiastical religion during the period of slavery was now merging into social and belief structures characteristic of full-fledged denominations.

Black churches served important social as well as religious functions. Like the parish churches of the Middle Ages, they were convenient community centers. There blacks could find fellowship without white intrusion and manage their affairs in their own way, and there men and women of talent could rise to leadership. As W. E. B. DuBois would later note, the black church was "the first social institution fully controlled by black men in America."

Commentators have described the black church in the late nine-

Billy Graham Center Museum

Worship services in an early black church.

teenth century as marked by overt emotionalism, theological naïveté, other-worldly escapism, and primitivistic superstition. Such features were, of course, present, yet a more important perception is this: the old spirit of evangelical revivalism flourished in black Christianity in America. Although exaggerated or distorted, the central core of the revivalistic movement was cultivated by the black church: a sense of divine immediacy, spontaneity of individual response, an urge toward personal holiness, and the redress of present injustices. These fellowships held unswervingly to the Bible as the sole source of religious certitude. Their leaders and ministers often knew little and cared less about creedal subtleties, alien philosophies, or the conflicting claims of science, but the basics remained anchored in orthodox Christianity.

Emancipation allowed the black man and woman to come out from under the condescending tutelage of white paternalism into the trying but promising realm of independent thought and action. Despite the obstacles the ex-slave fought hard to see himself or herself in a new light, as a person of worth, value, and potential. Some sought for identity by tracing their roots and urging a return to Africa because, as one wrote, "Africa is our home, and is the one place that offers us freedom and manhood." Others pursued education as a way to offer a uniquely black contribution to American society. The majority labored on farms or in factories and warehouses, seeking to make their peace with their adoptive country through the gradual effects of daily contact and common life. In the midst of these struggles the black churches became shelters, shielding their members from a hostile social climate and nurturing them in the desire for personal development as well as faith in the message of the risen Christ.

11

Evangelism and Holiness

The last three decades of the nineteenth century may well be termed the critical period that precipitated Protestantism's demise as the dominant influence in American culture. The new economic, social, and intellectual forces reverberating through the nation are now well recognized. Business and society consolidated into ever larger units. Industrial towns and cities burgeoned with new populations drawn from both the adjacent countryside and overseas. The Roman Catholic and Jewish faiths practiced by many of these new city dwellers increased religious pluralism. Unimaginable fortunes and equally generous philanthropy arose alongside unanticipated working-class squalor. At the same time the thoroughly orthodox and conservative theologies that undergirded most of the great American denominations came under attack by controversial ideas filtering in from Europe. This chapter discusses how American revivalism adapted to shifting parish circumstances while it continued the quest for holy living. Succeeding chapters will examine respectively the concurrent intellectual revolution and the response of the churches to urbanization.

Urban Parishes and City Revivalism

The concentration of upwardly mobile churchgoers in large, affluent city congregations led to a respectability and genteel piety that had not usually characterized Presbyterians, Methodists, and Baptists earlier in the century. The informality and crudity of frontier religion had metamorphosed into urban gentility. Robed choirs concertized beside robed clergymen, who were better educated and credentialed than their ministerial fathers and grandfathers. Hundreds of thousands of donated dollars underwrote large and beautiful downtown churches. Whether Romanesque, latter-day Gothic, or eclectic in architecture, these expensive masonry edifices graced the center of every city of even mild consequence.

Successful laymen assumed increasing initiative in leading congregational affairs. Administrative efficiency, the professionalization of denominational leadership, more extensive budgets and programs all regularized the ebb and flow of parish life. Even the old camp meeting gave way to the summer Bible conference with its culturally uplifting lectures, shuffleboard, and comfortable latticed cottages. Emphasis persisted, however, on the need for evangelical Christian conversion and purity of life. In fact, a new style of urban evangelism unfolded in the person and ministry of Dwight Lyman Moody (1837–1899).

In certain ways D. L. Moody epitomized his times: the hinterland childhood with his poor and widowed mother in Northfield, Massa-

The Illinois Street Church, founded by D. L. Moody. The church burned in the Chicago fire.

chusetts, where his education ended by age thirteen; his move as a late teen from village to city, first to his uncle's shoe store in Boston, and then on to the lusty Chicago of 1856; his quick prosperity in the business world as a salesman of shoes for the urban masses. His energetic and entrepreneurial personality probably would have insured him a tycoon's fortune, but his quiet conversion while he was still in the East motivated him to shun personal wealth and devote his enormous vigor instead to God's business. By age twenty-five, Moody's part-time avocation as a YMCA enthusiast and self-styled urban missionary became his full-time vocation; he never returned to selling shoes.

Throughout the 1860s Moody's ministry was not primarily preaching. He channeled his energies into recruiting up to fifteen hundred drifters and indigents off Chicago streets into his Sunday school, which in 1863 grew into the Illinois Street Church, nondenominational and independent. Working for the United States Christian Commission during the war years, he tirelessly served the encamped soldiers. As the driving force behind the Chicago YMCA he aggressively pursued a host of projects, financing his ventures by raising astonishing amounts of money from rich friends and supporters such as Marshall Field, Cyrus McCormick, and George Armour.

It was from a British rather than an American pulpit that Moody's evangelistic career was launched. As a substitute preacher while in London on YMCA business, he elicited overwhelming response to his closing invitation to faith. Invited to return to Britain, he and musician Ira D. Sankey (1840–1908) undertook what became a two-year evangelistic campaign through Scotland and England which reached upwards of three million hearers between 1873 and 1875. The pair arrived back in America as internationally acclaimed public figures. There followed five years of unparalleled revival meetings across America from Brooklyn and Philadelphia to San Francisco.

These years marked the peak of Moody's evangelistic ministry, for thereafter he concentrated on founding the Northfield (Mass.) Seminary for girls and, close by, the Mount Hermon School for boys, Moody Bible Institute in Chicago, and on conferences and student work. Although he raised the equivalent of several fortunes to fund his endeavors, his estate consisted of five hundred dollars he didn't know he had.

Moody's broad and nondenominational gospel message won the endorsement at one time or another of practically every denomination except the Roman Catholics, Unitarians, and Universalists. He cared not a whit for formal discussion of theological issues. "My theology! I didn't know I had any," he once exclaimed. "I wish you would tell me what my theology is." Unschooled since his thirteenth year, he never sought ordination or became a licensed clergyman. Yet, he and Sankey rejuvenated the fires of revival and conveyed God's love for sinners to millions through their urban, mass evangelistic crusades.

The manner and message of Moody appealed especially to the displaced country folk who were abandoning farms and villages for the lure of urban opportunity. Many, understandably, felt uncomfortable in the bustling, impersonal city. Moody's promise of salvation and eternal life, based on simple faith in Jesus Christ, provided a vital source of stability and comfort to thousands of converts. He spoke with great simplicity and directness, translating the gospel into the literary style of contemporary popular magazines, which were deeply tinged with Victorian sentimentality. His only goal was that sinners be saved. To continue in their new faith, converts were urged to join a church—any church. And join they did; church membership expanded more rapidly than the population.

Historians have noted that Finney's revivalism belonged to the age of Andrew Jackson and Lyman Beecher, whereas Moody's belonged to the age of Andrew Carnegie and P. T. Barnum. His preaching revealed both his own sales experience and the burgeoning business climate of Victorian America. He displayed remarkable skill in organizing his campaigns in accordance with urban conditions. Committees of prominent ministers and laymen took charge of planning; and it was the laymen, usually successful industrialists and business leaders, who headed the finance and executive subcommittees, leaving to the clergy the lesser functions.

Moody could sound like a businessman on the platform. At times he spoke like a salesman of salvation. A businesslike decorum characterized his campaigns; the impromptu emotional outbursts of the old-time revivals were now inadmissible under the watchful eye of the urban press. Moody thought nothing of interrupting his sermon to ask ushers to remove unrestrained enthusiasts.

The list of Moody's sponsors reads like a roster of tycoons: in Chicago, Field, McCormick, and Armour; in Philadelphia, Jay Cooke and John Wanamaker; in New York, Cornelius Vanderbilt II and J. P. Morgan; in Boston, Amos Lawrence and Joseph Story. One cannot judge the motives of these men and, doubtlessly, they were moved in part by simple piety. But the business community was also uneasy about the danger to social stability from what were often called "the unchurched masses" of the rapidly growing cities. Moody's own attitude toward economic and social problems was explicitly and vigorously conservative. Although he himself was a lifelong worker for good causes, especially Christian education, Moody, like his fellows, remained aloof from any discussion of the structural ills of society. He optimistically believed that the improvement of society would be effected by individual conversions.

From an alcoholic past in rural Georgia emerged Sam Jones (1847–1906), to become Moody's southern counterpart. After promising his dying father that he would reform, he was converted under his Methodist grandfather's preaching and became a circuit rider for the North Georgia Conference of the Methodist Episcopal Church, South, in 1872. Eminently successful in winning converts in Georgia before 1880, he was thereafter invited to conduct revivals in major southern cities and became an evangelist of national prominence, the "Moody of the South."

Jones's messages, expounded in the colorful language and style of southern hill country, proved highly entertaining to city audiences unaccustomed to the jargon and nuances peculiar to his locality. Like Moody's, his was the simple gospel, shorn of theological elaboration and radically practical in its impact: turn from sin, be saved, and join the crusade against urban wickedness. Jones's revivals were a significant factor in the urban recovery of the Methodist Episcopal Church, South, especially after E. O. Excell joined him as choirmaster and gospel song writer.

Moody and Jones were but two of a host of professional evangelists promoting revival during these years. Reuben A. Torrey (1856–1928) and J. Wilbur Chapman (1859–1918) had Moody's personal approval of their mass revival meetings. Torrey, an ordained Congregational minister, was something of an oddity among revivalists at the time. His strict theological conservatism belied his university education at Yale and his studies in historical criticism of the Bible at Leipzig. He later became superintendent of Moody Bible Institute. Rodney "Gypsy" Smith, an English-born revivalist, delighted in capitalizing on his gypsy origins, attracting curious crowds and appearing with his songstress daughter in native costume. In a series of meetings held in Boston in 1906, he is said to have won 2,550 "decisions" for Christ. It was becoming customary to judge a revivalist's success by the number of "decision cards" turned in during the campaign.

As a whole, this new revivalism represented a significant deviation from the theological content of preceding revivals. Whether this was due to the urban setting or the general antisupernatural drift of American thought, one cannot judge. But the change of motif was apparent, even to outside observers. In an 1876 editorial for *The Nation* entitled "Moody and Sankey," Arthur Segwick, a sympathetic observer, pondered what was "new" in the new revivalism:

> The only peculiarity that we have been able to detect in it is, that in the present case the revivalists, accommodating themselves to the spirit of the times, have left out of their programme the use of the awful warnings of future damnation which used to play such a prominent part in their appeals. In the services at the Hippodrome [a large Brooklyn auditorium rented from P. T. Barnum] the sinner is not frightened or browbeaten. He is affectionately entreated to enter into the Kingdom of heaven. It is represented to him to be an easy matter—a matter not of ritual or works, but of exertion of the will. The revivalists' God is not the just Jehovah of the Puritans, holding the scales even and meting out rewards and punishment with an impartial and unpitying hand . . . He is, on the contrary, a mild and loving God, forgiving and pardoning to the last; a God who cares little for corrections of dogma so that the heart be pure. . . .

To the lonely crowds of America's urban centers the revival service offered a welcome release from monotony without the penalty of undue reprimand. The crowds, the hymnbook vendors, the singing, the general hubbub and excitement encouraged many to come and be warmed by an evening of participation. Revivalists often advertised in the amusement pages of the newspapers. Although they were deeply concerned with the evils of city life, their primary burden was to evangelize the unchurched. The Christian social vision, once so pervasive throughout Protestant evangelicalism, faded quietly into the background until its reassertion in the social gospel toward the century's end.

Holiness: Reviving an Old Tradition

A parallel force to the urban revivals in the late nineteenth century was the wave of Holiness teaching that rippled across the denominations, creating complicated crosscurrents and distinctions, which profoundly affected evangelical theology and alignments. An accompanying interest in the Holy Spirit is evidenced by the prolific writing on the subject.

From the time of John Wesley, revivalism in the English-speaking world had been periodically accompanied in varying degrees by his teaching about Christian perfection: the view that it is possible for the Christian to live free from all *known* sin. Wesley's unique theological contribution was his doctrine of entire sanctification or the "second blessing." Conversion, as with all evangelicals, was the first and indispensable step in salvation. However, the Christian could and should move onward to a state of purity of life in which all temptation

Jenks Memorial Collection, Aurora College Library

Traveling evangelists spread the message of salvation.

United Methodist Church, General Commission on Archives and History

A Methodist camp meeting at Sing Sing, New York.

Jenks Memorial Collection, Aurora College Library

The practice of holding camp meetings continued into the twentieth century. Pictured is an Adventist camp meeting in the early 1900s.

to sin would be not only conquered but also removed, usually through a dramatic experience giving power to then maintain a condition of sinless perfection. Wesley's circuit riders spread these ideas and Finney gave them systematic and institutional expression, if somewhat qualified.

These Holiness teachings were a radical departure from the Reformed and Puritan roots of evangelicalism, which denied the possibility of earthly perfection and declared the Christian life an intense warfare between the old sinful nature and the new regenerated nature. The doctrinal combination of Arminianism, which allowed a measure of free cooperation on the part of the individual in the process of salvation, with entire sanctification, perhaps provided an irresistibly optimistic package to the many Americans who were inclined to think rather extravagantly about both their own and their nation's possibilities. Church historian Vinson Synan sees even a similarity between the ethical ideals of Ralph Waldo Emerson and Henry David Thoreau and those of the early Holiness groups. In his view, Holiness was a kind of "evangelical transcendentalism" that thrived in the idealistic and growing America.

Within Methodism, both North and South, arose a desire for a new Holiness revival to relieve the spiritual stagnation of the post-Civil-War

HANNAH WHITALL SMITH.

Presbyterian Historical Society

period. In 1870, the bishops of the southern branch called for a reassertion of sanctification. A similar conviction led Methodists in the North to reorganize camp meetings. The National Camp Meeting Association for the Promotion of Holiness was founded at Vineland, New Jersey, in 1867, inspired by Phoebe Palmer. Although sponsored primarily by Methodists, the movement was interdenominational in character and became national in scope.

Reformed circles, from which the spontaneous revival of 1857 and 1858 had received impetus, continued to be affected by Holiness teaching. Two 1858 converts, Robert Pearsall Smith and his wife Hannah Whitall Smith, became Presbyterians and worked to spread Holiness ideas on both sides of the Atlantic. With William E. Boardman, a Presbyterian clergyman and author of *The Higher Christian Life* (1859), the Smiths went to London in 1873 during the Moody-Sankey revival. In its wake, they organized a remarkable series of meetings culminating at Oxford in 1874, in which they taught the need for a second work of grace, sanctification, following salvation. Mrs. Smith's book, *The Christian's Secret of a Happy Life* (1875), became a classic on the subject. From this beginning the English Keswick movement was born, but with its own style of Holiness teaching; sanctification is a *process* beginning in the absolute surrender of self to be filled with the Holy Spirit at all times (or perhaps many times)—the "victorious" or "higher" life—but not the eradication of the sinful nature in the Wesleyan sense.

The Keswick teaching traveled back across the Atlantic to have pervasive influence on American evangelicalism for many decades. Indeed, the personal experience and preaching of Moody, Torrey, and other prominent evangelical leaders reflected much of the Keswick Holiness motif.

Predictably, the Holiness movement drew criticism from leaders of organized Protestantism, many of whom were identified with the Methodist church. As the century closed, moderates among the Methodists became inclined toward the "churchly" position that sanctification is a gradual process, a notion somewhat akin to Horace Bushnell's concept of Christian nurture. Others were strongly attracted to the more radical position that sanctification, like traditional evangelical conversion, is a dramatic experience that leaves the individual purified and transformed in no uncertain fashion. It was natural that advocates of Holiness, finding themselves ignored or rejected, should retreat into increasingly exclusive fellowship. By the 1890s, many of Holiness persuasion were organizing themselves into separate denominations. Interestingly, members of these new denominations were predominantly from the lower economic classes, just as the Methodists had been when they seceded from the more privileged Anglican church.

Typical of the emergent Holiness groups was their stated desire to be "nondenominational," stressing what they believed to be basic apostolic Christianity. From Methodism came Phineas Bresee, a minister, and J. P. Widney, a wealthy layman, to develop such a Holiness movement in southern California. This movement centered in the Church of the Nazarene, which opened in Los Angeles in 1895. From this congregation came numerous satellite churches, which ultimately united with several small sects to become a new national denomination by 1908. The Nazarenes reflected their Weselyan roots in their conservatism, revivalism, and perfectionism. Another nondenominational fellowship in New York, stressing missions, Holiness, and divine healing, was created by former Presbyterian A. B. Simpson in 1881. In time it also became a new denomination, the Christian and Missionary Alliance. A similar pattern of evolution is identifiable in the history of the Church of God (Anderson, Indiana), the Missionary Church Association, the Metropolitan Church Association, and other Holiness sects. The schismatic tendency precipitated before 1900 by the issue of sanctification was to be exacerbated immediately after 1900 by the new movement within Holiness marked by glossolalia—speaking in tongues as evidence of baptism by the Holy Spirit.

Holiness teaching received tremendous impetus from the migration of the Salvation Army from England to America in 1880, only two years after its founding by William Booth. Led first by Ballington Booth and

Nazarene Publishing House

Interior of the first Nazarene tabernacle, Los Angeles.

later by his sister Evangeline, both children of the founder, the American Army grew rapidly as it both aided and evangelized the urban poor. It too evolved from religious welfare agency into another denomination based on Wesleyan perfectionistic doctrine, expounded in the writings of the Booths, especially Catherine, William's wife.

The piety that emerged in the contexts of the Holiness movement and urban revivalism was best expressed not in formal theology, but in

Salvation Army Archives and Research Center

William Booth, founder of the Salvation Army.

Aurora College Library

The Advent Christian Church of Mount Vincent, Oregon, in 1888—a contrast to the trend of urbanization.

the new hymnody of this period, accessible to all through a series of published gospel songs which gained rapid popularity and tremendous sales. Besides Sankey's compositions for the Moody meetings, the more than two thousand hymns of the blind Fanny J. Crosby seemed to be on every lip. In simple lyrics, her themes of consecration and surrender to the rapturous love of Jesus presented the gospel and its consolations in romanticized images centering on the emotions of the singer. In association with William H. Doane she produced "Safe in the Arms of Jesus," "Near the Cross," and "Draw Me Nearer"; with William J. Kirkpatrick, "Redeemed" and "He Hideth My Soul"; with John R. Sweney, "My Savior First of All" and "Tell Me the Story of Jesus"—great favorites all. Philip Bliss and England's Frances Havergal also contributed heavily to the popular hymnody.

Post-Civil-War America saw the first overt signs that its spiritual foundation, once provided by a confident and aggressive Protestant majority, was shifting in new directions. After 1865, the problems of Reconstruction, immigration, urbanization, and natural science consorted to erode the reigning evangelical consensus, creating a climate in which dissenters found no united front to attack and participants were increasingly pressed into arenas of noninfluence. The public gradually began to recognize that a nation supposedly agrarian was, in fact, irrevocably committed to an urban-industrial motif. The old simplicities were gone, or going, and complexity characterized the era. It was an age of change; change in population, economic structures, political policies, and growing change in belief. The modern American mind was awakening.

12

The Churches and the New Intellectual Climate

Astute observers of human behavior have long recognized that ideas have consequences. Perhaps at no time in its long and varied history did the church face such a barrage of new and unsettling intellectual formulations as in the nineteenth century, and for American Christianity, the last third of that century in particular.

When we discuss the role of ideas in history it is important to recognize their place in affecting the larger society. Novel ideas usually originate among the educated elite, for they have the literacy and leisure to entertain thought as an activity for its own sake. At first these ideas affect only "intellectuals." But being of dynamic rather than static quality, the ideas begin to percolate from the intellectuals to the middle masses as the media take up their propagation. Eventually the original idea is modified and sometimes even vulgarized. For example, the typical man on the street may be unable to quote a line from Jean-Paul Sartre or Albert Camus, but the *idea* of existentialism which they expounded and its attitudinal implications have reached the common man and affected the way he views life and the universe. This tendency is also clearly shown by the manner in which many nineteenth-century businessmen applied the idea of evolution to the economic sphere of life.

America has been remarkably accommodating to new ideas

throughout its history. While the church denominations maintained their distinct theological traditions they also learned to tolerate other perspectives, for America has a unique heritage of religious pluralism. European-born Enlightenment thought found its initial American home in the minds of many of the founding fathers. But they affirmed a generally moderate Enlightenment rather than a skeptical view, as prevailed in France. As more radical strains of modern thought continued to flow from Europe, the first quarter of the nineteenth century became something of a watershed for theological and philosophical influences in America. Previously, British sources were by far the most important. After 1815, however, German influences increased, and were not lessened for being mediated by English and Scottish thinkers like Samuel Taylor Coleridge and Thomas Carlyle. In addition, many students, unwilling to settle for second-hand German philosophy, undertook the long trip to Germany to study in its renowned universities. In all, some ten thousand Americans matriculated in German schools between the War of 1812 and the First World War. The German ideal of detached, rationalistic scholarship was thus imported to American colleges and helped undercut confidence in the Scriptures and orthodox theology.

Furthermore, German romanticism, with its emphasis on subjective and intuitive truth, directly contributed to the rise of American theological liberalism. No one had previously conceived the knowing process except in terms of the object known; now the *subject* or knower came powerfully into the picture. Subjectivism holds that the mind partly creates the external reality it grasps. Consequently, truth, as reality, differs for each person perceiving it. Such romantic ideas frequently found resonance with the nineteenth-century ideals of American individualism and freedom.

Of the many religious and idealistic American philosophers Borden Parker Bowne (1847–1910) probably generated the most influence as far as the churches were concerned. Theology for the German-educated Bowne was an extrapolation from the facts of religious experience and the interpretation of moral obligation. Although he was a philosopher by training, his impact on many generations of seminarians was great.

Alongside romanticism and its variants stood a growing faith in science as an authoritative and comprehensive world view. Since the seventeenth century, western science had been moving increasingly toward a rigid empiricism that closed off the universe from any spiritual realities and regarded "religion" as an outdated and hidebound superstition. The traditional declaration, "the church says . . . ," was now usurped by the modern, "science says . . . ," and the natural scientist became the modern priest. English-born John William Draper (1811–1882) early championed the claims of science over the supernatural. In 1838 he joined the scientific faculty of New York University and from this post became a popular apologist for a unified, intelligible, altogether natural world. In his famous *History of the Conflict Between Religion and Science* (1874), Draper insisted that religion and science were in fundamental conflict, for religion perpetuated its power through the organized church, whereas science sought to destroy the church's pretensions by indicating the *human* origins of all religious institutions. Draper concluded that Christianity would disappear, as Roman paganism had done, leaving science with its "grander views of the universe, more awful views of God." Not all scientists went as far as Draper, but although traditional Christian vocabulary was still used by most scholars, the foundations of biblical supernaturalism were being quietly eroded.

Darwinism in American Thought

With the publication in 1859 of Charles Darwin's *Origin of Species* a new era in scientific thinking began. The idea of development in the physical world had early been present in the history of western thought but had remained largely dormant. More revolutionary to the thought of the late nineteenth century was the concept of organic evolution. Those whose theology was very detailed, especially the Catholics and Calvinists, soon saw the implications of the new biological theories for time-honored doctrinal views. The argument of design in the universe, as popularized by the English theologian William Paley (1743–1805), had long been accepted in Protestant circles as a basis for definite proof of theism. This confidence now seemed imperiled, as did the established views of Adam's fall, man's depravity, the atonement, and immortality. According to one present-day authority, by undermining the fixity of concepts regarding species—plant, animal, and human—Darwin exposed mind, morals, and therefore the whole scope of social relations to change and ultimately to naturalism.

At first, Darwin's views were of interest primarily to scientists. Yet, his ideas came to have great effect on theologians and churchgoers in general, who were in many instances unwilling to ignore the scientific viewpoint.

In the early stages of the controversy churchmen attacked Darwinism on scientific ground, claiming lack of proof that species had really evolved; no record in geological remains of the fossils of the missing links; the sterility of hybrids; the inability of manmade varieties to survive in nature; and, for believers, the more plausible explanation of natural phenomena provided by the idea of special creation. At first these critics did not accuse Darwin of a definite attempt to further atheism. Very early, however, some asserted that atheism, although unavowed, was really implicit in Darwin's work.

In the United States, George Frederick Wright (1838–1921), Oberlin professor of science and religion, and Asa Gray (1810–1888), distinguished Harvard botanist, championed a view that harmonized Darwinism and Christian theism. This came to be called theistic evolution. They endeavored to defend Darwin's own theism and the compatibility of natural selection with the argument from design, and although both were deeply religious men, they refused to agree that explanations of the origin of species should be left exclusively in the realm of the supernatural. Their essays were published in Gray's *Darwiniana* (1876).

For those who put firm trust in the literal truth of the Bible, the Genesis creation story itself was an effective answer to the new theory. Some claimed that if the literal creation story was rejected, along with it would go the rest of the biblical revelation. This concern motivated one of the most noted theologians of the period, Charles Hodge (1797–1878) of Princeton Seminary, to bring forth, at the age of seventy-seven, a popular exposition on the theme that theism and natural selection could not be reconciled. Published as *What Is Darwinism?* (1874), it attempted to overthrow the evolutionists by proclaiming that the Bible asserts that those who reject Holy Writ are lost to reason or morals, or both. In his zeal Hodge, according to some, had abandoned the attitude of fairness for which he was known, asserting that any acceptance of evolution inevitably leads to atheism.

Throughout the remainder of the century, the theory of evolution held a prominent place in preaching and the clash between science and religion continued to be a favorite topic among lecturers. Many educational leaders of Christian background came to accept the principle of evolution as no more uncertain than the law of gravity. As early as 1891, a prominent Methodist science professor asserted that one could easily count on the fingers of one hand "all anti-evolutionists who are competent to have an opinion on the subject." Some church leaders and the rank and file of the laity, however, took their stand against the new ideas and condemned them as destructive of the truth. This opposition was markedly strong in the South, where the state legislatures of Texas, Tennessee, Arkansas, and Mississippi passed statutes outlawing the teaching of evolution in the public schools. In seven other states similar legislation was rejected.

Trends in Biblical Study and the New Theology

The new methods of finding truth were soon applied to the fields of biblical and theological study. From the time of the Reformation writers had occasionally challenged traditional views regarding certain aspects of Holy Writ, and modern Old Testament criticism was definitely emerging in Germany by 1780. During the 1880s the writing of Julius Wellhausen, a leading German scholar of the Old Testament, received recognition in the United States. Following the canons of the new higher criticism, Wellhausen believed that one might be able to reconstruct the history of the development of biblical concepts by dating the books of the Bible. Through this approach he proposed an evolution of thought in the Old Testament, starting from primitive polytheistic origins and progressing to ethical monotheism; among other conclusions, this cast doubt on the Mosaic authorship of the Pentateuch. At about the same time new questions were being asked about dates, reliability, and related topics concerning the New Testament.

Both liberal and conservative scholars placed great emphasis on lower criticism, which dealt with the Scripture text itself. Great strides were made in determining the most reliable Hebrew and Greek texts for understanding the original languages of the Bible. Vigorous research efforts provided a foundation for more accurate exegesis and translation work. Extensive archaeological excavations in the area around the Mediterranean expanded knowledge of Bible times.

In answer to the troubling questions numerous critics raised about the Bible, conservative scholars explained some seeming inconsistencies as the mistakes of copyists or translators and claimed, at the same time, that only the *original* autographs (no longer extant) had been directly inspired and thus were free from error. The essays of Professor B. B. Warfield of Princeton Seminary supplied a widely adopted argument defending the full inspiration of the Scriptures and the accuracy of the original manuscripts of the Bible. Some evangelicals, such as Scotsman James Orr, editor of the *International Standard Bible Encyclopedia* (1915), and Baptist theologian Augustus H. Strong, held that the Bible is true and authoritative in all it affirms and teaches but as an ancient document is not necessarily inerrant in every historical allusion.

The new emphasis on reason, biblical criticism, intuition, science, and evolutionary thought had important consequences for generally accepted ideas of God, Jesus Christ, man, and history in the American churches. Radical attempts to restate the essence of theology and religion were often influenced by the religious heritage of the past, but were fundamentally determined by modern modes of thought. Familiar terms might be employed, but invested with quite new meanings. Although they were contributors to each other's thought, the exponents of theological liberalism were by no means a homogeneous group. Some had no intention of breaking with inherited faith and never agreed they had. Others among the radicals did intentionally break with the Christian heritage. Between these extremes, theological liberals occupied a wide spectrum of viewpoints, but all were in some sense reconstructionists in religion. They rejected traditional orthodoxy and full biblical authority.

Three primary streams of thought merged during the nineteenth century to influence American theological liberalism. From the German philosopher–theologian Friedrich E. D. Schleiermacher (1768–1834) came the idea that religion is based on feeling or intuition and that the essence of salvation is to be found in love for one's fellow man, not in intellectual adherence to creedal formulae. A second stream of thought was the idealism of Georg W. F. Hegel (1770–1831), reinterpreted for Americans by Josiah Royce (1855–1916) at Harvard and George T. Ladd (1842–1921) at Yale. Idealists defended a "spiritual monism," that is, the view that all existence is spiritual, for it is the offspring of God and expresses God who alone is the perfect personality, acting himself out in the universe and training human personalities through ethics and religion for divine fellowship. German theologian Albrecht Ritschl (1822–1889) provided the third creative force, holding that Christianity is an experienced fact, verified in the consciousness of the believer and incapable of being disturbed by metaphysical or natural science. God is love revealed through Jesus Christ, the first and only sinless man. Divine anger, original sin, and mysticism are repudiated, Christ being viewed as a man by nature. Ritschl's views were mediated to America by Adolf von Harnack, the renowned church historian and theologian who taught the fatherhood of God and the brotherhood of man, but rejected the full deity of Jesus Christ.

The closing decades of the nineteenth century saw a growing effort on the part of certain American thinkers to evaluate and adapt these concepts to form a theology that stressed the immanence of God in the world and the progressive moral improvement of man. The theological result was an identifiably structured religious movement whose major contentions can be summarized even though the emphases varied from man to man. At its foundation was a revised and favorable estimate of human nature, coupled with an optimistic view of human destiny that paralleled the secular idea of progress. Consonant with this, the churches increasingly saw their task in terms of moral uplift, ethical counsel, and education. Ecclesiastical and doctrinal concerns yielded to a man-centered emphasis on moralism and religious experience, while philosophical theology in a complementary fashion moved toward affirmations of the unity of interpenetration of God, man, and nature. Christ and his work were in this manner "naturalized," but nature, including human nature, was seen as infused with the divine.

In *The Kingdom of God in America* (1937), H. Richard Niebuhr has traced the process by which the liberal movement in American theology gradually divorced itself from its roots in the Reformation tradition. The moralism of William Ellery Channing or the experientialism of Horace Bushnell remained proximate with traditional piety; the next generation, at another remove, manifested a decline of vitality; and the following generation a still greater loss of dynamic. Niebuhr then thoughtfully summarizes the outcome: "A God without wrath brought men without sin into a Kingdom without judgment through the ministrations of a Christ without a cross."

Accommodation and Dissent

As denominational leaders confronted these new issues and decided for and against, controversy swept the churches. Issues were so hotly contested that some ministers were accused of heresy before ecclesiastical courts and were disciplined by their communions. The conflict appeared most severe among the Presbyterians. An outstanding example is the case of Charles A. Briggs, professor of biblical theology at Union Seminary in New York. An early enthusiast of biblical criticism and a keen student of German theology, Briggs clashed with Princeton conservatives A. A. Hodge and Warfield in 1881 over the questions of verbal inspiration of the Bible and Mosaic authorship of the Pentateuch. When Briggs boldly disavowed biblical inerrancy in an inaugural address delivered at Union in 1891, his opponents decided to take action. He was prosecuted before the Presbytery of New York and, after initial decisions in his favor, was brought before the General Assembly and, in 1893, found guilty of heresy. Briggs was suspended from the ministry and, in 1899, received priest's orders in the Protestant Episcopal Church. Congregationalists, Baptists, and Methodists all experienced similar incidents. Although the penetration of higher criticism into the Roman Catholic Church caused serious internal strife in Europe, the effect was considerably less in the United States. Leo XIII's critique of "Americanism" in 1899, however, struck a heavy blow at the liberal movement in the United States, still in its infant stage. This was followed by the issuance of Pius X's encyclical *Pascendi Domini gregis,* in 1907, in which the pontiff specifically condemned

The First Church of Christ, Scientist

The "Mother Church" (the First Church of Christ, Scientist) in Boston, world headquarters of the Christian Science movement.

The First Church of Christ, Scientist

Mary Baker Eddy, founder of the Church of Christ, Scientist, in 1886.

"modernism" and directed that professors tainted with heresy be dismissed from their posts.

Many of the same currents that bred theological liberalism led similarly to the emergence of a number of novel religious and philosophical movements in late-nineteenth-century America. Grounded in philosophical idealism and emphasizing the attainment of right states of mind, these groups were encouraged indirectly by New England Transcendentalism, particularly as expressed by Ralph Waldo Emerson and Bronson Alcott in their attacks on materialism and their proclamation of divine immanence and the essential goodness of human nature.

In the closing years of the Civil War, Mrs. Mary Baker Eddy (1821–1910), a frail woman of forty-four, believed that she was receiving direct physical help from a rather remarkable and unworldly faith healer, Phineas P. Quimby (1802–1866). After his death she taught and practiced the new method of religious healing. Although unschooled in philosophical concepts, she composed *Science and Health with Key to the Scriptures* (1875). Her strategy for combating individual and societal disease was that of denial. If both the microcosmic physical body and the macrocosmic social body were problematical and the sources of aches and strains, she would deny their very existence, not merely tinker with trying to improve them. Mind would be all, and matter nothing. Death and sickness were simply illusions, which could be overcome through neither prayer nor medicine but through a new *gnosis* (knowledge), a new method of interpreting Scripture which produced hitherto unrealized insights about the true nature of the metaphysical realm and its application to immediate human problems.

At once small groups using *Science and Health* as a study book began to call themselves Christian Scientists, and by the summer of 1879 The Church of Christ, Scientist had been organized, with headquarters in Boston. The "Mother Church" in Boston remains the strong center of the movement; other churches of Christian Science are "branches." By 1926 the church had more than two hundred thousand members.

A number of other religious movements originated during these years. "New Thought" emerged out of the "mental healing" doctrines of Quimby, as did Christian Science. It had considerable influence within many Protestant churches and also led to the formation of several new religious bodies. In 1889, for example, what came to be known as the Unity School of Christianity was founded by Charles and Myrtle Fillmore. Unity's theology was essentially practical, a guide to good living. Its view of God was like that of Christian Science, but it differed in affirming the reality of the material world and sickness and death. The Watch Tower Bible and Tract Society, commonly known as Jehovah's Witnesses, was founded by Charles Taze Russell in Pittsburgh, in 1872. Its view of the imminence of the apocalypse and of the Witnesses as the sole "righteous remnant" made a strong appeal to those alarmed or alienated by the rapid changes in society.

Blacks were also affected by the general movement away from traditional religious affiliations and beliefs. The combination of Jim Crow laws and lack of economic opportunity in the rural South resulted in a massive exodus of southern blacks to the urban centers of the North, which continues to the present. The consequent sense of cultural displacement created a religious vacuum among migrant blacks that was filled by proliferating storefront churches, often of the Pentecostal-Holiness variety. Pentecostalism as a movement was pan-racial in its beginnings. Its unstructured worship and emphasis on religious experiences fit with the expressive character of black religion in general.

Many blacks, however, were not comfortable with Christianity. As did many American Indians, they regarded it as a "white man's religion." Accordingly, a series of urban movements arose, usually around charismatic figures of obscure origin, which provided non- or anti-Christian ideologies that could serve as a basis for racial identity and pride. Among these was the Father Divine Peace Mission Movement. Father Divine was born George Baker, probably around 1880, on a rice plantation in South Carolina. After an early career as an itinerant gardener and preacher, he arrived in New York City in 1915 and gradually began to acquire a following. Never modest, Father Divine claimed to be God and lived in a corresponding style. He demanded total loyalty from his disciples (including some well-to-do whites), and received it in an extraordinary measure. In many ways the movement represented a withdrawal from the logic and mores of everyday American life into a separate world with a communistic economy and a regimen of asceticism, governed by a leader whose behavior stood in dramatic contradiction to the expectations of conventional Christianity. In another sense, however, the movement represented a powerful (if eccentric) political protest against white racism, and the life of its members in interracial community was a literal expression of the "kingdom beyond caste."

Pentecostalism and Incipient Fundamentalism

Two additional religious currents, apart from both the new theological liberalism and the cultish groups, took shape during this period.

Assemblies of God

The Azusa Street Mission.

Both Pentecostalism and fundamentalism are extremely significant in light of recent trends in American religious life. Whereas nineteenth-century revivalism and Methodist Holiness took a relatively optimistic view of the believer's place in the world, Pentecostalism and early fundamentalism were, in considerable measure, "other-worldly" in their orientation and often pessimistic about the course of their own times.

Pentecostalism and its offshoot, the faith-healing movement following World War II, found its most natural, although not exclusive, constituency among the urban and more especially the rural poor, for these movements were the successors, in many ways, to the enthusiastic religion of the first two Awakenings. More direct impetus flowed from Methodism and the Holiness movements. Throughout church history experiences of intense religious fervor have been interpreted by those involved as fulfillments of Peter's classic Pentecostal message (Acts 2:1–20). On January 1, 1901, the "gift of the Spirit" came to Agnes Ozman, a student at Bethel Bible College, recently founded in Topeka, Kansas. Soon other Bethel students were speaking in "tongues" they could not understand, and the movement spread rapidly to other Holiness groups. In 1906 Pentecostalism reached Los Angeles, and the Azusa Street Mission, under the leadership of William J. Seymour, became a center for the new movement.

Speaking in tongues, or glossolalia, is perhaps Pentecostalism's most distinctive feature. The experience somewhat resembles the intense ecstasies associated with Awakening revivalism. It is essentially an unstructured form of expression in which individuals relinquish rational discourse for an unmediated and uncontaminated flow of syllables from on high. For believers this is evidence of God's active participation among his people. Theologically, Pentecostals held to conservative biblical infallibility. Usually marked by belief in dispensational premillennialism, they have interpreted their experiences of the Holy Spirit as an outpouring in fulfillment of prophecy, and a sign of the last days pointing to the imminent return of Christ. Out of a need to coordinate the various activities of American Pentecostals, a new fellowship, called the Assemblies of God, was formed in 1914.

"Fundamentalism" is an amorphous term used to designate an early–twentieth–century antimodernist movement that sought to affirm the traditional tenets or fundamentals of the Christian faith in the face of an eroding supernaturalism.* The fundamentalist high tide in the 1920s will be dealt with in a later chapter. Only its early stages and shapers receive comment here.

*The term *fundamentalist* apparently was first employed in the independent Baptist weekly, the *Watchman-Examiner*, in 1920.

Assemblies of God

General Council of the Assemblies of God, 1914.

The fundamentalist style of Christianity grew out of the vast interdenominational movement made up of evangelicals troubled by the advance of theological liberalism and the decline of traditional morality in the closing quarter of the nineteenth century. During the 1870s and '80s a group of ministers, predominantly northern Presbyterian and Baptist, convened a series of annual meetings for Bible study, out of which grew widely publicized prophecy conferences. Animated by the conviction that the last days were approaching, the church was apostate, and scriptural preaching was sorely needed, these ministers searched out God's whole "pattern for the ages." They gradually constructed a distinct system of dispensational premillennialism built around the views of J. N. Darby (1800–1882), an English Plymouth Brethren Bible teacher.

Very soon various American dispensationalists began to modify and improve upon Darby's rather loosely-defined scheme. Nowhere did Darbyism fall on more fertile ground than when it reached C. I. Scofield (1843–1921). After serving in the Confederate army and as a lawyer after the war, Scofield experienced a religious conversion in 1879 and entered the ministry. By 1907 Scofield was ardently propagating his scheme of dispensations and convenants through public lectures and his Correspondence Bible School (which later became Dallas Theological Seminary). His most lasting legacy has been the

Scofield Reference Bible, first published in 1909. It expounded the basic form of American dispensationalism, and for millions of church-goers its dogmatically phrased annotations became a constant guide to God's Word. According to this scheme of interpretation, the sacred history of both Jews and Gentiles can be divided into a number of discrete periods, or dispensations, each of which has been placed under a separate covenant, handed down by God, through which men would relate to him. The last of these, which is yet to come, is known as the Fullness of Time or the Kingdom, the millennium in which Christ will restore the Davidic monarchy and rule for a thousand years. This theological scenario was elaborately explicated in charts and graphs and acceptance of it quickly became a mark of many fundamentalists, especially in areas outside the South. For numerous earnest lay persons the approach of the Scofield Bible made sense and seemed to answer the criticisms of the Scriptures posed by liberal scholars.

It should be remembered, however, that not all who came to be termed fundamentalists adopted the dispensational approach. Also, numerous ministers and scholars across America and Britain, who considered themselves evangelical in faith, were not heavily involved with either dispensationalism or the growing fundamentalist coalition.

The desire to thwart the progress of theological liberalism led to one other major event in the early history of fundamentalism—an event, it seems, that actually gave the movement its name. With the financial support of two wealthy Los Angeles oilmen, Lyman Stewart and his brother Milton, a series of twelve booklets, called *The Fundamentals,* was written and distributed to "every pastor, evangelist, minister, theological professor, theological student, Sunday School superintendent, YMCA and YWCA secretary in the English-speaking world." These essays, the first appearing in 1910, addressed the theological issues of the day from a conservative Protestant viewpoint; before the twelfth volume was issued three years later, a total of three million booklets had been distributed. Despite their differing interpretations of countless scriptural passages, the authors succeeded in forging an uneasy alliance to defend the doctrine of the Bible's literal veracity, thus achieving a commendable interdenominational witness. The tone of *The Fundamentals* was primarily scholarly and moderate. The project spawned links between evangelical scholars and pastors in the denominations and the emerging Bible-institute movement with its dispensational orientation.

Fundamentalism as a movement would eventually reflect as much a state of mind and a cultural configuration as a set of theological propositions. Its adherents came to be associated with a cluster of cultural attitudes that looked upon "sophistication" with suspicion or hostility. They tended to regard themselves as a "saving remnant," loyal to traditional American Christian values and scornful of "modernism" in thought and behavior. The most basic thrusts of the movement were toward maintaining boundaries against external pollution, and rigidity in all categories of both "religious" and "secular" life. Some historians have suggested that the historical context for this characterization is rooted in the clash between urban and rural values that polarized Americans during the rise of the pluralistic, urban-industrial technocracy in the early twentieth century. Other interpreters have maintained that fundamentalism must be viewed as a religious movement that attracted a considerable variety of supporters, all of whom rejected the claims to truth of the new psychology, the new theology, and Darwinian science, claiming instead strict biblical piety and orthodox doctrines.

13

The Churches and the "Incorporation" of America

The America of 1860 would have been recognizable in many important ways to a revisiting founding father. Not so the America of 1918. During these sixty years the expansive tendencies of American society began to reverse their direction; centrifugal force gradually became centripetal. The Department of the Census announced that the frontier had come to an official end in 1890—there was no longer any significant amount of arable land left to be claimed for settlement. Consequently the late nineteenth century in the United States, the time of the first large-scale confrontations with industrial and urban conditions, deserves to be looked at briefly both as a backdrop to the history of the American churches in the twentieth century, and as an example of a society undergoing changes it understood so poorly that it unwittingly provoked within itself a deep crisis of values.

Industrialism and Urbanization

Although most historians and economists agree that America's industrial revolution had begun in pre-Civil-War days, the postwar years were marked by astounding industrial development. Older industries expanded, and new industries—oil, electricity, and steel, to name only three of the most significant—grew into giants by the early decades of the twentieth century. Industry, mainly concentrated in the Northeast before the Civil War, rapidly spread westward after 1865. Heavy industry gradually became more important in terms of the value of its products, and large-scale production came to dominate American industry, outstripping the industrial production of Britain by 1900. America would never again revert to a predominantly agricultural economy.

The results were profound. Large-scale production required heavy capital expenditures and skilled leadership. A huge working class and a large middle class of professionals congregated in rapidly growing industrial urban centers. Although rural Americans during these years increased in absolute numbers due to westward expansion, they declined in relative terms. In 1860 only 20 percent of Americans lived in cities of more than twenty-five hundred inhabitants. In 1900 the figure was 40 percent and the trend continued. Almost thirty-nine million people immigrated to the United States between 1820 and 1920, mostly before World War I. Few nations could have absorbed such a staggering influx, and America handled it only with difficulty. Urban migrants suffered all the hardships of cities growing too fast to provide adequate housing, streets, sewers, police, and transportation. One group of native migrants, the blacks, suffered additionally because of racism.

America, with its abundant coal and ore deposits, resources for steam and power, and a labor force swelling with immigrants, was endowed with one additional critical element: an inventive business leadership that found ways to operate efficiently and profitably very large enterprises. By the late nineties, "big business," in the recognizably modern form of the multimillion-dollar corporation, was an established part of American life, and apparently a necessary one from the standpoint of continued economic development.

All of these external transformations in American life had significant social and cultural consequences. Paramount was the decline in social importance of the traditional middle class. The new plutocracy, the masters of the great corporations, by-passed the old gentry, the merchants, the small manufacturers, and the established professional men of an earlier era. The old-family, college-educated classes were overshadowed and edged to a marginal role in the making of basic national and economic decisions. They were not growing financially poorer as a class, but their influence and fortunes were dwarfed by comparison with the new eminences of wealth and power.

Related to this "disinheritance" is another major social consequence of the changing order: the enthronement of wealth as the sine qua non of power and prestige. Birth, breeding, and morality mattered less, and the way was open for the ambitious and clever to claw their way up the social ladder. The vast concern with social climbing between 1870 and 1920 was a new phenomenon and it assumed the existence of a social ladder not previously recognized. The increasing emphasis on wealth and opulence that characterized the Gilded Age rendered it vulnerable to charges of hollowness and social injustice.

A third social and cultural consequence, integrally linked to the second, was the emergence of "business thinking" as the dominant mode of American thought and praxis. In government, in education, in fields far removed from the sphere of the marketplace, business thinking came to be the criterion of sound thinking. Concomitant with this was the rise of a new American hero: the smart man. In the seventeenth century America had looked up to its ministers; in the eighteenth to its statesmen, patriots, and pioneers. Now, with all the veneration that once marked its religious devotion, and with all the vitality that had leveled its wilderness, it turned in a new direction: money made the national pulse beat faster and the businessman led the way.

This frenzied quest for wealth received an almost metaphysical legitimation in the short-lived theory of social Darwinism, an attempt to apply the biological ideas of Darwin to the socio-economic culture. These views, in essence, rationalized the harsh facts of social stratification and justified unfettered competition and consolidation into monopolies and trusts. Social evolution was seen as more or less an automatic slow process not to be tampered with. Although the theory was challenged and modified, it nevertheless cast its spell on Americans in high places throughout these years.

A general consequence of the new wave of immigration, which is particularly relevant to the study of American religion, is the further erosion of the Protestant establishment. As the American population grew more racially mixed through the eighties and nineties, the attitudes of many "older" Americans grew less friendly. They applied clichés about inferiority to the new outsiders. Not surprisingly, the post-Civil-War generation that ultimately failed to protect and provide for the millions of emancipated slaves also attempted to exlude specific immigrant groups out of prejudice. Anti-Semitism often accompanied anti-Catholicism. The American Protective Association, strong in the 1890s, crusaded against Roman Catholic, Jewish, and non-Anglo-Saxon ideas and immigrants.

A final social consequence of the new urban-industrial complex is the highly significant effect it had on the American family and

American views of work. The nation was shifting from a producing to a consuming society or, in slightly different terms, from predominantly cottage production to predominantly industrial production. By 1920, two-thirds of the national income crossed the counters of retail establishments selling goods that less than a century before had been part of the daily production of many homes. The rise of the wage system as a dominant mode of survival meant that a "living" was to be bought and that the social function of work was now mediated by an exchange process: selling labor and buying goods.

For many Americans the changes opened doors to expanded opportunities: provincialism was broken down by railroad and steamship travel; telephones and transoceanic cables linked places near and far; mass-circulation newspapers and magazines, despite sensationalism, widened access to information; newly established art museums and symphony orchestras, financed by business philanthropy, brought "high" culture to thousands; emerging modern medicine and new insights about hygiene added to life expectancy; laborsaving devices entered the home, which would be further affected, first by gaslights and later by electrification; canned and prepared foods saved time in the kitchen and added variety to diets.

The role of women was particularly affected by the dramatic transitions precipitated by urbanization and industrialization. Middle- and upper-class women sought more access to educational, professional, and political participation outside the home; women on society's lower rungs competed with men and boys for employment, often unsuccessfully when times were difficult.

The Churches and the New Social Climate

The American churches, both Protestant and Catholic, were at first singularly unprepared to deal with the moral dilemmas of the new industrial era. Protestantism had long before yielded to the compartmentalizing and secularizing of life initiated by the Renaissance and infused with a special character in America by the separation of church and state. The subsequent heritage from the frontier ethos and revivalism had made Protestants of the late nineteenth century individualistic to an unusual degree at the very moment when a corporate understanding of emerging industrial and societal problems was appropriate. Although Catholics were heirs to the medieval ideal of a Christian society under the influence of the church, they belonged to a communion that in America and other parts of the world had large vested interests.

The wealth and optimism that characterized the larger society were

Phillips Brooks.

T. DeWitt Talmage.

Washington Gladden.

displayed in like manner in all the denominations. At one time churches such as the Methodist, Baptist, and Disciples had prided themselves on their ministry to the poor; they now noted with satisfaction their social status, soaring budgets, and wealthy and influential communicants.

This was the age of the golden-tongued orators, the "princes of the pulpit," who held their audiences spellbound and explicated the Christian message in eloquent but accessible language. Located mainly in large urban centers, these preachers included men like Henry Ward Beecher and T. DeWitt Talmage in Brooklyn; Phillips Brooks, George A. Gordon, and Adoniram J. Gordon in Boston; David M. Swing and Frank W. Gunsaulus in Chicago; Russell H. Conwell in Philadelphia; and Washington Gladden in Columbus. In the large cities congregations competed with each other for the distinction of having the most popular and sensational preacher. To be able to emotionally enthrall one's audience became a standard criterion of ministerial success.

For the millions of immigrants from southern and eastern Europe, the Roman Catholic Church provided the one familiar landmark in a strange and alien land. In the parishes and religious societies of Catholicism they found both a link with Europe and a bond with America. Besides Italians and Poles, in lesser proportions were Catholic Czechs, Yugoslavs, Croatians, Magyars, Portuguese, Lithuanians, and Ukranians. In their churches they found help in adjusting to their new life. But in another sense the ethnic churches impeded Americanization by preserving, particularly in the language, the diverse cultures brought to American shores. The Catholic presence was now vast and Protestants were forced to accommodate themselves to it.

Religious diversity was further enhanced by the arrival of numbers of ethnic Protestants, many of whom perpetuated native-language worship in their respective parishes well into the twentieth century. The list and variety of denominational groups, which drew from both state-church and pietistic free-church traditions, is too extensive and complex to treat in this narrative, except to mention a few examples.

The Midwest received a large concentration of German-speaking Lutherans, especially the Saint Louis area where the conservative German Evangelical Lutheran Synod of Missouri, Ohio and Other States centered after its start in Chicago in 1847. It grew under the leadership of Carl F. W. Walther (1811–1887) to be the largest among the Lutheran synods in America by 1914.

The Dutch Calvinist heritage was consolidated throughout Michigan and the surrounding region by thousands of immigrants who made up the constituency of the Christian Reformed Church of America, which absorbed the smaller True Reformed Church in 1889.

Methodist and pietistic Holiness was advocated by the German-

Concordia Historical Institute, Saint Louis, Missouri

Carl F. W. Walther.

Concordia Historical Institute, Saint Louis, Missouri

Interior view of Saint Lorenz Church in Frankenmuth, Michigan, one of the early Lutheran churches in Michigan.

speaking Evangelical Association and United Brethren in Christ. German and Swedish Baptists planted congregations in city and countryside throughout the upper Mississippi Valley and German Mennonites settled in Kansas and the northern plains. In 1885 Swedish Lutheran pietists formed the Evangelical Mission Covenant Church centered in Chicago and the upper Midwest. Although the first Eastern Orthodox parish in the United States was founded in New Orleans in 1866, the growth of the Greek, Serbian, Romanian, Syrian, Russian, and Ukranian Orthodox churches is tied to twentieth-century immigration patterns.

In the large industrial communities, many in the laboring classes, particularly the city-born, were impervious to the ministry and message of the churches. It was not that the churches let these people slip away; they never really had them. This group of people was to constitute a continuing challenge to the churches. How were they to be reached? How were those of middle-class values to deal with the squalor and blight of the poor?

Christians were by no means united in their approaches to contemporary social problems. Many adhered to the old pattern of ameliorating social evils by fighting sin and dispensing charity; a few advocated complete reconstruction of economic and political organization along socialistic lines; still others were dissatisfied with the present social structure but were more conservative in their approach to change. The first of these approaches predominated in the thirty years following the Civil War. For instance, many "skid row" missions were founded, along with shelters for indigent women. Prosperous urban churches built gymnasiums and sponsored neighborhood social programs. In spite of the efforts of earnest churchmen, however, particular groups of Americans were mercilessly squeezed: blacks in southern fields, immigrants in northern slums, farmers on western homesteads, children in eastern factories, and laborers in every quarter. They were

Salvation Army Archives and Research Center

An open-air Salvation Army meeting in the Bowery.

often trapped without protection between the harsh realities of the new order and the inadequate social theories of the old.

The southern and western farmers, mostly evangelical Protestants in their small-town and rural parishes, politically and morally challenged the emergent industrial society. They advocated abandonment of the monetary gold standard and urged the institution of a federal income tax as well as government ownership of railroads and telephone service, direct election of senators, postal savings banks, legislation of the eight-hour workday, and other government action to offset the concentrated power of the industrial and banking communities.

A devout Presbyterian layman from Nebraska, William Jennings Bryan, championed this crusade as leader of the agrarian Populist Party, which joined with the Democrats in 1896 to nominate Bryan for the presidency. Destined to run twice again for president, Bryan, more than any other person, represented the aspirations and agendas of rural Protestant America during an era when it was losing influence in the larger economic and social order.

With the exception of some, such as Adoniram J. Gordon in Boston, the prestigious urban preachers generally reflected a fundamentally conservative social outlook and sometimes a puzzling naïveté. Phillips Brooks (1835–1893), born into social and economic security, could write in 1887, "Excessive poverty, actual suffering for the necessities of life, terrible as it is, is comparatively rare." Such a statement said more about Brooks's own social insulation than the realities of poverty in America. Henry Ward Beecher (1813–1887), who enjoyed a large salary from Plymouth Church in Brooklyn and enviable revenues from royalties, newspaper syndicate fees, and lecture appearances, could point out to strikers in 1877 the virtue of patient acquiesence in poverty: "It is said that a dollar a day is not enough for a wife and five or six children. No, not if the man smokes or drinks beer. . . . Water costs nothing; and a man who cannot live on bread is not fit to live." And D. L. Moody, preaching to a New York crowd during the depression of the 1870s, proclaimed: "It is a wonderful fact that men and women saved by the blood of Jesus rarely remain the subjects of charity, but rise at once to comfort and respectability." Underlying these statements was the firm belief that the American system was basically sound and that urban and industrial problems were only minimal and temporary.

In 1878 the *Congregationalist* branded the wandering unemployed "profane, licentious, filthy, vermin-swarming thieves, petty robbers, and sometimes murderers, social pests and perambulatory nuisances" and suggested the revival of whipping for them. Gradually, however, the religious press took a more favorable attitude toward industrial workers and unions. Stirring books by an optimistic Congregational clergyman, Josiah Strong, stressed the alternative of social regeneration in a spirit of fervent evangelism. His best-selling *Our Country* (1885) became a veritable *Uncle Tom's Cabin* of city reform. Concrete details of revolting conditions in urban life shocked many people who read books like Helen Campbell's *Prisoners of Poverty* (1889) and Jacob Riis's *How the Other Half Lives* (1890). The conscience of churchgoing America was stimulated by such disclosures to expand missions in the slums, increase support to the Salvation Army (imported from Great Britain in 1880), and build more recreational facilities and social settlement homes.

Soon there arose clergymen who were not satisfied with a defense of existing institutions only moderately changed to stave off radical demands. These new thinkers were definitely searching for an improved social order. To them, individual regeneration was not enough, and they endeavored to find specific proposals to improve the life of organized society. Optimistic and retaining much of traditional American individualism, they appealed especially to middle-class people who gradually abandoned the rigid economic views of mid-nineteenth-century social thought. Especially congenial to the growth

Dargan-Carver Library, Sunday School Board of the Southern Baptist Convention

Every-day Bible school, sponsored by Epiphany Baptist Church and held at the Knox Presbyterian Church in New York City, 1904.

of this progressive type of Christianity were three viewpoints of liberal theology of the period: the immanence of God; the organic character of nature and human life; and the ideal of the kingdom of God on earth. This outlook came to be called the social gospel.

The social gospel was not a revolutionary attack on capitalistic society from the outside, but a reforming effort from within. Its ideal of the kingdom of God had a striking resemblance to bourgeois, post-Civil-War America. In fact, leaders of the theological revival of the 1930s later charged that this particular form of social Christianity, with its confidence in the rationality and disinterestedness of man's conduct, was less realistic than either proletarian radicalism or biblical prophetic religion. But proponents of the social gospel showed timely awareness that society is more than the aggregate of individuals composing it; they realized that Christianity has deep ethical obligations to its immediate community; and they sought to state these obligations in terms of their own theology.

Perhaps most influential was Washington Gladden (1836–1918), after 1882 for more than thirty years pastor of the First Congregational Church of Columbus, Ohio. Owing much to the thought of Horace Bushnell, Frederick W. Robertson, and John Ruskin, he began with no preconceived economic theories, but asserted the validity of Christian principles for the whole of life. Gladden's ideas gradually developed so that he came to a firm insistence on labor's rights of collective bargaining and moved to advocate some adequate form of profit sharing to resolve the tension between capital and labor. Finding no ultimate solution for the problem either in the older individualism or in socialism, he gradually recognized the need for greater governmental intervention. His personality, his plain speaking with the use of practical illustrations, and his genuinely religious spirit brought him extraordinary influence.

Also of outstanding significance was Walter Rauschenbusch (1861–1918), who as a young clergyman in 1886 accepted the pastorate of the small Second German Baptist Church near the tough Hell's Kitchen area of New York City's west side. Working on a meager salary in the midst of struggling German immigrants, he acquired invaluable experience in meeting the needs of men in a most unpromising environment. There, he supported Henry George for mayor of New York and worked with the journalist-reformer, Riis, in behalf of playgrounds and fresh-air centers for tenement children. Through study of the works of Leo Tolstoi, Giuseppe Mazzini, Karl Marx, Edward Bellamy, and others, he began to emphasize the ideal of the kingdom of God on earth. "As the idea of the Kingdom is the key to the teachings and work of Christ," Rauschenbusch said, "so its abandonment or misconstruction is the key to the false or one-sided conceptions of Christianity." He found that many churchgoers, caught up in the American ethic of rugged individualism, regarded social issues as a nonessential area of Christian service:

> Because the Kingdom has been dropped as the primary and complete aim of Christianity and personal salvation has been substituted for it, therefore men seek to save their own souls and . . . the individualistic conception of a Kingdom of God on earth, and Christian men . . . are comparatively indifferent to the spread of the spirit of Christ in the political, industrial, social, scientific and artistic life of humanity.

In his own study of the Bible Rauschenbusch came to feel that he needed to devote more attention to economic and social problems and less to theological issues in preparing for greater usefulness to the cause of Christ. In 1897 Rauschenbusch became a professor at Rochester Theological Seminary, and there over a period of years he developed wide influence as he crystallized the social theory associated with the social gospel. The more radical wing of the movement, led by Rauschenbusch, included Jesse H. Jones, William Bliss, and George Herron and sometimes moved close to Christian democratic socialism. Moderates closer to Gladden's ideas included Bishop Henry Codman Potter, Frederick Huntington, Charles Stelzle, and Samuel Batten.

However, these social gospelers' vision, conceived in terms of social redemption, lacked broad appeal because of its liberal stance, both theological and social. Although what we might call the high social gospel of Rauschenbusch and Gladden may have had considerable impact on seminary education and the higher echelons of ecumenical bureaucracies, it fell short of becoming the stuff of popular Protestantism for most neighborhood congregations.

In 1897, Charles M. Sheldon, a Congregational minister from Kansas, published a novel that sought to reach the Christian masses with social concerns. *In His Steps* revolves around a conscientious minister's attempts to rouse his rather placid and comfortable parishioners by asking them to consider what Jesus would do if confronted with their moral decisions. Sheldon's vision of reform merged evangelical morality and conservative political progressivism, and nowhere approached what were then quite radical calls for social legislation—which other social-gospel spokesmen were advocating.

While social-gospel views gained importance in American Protestantism, especially in areas where "Yankee Reformers" were active, in those same areas both clerical and lay Roman Catholics were almost wholly indifferent to social reform. For example, in Boston, Catholic leaders deemed voluntary poverty to be a virtue and involuntary poverty a consequence of disobedience to God's law. Many Protestants also remained inimical to social issues. Although evangelicals had inherited a glowing tradition of social reform, these years represented what sociologist David Moberg (citing historian Timothy L. Smith) has termed a "Great Reversal" in social orientation. As George Marsden writes:

> When fundamentalists began using their heavy artillery against liberal theology, the Social Gospel was among the prime targets. In the barrage against the Social Gospel it was perhaps inevitable that the vestiges of their own progressive social attitudes would also become casualties.

Besides, for some evangelicals the increasing appeal of dispensationalism, with its emphasis on worsening societal conditions in the end times, worked against political involvement beyond charitable acts and opposition to vice and liquor.

The church has always lived with a degree of tension toward the surrounding social order. It hearkens to the gospel call which urges people to look heavenward and live redeemed lives marked by just and unselfish behavior. Yet, the churches are human organizations subject to many of the economic and social values of earthly culture. Whenever Christians adopt a hands-off policy toward efforts for amelioration of social problems, they unconsciously affirm the injustices of the moment and sanctify the status quo as God's will, thus compromising ideals and losing moral credibility. On the other hand, if Christians challenge too strongly the prevailing economic and social forces, they may have to withdraw to sectarian roles and correspondingly eschew opportunities for genuine cultural and social influence.

As institutions the American churches faced real dilemmas amidst the swirling tides of the late nineteenth century. Most Christian believers were confident, however, that honest efforts by government and individuals of good will would eventually correct social problems and both the nation and the churches would fulfill their destinies. In fact, this confidence and hope helped launch a major missionary movement to earth's remotest corners. The churches were entering an era of crusading international outreach.

14

A New American Empire and the "White Man's Burden"

After 1897, vigorous expressions of national pride became popular and rather common in the United States. America went to war with Spain in 1898, primarily to assist the Cuban people in their battle against Spanish despotism. But whatever the initial motives, the "splendid little war" gave the United States the opportunity to govern or temporarily occupy large tracts in the Caribbean region and to obtain outright Puerto Rico and the Philippine Islands. American annexation of noncontiguous lands had precedents (e.g., in Alaska, Samoa, Midway, and other Pacific islands). Still, the Philippines were so distant and so large that annexing them was a departure. Majorities in Congress supported it, and despite a strong anti-imperialist minority, which included William Jennings Bryan and numerous churchmen, many Americans thought the expansions of 1898 and after were entirely appropriate ventures for a great new country.

Some expansionists exploited traditional notions of America's holy "mission" and "manifest destiny" to vindicate imperialistic interests. Senator Albert Beveridge of Indiana explained in 1900 that the question of annexing the Philippines was

> elemental . . . God has not been preparing the English-speaking and Teutonic peoples for a thousand years for nothing but vain and idle

> self-contemplation and admiration. No! He made us the master organizers of the world to establish system where chaos reigns. . . . He has marked the American people as his chosen nation to lead in the regeneration of the world.

This genre of argument gave Americans a rationale for competing with other colonial powers. It offered a new frontier, a sense of purpose, a way out of the drift and divisiveness of the 1890s.

As the comments of Beveridge reveal, imperialistic nationalism rested in part on the academically respectable view of the time that the Anglo-Saxon peoples, construed to be the British, Germans, and Americans, were morally and racially superior to others, especially Latin Americans, Asians, and blacks. This superiority was accompanied by a duty, called "the white man's burden" by Rudyard Kipling, to bring Christianity, civilization, and commerce to the lesser peoples whether they welcomed these or not.

American Christianity often reflected this larger national ethos as it promoted the cause of overseas missions with unmitigated vigor. The extent of voluntary lay support for missionary causes reached record levels as denominations sought to engage every member in some way or other in home and foreign evangelism. The dynamic concept of the church-as-mission motivated denominational self-consciousness, energy, and resources toward presenting to the entire globe the saving grace of the Christian gospel. Of this new impulse Yale church historian Kenneth Scott Latourette wrote: "Never before in a period of equal length had Christianity or any other religion penetrated for the first time as large an area as it had in the nineteenth century."

The Extension of World Missions

As we noted in chapter 8, the Second Awakening spawned an array of state, regional, and national mission societies, with the American Board of Commissioners for Foreign Missions leading the way abroad in 1812. Denominational missionary agencies greatly expanded throughout the century. The turn of the twentieth century marked the emergence of three important new movements destined to have overwhelming impact on the course of Christian missions: the faith missions, the Bible institutes, and the Student Volunteer Movement. All three originated in the second half of the nineteenth century but did not achieve maturity until the 1900s. The first two remain vital; the third dissolved in the 1930s.

The faith-missions movement entitles that cluster of interdenominational agencies which, because they have no guaranteed income from a denominational constituency, must to an unusual degree rely on God to move the hearts of individuals to support their work. The faith missions view their relationships to the denominations as cooperative and complementary rather than competitive, although mainline churches have often regarded the movement as sectarian and potentially divisive. If time is an accurate indicator of validity, then the faith missions have succeeded grandly: not a single nineteenth-century mission has collapsed. They not only have endured but also have grown dramatically and are today among the largest in the world; some, like the Wycliffe Bible Translators, have a membership of three thousand or more. They have pioneered the use of radio, aviation, Bible correspondence courses, and theological education by extension. In the twentieth century their support has derived mainly, but not exclusively, from independent, Baptist, Bible, and "community" churches and their recruits have come primarily from the Bible institutes and evangelical colleges. Also, there have always been persons within the mainline denominations who have been contributors to the faith missions.

The Bible-institute movement, born in the 1880s, has remained an overwhelmingly North American phenomenon. It represents a pietistic response to secularism, a theistic reaction to humanism and agnosticism, a resurgence of spiritual dynamic in Protestantism, a restoration of biblical authority and direction in education, and a focus on the implementation of Christ's Great Commission: "Go ye into all the world." The earliest schools were the Missionary Training Institute of Nyack (1882), now Nyack College (N.Y.); Chicago's Moody Bible Institute (1886); Boston Missionary Training School (1889), now Gordon College and Gordon-Conwell Theological Seminary; Toronto Bible Institute (1894), now Ontario Bible College; and Providence Bible Institute (1900), now Barrington College. At present there are more than three hundred Bible institutes and Bible colleges in North America and they continue to prepare a majority of candidates for the faith missions. Exemplary is Moody Bible Institute, which has sent more than five thousand alumni to the mission field since 1890 and accounts for nearly 8 percent of all missionaries in the world today. Always practical in training, and geared more toward spiritual than broad intellectual development, the Bible institutes have supplied the foundation of ministerial preparation for many evangelicals throughout the twentieth century.

The Student Volunteer Movement was spearheaded by Robert P. Wilder, a graduate of Princeton University, John R. Mott, a student at Cornell, and the evangelist D. L. Moody. At an international student conference held at Mount Hermon, Massachusetts, in 1886, a group of

Architect's drawing of Moody Bible Institute.

some 250 college men and women found their attention arrested by an enthusiastic minority of missionary-minded students. Following the famous conference, Wilder and an associate toured American colleges, taking as their motto *The Evangelization of the World in This Generation.* As a result, two thousand volunteers were enrolled, of whom about five hundred were women, a significant indication of increasing roles for women in Protestantism. Eventually more than twenty thousand volunteers had served overseas as a direct response to the movement's call. The Mott-Wilder-Moody group was additionally instrumental in bridging gaps between conservatives and liberals in mainline churches both here and abroad. The thousands of lay people awakened by the movement became powerful agents in other crusades and campaigns throughout World War I and the twenties, illustrating what has always been the most important aspect of the entire foreign-missions impulse: its reflective effect on the life and church activities of Christians at home. As Sydney E. Ahlstrom writes:

> The missionary on furlough was the great American window on the non–Western world. Through him, the aims of the missionary movement, as well as the cultural stereotypes which underlay it, became fundamental elements of the American Protestant's world outlook.

Ecumenical Beginnings

The ecumenical (from the Greek *oikoumene,* the inhabited world) movement of our day is the direct result of the missionary enterprise of the nineteenth century. It may be defined as that process whereby Christian communions in every part of the world strive to discover and express a common faith and life centered in commitment to Jesus Christ, their common Lord.

During the nineteenth century Protestant leaders in America and Europe began to realize that if the world missionary movement was to be effective there would have to be interdenominational teamwork. The challenge was particularly acute in America with its ever increasing array of Protestant styles of church life. In the United States alone almost three hundred denominations, large and small, could be identified. Because American believers found it difficult to cooperate across denominational lines, they sensed the need for denominations within the same "confessional family" to attempt federation on a worldwide basis.

To this end, interdenominational meetings were convened in large cities in both Europe and America from 1854 onward. These were interecclesiastical exchanges—in contrast to the Evangelical Alliance, formed in England in 1846 and America in 1867, which enrolled individual believers. Deeply significant was the World Missionary Conference of 1910 in Edinburgh. Consisting of delegates appointed by several missionary societies, the conference enjoyed a more official character than previous assemblies. The participation of delegates from the "younger churches," whose origins were the direct result of missionary endeavor, added special inspiration. Two significant outcomes of the conference were the formation of a continuation committee, presided over by American Methodist leader Mott, and the founding of an *International Review of Missions*. Following the conference Mott made a world tour in the twin interests of missions and unity. In India, China, Japan, and other Asian countries he organized national and regional councils which later developed into the present-day Christian councils. When the International Missionary Council came into existence in 1921 these joined the IMC.

An outstanding delegate to the 1910 World Missionary Conference was Charles Brent, Protestant Episcopal missionary bishop to the Philippine Islands. Inspired by the idea of a reunited Christendom, he and two other leaders persuaded the General Council of their denomination to call a World Conference on Faith and Order. All churches that "accept our Lord Jesus Christ as God and Savior" were invited to send representatives, and the conference convened in 1927 at Lausanne. All major Protestant denominations dispatched delegates, as did the Eastern Orthodox Church. Pope Pius XI, in the interest of orthodoxy and church authority, forbade Roman Catholic participation in the ecumenical movement. Although theological differences repeatedly surfaced, a spirit of Christian charity prevailed. The noteworthy agreements to come out of the conference were that the faith of the church universal was that expressed by the Apostles' and Nicene creeds, and that congregational, episcopal, and presbyterian forms of government all had appropriate places in a reunited church. Although the archbishops from the Eastern Orthodox Church withdrew, much to the disappointment of the conference as a whole, the majority opinion was that something of permanent value had been accomplished, which would point to the eventual achievement of Christian unity throughout the world. On the other hand, many evangelical and fundamentalist church leaders, fearful of theological dilution or bureaucratic control, opted out of the ecumenical movement on principle.

The rise of councils of churches, world conferences, and other cooperative agencies at local, state, national, and international levels constituted Protestant efforts to deal with the fracturing pressures of modern life. The councils undoubtedly contributed to the razing of old walls of separation between church communions and fostered a genuine spirit of ecumenicity. At the same time a nascent western pride was implicit in many ecumenical plans. The relationship between Christianity, civilization, and commerce appeared close in the minds of missionary and early ecumenical leaders. As one minister wrote in 1898:

> American imperialism, in its essence, is American valor, American manhood, American sense of justice and right, American conscience, American character at its best, listening to the voice of God and His command, nobly assuming this republic's rightful place in the grand forward movement for the civilizing and Christianizing of all continents and all races.

For many European and American Christians the desire to "convert the heathen" ran in tandem with a desire to impart western manners and mores or, in short, western culture. This would help account for much of the hostility toward the Christian faith expressed by many non-westerners later in this century for, in their minds, it was difficult to separate Christianity from other expressions of western power and hegemony.

It is unfortunate that the heroic, altruistic, loving, and contributory aspects of Christian foreign missions have not been accorded more positive treatment in the media and secular scholarship. Many of the educational and medical facilities operating in the Third World today derive from missionary efforts. Certainly the self-sacrifice demanded to carry the gospel to those "who sit in darkness and the shadow of death" cannot be easily appreciated by an increasingly hedonistic society.

The Surfacing of the Peace Movement

Among the many crusades that gained momentum during the first decade of the present century was the peace movement. As we suggested in chapter 8, the peace movement was not of recent origin but began among the Quakers, Moravians, and German pietistic groups in colonial times. As religious bodies these groups have remained faithful in their testimony against war from that day to this. By 1826 there were some fifty peace societies throughout the several states, devoted to a variety of benevolent enterprises and supported by ministers and pious laymen such as Lewis and Arthur Tappan and David Low Dodge. The peace societies prospered as long as the churches gave aid. During the Civil War, however, churches withdrew their support, and the societies waned until the end of the century.

The peace movement's period of greatest vitality occurred between the Spanish-American War (1898) and the outbreak of World War I (1914). After the Spanish-American War, proponents of peace rapidly multiplied and yet remained a small minority in the entire nation's social and political life. The crusade for peace was closely identified with the campaign against American imperialism. Churchmen joined hands with other anti-imperialists such as William Graham Sumner, Mark Twain, and William James for the advancement of their mutual interests.

The activities of the American Peace Society were supplemented after 1866 by the Universal Peace Union and after 1889 by the

Billy Graham Center Museum

Billy Sunday.

Department of Peace and Arbitration of the Women's Christian Temperance Union (WCTU). The Quakers, always pacifists, held a Conference of Friends in Philadelphia in 1901 solely for the purpose of discussing peace. A direct outgrowth of these annual conferences was the movement for international arbitration, which also received endorsement by a number of American statesmen. In 1899 representatives of twenty-six nations met at the Hague to discuss plans for the promotion of international peace; a second conference with delegates from forty-nine countries convened again at the Hague in 1907.

In 1902 a group of clergymen meeting in New York City organized the American Association of Ministers for the Advancement of Peace. Thereafter the peace movement in the United States took the offensive. Through its Department of Peace and Arbitration, the WCTU published a study course entitled "World Peace" for use in Sunday schools, youth groups, and women's organizations. It reported in 1905 that more peace sermons had been delivered that year than at any time previously. The American Peace Society more than doubled its membership and took on new vigor as it re-established its headquarters in Washington in 1912.

While peace enthusiasts in the American churches were optimistically assuring themselves of the certain triumph of their cause, the European political scene was taking an ominous turn toward disaster. Although initially committed to a policy of neutrality at the outbreak of war in 1914, many Americans suddenly found themselves favoring intervention as word of German "atrocities" in Belgium and in the waters surrounding Britain began to be heard. The change in religious thinking is perhaps best illustrated by evangelist Billy Sunday. At first he opposed American involvement in European affairs, but his attitude shifted 180 degrees when the sinking of the *Lusitania* (1915) was reported and American lives were lost. Suddenly Sunday became an ardent interventionist, helping to raise thousands of dollars in war bonds to aid the crusade againt "the Hun." In a more acrid mood he once suggested that if one were to turn hell upside down he would find the words *Made in Germany* written there. By April 1917, Americans had been persuaded that, in the words of their president, "the world must be made safe for democracy," and that the war was not an imperialistic conflict but a just crusade for the triumph of good over evil. And so, as America entered the international struggle, justified by a sense of divine calling, the peace movement in the United States submerged once again.

Part 5

The Churches in Modern America

(1917–present)

15

The Churches in War, Prosperity, and Depression

Few American Christians would have taken issue when evangelist Billy Sunday prayed in the House of Representatives in 1918:

> Thou knowest, O Lord, that no nation so infamous, vile, greedy, sensuous, blood-thirsty ever disgraced the pages of history. Make bare thy mighty arm, O Lord, and smite the hungry, wolfish Hun, whose fangs drip with blood, and we will forever raise our voice to thy praise.

The nation had launched a holy war to punish evil and end all wars, a "Great Crusade" in which the churches overwhelmingly enlisted. It is difficult for the late-twentieth-century reader to perceive the idealism, even naïveté, that characterized the rapid change of churchly opinion from the isolationism and neutrality of 1914–1916 to the enthusiasm and mobilization for military combat of 1917–1918.

The American Churches and World War

Although all ministers did not employ Sunday's graphic language, most denominations passed resolutions similar to that adopted by the Troy Conference of the Methodist Episcopal Church in 1918:

> We see the trembling lines above which float the Tricolor and the Union Jack, as the hellish Hunnish hordes beat against them to seize the panting throat of the world. We hear the cry 'Hurry up, America,' and we go with fierce passion for world freedom to twine with Union Jack and Tricolor the Stars and Stripes and say to the sinister black eagle flag of Germany, 'You shall not pass.'

Such vitriol against Germans, catalyzed by a flood of propaganda, extended even to the language: several states passed legislation banning the use of German in public services, resulting in a rapid shift to English among German-speaking Lutherans.

With the nation bending all its energies to winning the war, the churches bordered on becoming government agencies. Local Red Cross units met in church sanctuaries, as did other wartime agencies; the purchase of Liberty bonds was urged in religious periodicals; ministers preached from outlines supplied by the government propaganda office and helped circulate stories of enemy atrocities. The large denominations organized war commissions to direct their special activities in support of the war, while the Federal Council of Churches (founded 1908) created a General Wartime Commission to act as a clearing-house. Clergy from both the Protestant and Roman communions were recruited to the chaplaincy. The YMCA, Salvation Army, Red Cross, and Knights of Columbus each provided invaluable service in medical assistance, recreation, entertainment, and education. Most congregations were beehives of activity supported by the tireless work of ladies' groups and the men who were left behind.

Unfortunately, there was also widespread contempt for members of the pacifist denominations such as the Friends and Mennonites. Although exempted from military service by law, conscientious objectors were victims of confusing and inconsistent treatment; many were thrown into prison camps. The fewer than one hundred clergymen known to be pacifists were also persecuted. A prominent Unitarian minister in New York, the Reverend John Holmes, was maligned for his views and was eventually repudiated by his congregation. The emotional climate of the war years even created incidents in which pacifist ministers were mobbed, beaten, tarred and feathered, or otherwise mistreated by the overzealous.

In the midst of the campaign to defeat the kaiser, many churchmen seized the opportunity to subdue also John Barleycorn, a reform sought by many Christians for decades. Support for prohibition was strongest among Methodists and Baptists, but practically all Protestant groups of every theological stripe (with the exception of some Lutherans and Episcopalians) championed the antisaloon effort. When war

Billy Graham Center Museum

The "women's whiskey war" in Ohio, as sketched by John R. Chapin.

was declared prohibition was already the law in twenty-six states. Wartime conservation of alcohol and flour led to Congressional passage of the Eighteenth Amendment and other restrictive legislation concerning liquor. Ratified by the states in October 1919, the Amendment took effect on January 16, 1920. For the next dozen years a Protestant coalition labored to make a success of the "noble experiment," as President Herbert Hoover later termed it.

Historical Committee of the Mennonite Church

Mennonite postwar relief work in the Ukraine.

The armistice signed on November 11, 1918, represented the triumph of only the first of America's two righteous causes: to defeat Germany and outlaw war. Indeed, the justness of the first rested squarely on ethical commitment to the second. Protestant churchmen, assuming the sustained momentum of wartime enthusiasm, launched vast fundraising schemes to bring in the new world order of peace and democracy under the banner of the Interchurch World Movement. They did not foresee the postwar letdown and resulting disillusionment, which along with other forces would bring their heavenly construct crashing back to earth. In retrospect, historians have come to see that the war and its aftermath marked passage from nineteenth-century confidences and visions to twentieth-century complexities and perplexities.

The intensity of the war ideology itself helped unleash latent nativist tendencies which repressed thoughtful dissent and demanded conformity. Buttressed by the fear of worldwide communist revolution and the dilution of "Anglo-Saxon democratic institutions," many Americans, in and out of the churches, harbored deep prejudices against blacks, Jews, Catholics, and other immigrants. The way was paved for a resurgence of the Ku Klux Klan mentality in the 1920s (in both the North and South) built on defense of Protestant America against alien peoples and programs. In short, the tendency to project Christian and American ways as identical led to an idealized picture of America that did not fit the experience of black Christians and other victims of prejudice.

The Retreat to "Normalcy"

Church historian Sydney E. Ahlstrom well summarizes the significance of the postwar decade in relation to the churches' continuing concern to define the ethos of American culture:

> One wonders if any decade was *less* normal, for it was a time of crisis for both the Protestant Establishment and the historic evangelicalism which undergirded it. It was the critical epoch when the Puritan heritage lost its hold on the leaders of public life, and when the mainstream denominations grew increasingly out of touch with the classic Protestant witness.

The mutually enhancing amalgamation of church and state in the Great Crusade gave no hint of its transitoriness. The end of the war was followed by a decade of steady decline (in spite of financial prosperity) in all tangible aspects of church life and also in certain crucial intangibles. Peacetime normalcy accommodated and accelerated the trend toward secularization in American society, of which the twenties are replete with examples.

Skepticism was widely expressed by intellectuals in their writing and by the common man in his behavior. While H. L. Mencken and Clarence Darrow charged that the churches were behind the times, religion as a subject of serious and intelligent discussion all but disappeared from the literary monthlies. The anonymity of urban life contributed to a casual attitude toward church attendance; Sunday took on a more recreational, holiday mood. Family devotions became old fashioned.

In addition to an overwhelming confidence in science to solve mankind's problems, Freudianism in psychology and pragmatism in philosophy exacerbated the drift toward a naturalistic approach to man. After Sigmund Freud's lecture visit to Clark University (Mass.) in 1909, the number of adherents to his views grew exponentially. This trend was aided by scores of popularizing books on the new psychology with its emphasis on human irrationality and animality. On the other hand, the advances Freudianism contributed to the mental-hygiene movement and the treatment of psychoneuroses should not be overlooked.

Pragmatism, particularly as stated by John Dewey (1859–1952) of Columbia University, postulated that the sense, or truthfulness, of an idea derives from its consequences or uses. Put simply, what works is what is true. More a methodology than a systematic philosophy, pragmatism concerned itself with immediate results rather than ultimate ends. As such, it heavily influenced education, pedagogy, and curriculum in the schools. Christian theism was further eroded by pragmatism's relativistic approach to truth.

On a more practical level vast numbers of American lives were dramatically shaped by the new merchandising, mass media, and leisure industries. Automobiles, cheap and efficient, came within reach of many beneficiaries of the suddenly higher wage and shorter work week after 1917. Installment buying and wild business speculation, traditionally frowned upon in religious circles, now offered an avenue to enjoyment, extravagance, and status, paid for only in part.

Sophisticated advertising techniques created desires for dazzling consumer products as the movies and radio created a new celebrity class that set the trends for both clothing and behavior. The upwardly mobile lifestyle, which often included a move to the suburbs, regular family vacations, and Sundays on the golf course or driving to the seashore, easily relegated religion to a minor sector of life.

Except in certain rural regions, largely in the South, the churches no

Noonday public preaching attracted an audience at Saint Paul's Cathedral (Episcopal) in Boston, 1919.

longer provided that singular formative role in community, family, and individual life that had been so evident in nineteenth-century America. Even after the turn of the century, during the decade and a half of intensive reform efforts known as the Progressive Era, Protestants of every outlook supplied the broad evangelical ideals and rhetoric from which most reformers drew inspiration. President Woodrow Wilson's wartime appeals exuded the same values. During the 1920s, however, the forces of Protestantism turned against each other at the very time when the pluralization and secularization of America took on new intensity. There is no doubt that the fundamentalist controversy debated foundational theological and social issues. The resultant polarization and extremity of positions, the eventual acrimony and schisms, mark the demise of Protestant hegemony in the United States. By 1933 Alfred North Whitehead could remark about Protestantism: "Its dogmas no longer dominate; its divisions no longer interest; its institutions no longer direct the patterns of life." Despite Whitehead's observation, however, it should be remembered that the societal value base for legally determining public and private morality continued to be drawn from the Jewish-Christian tradition. The full impact of pluralization and secularization would not be felt for another generation, especially as regarding the issues of pornography, homosexuality, abortion, and religious observances in the schools.

The Fundamentalist-Modernist Controversy

Fundamentalism has too often been caricatured by popular historians as the last gasp of a bigoted Protestant establishment. Neglecting to note the varied nature of the fundamentalist movement, scholars have often presented it as a belligerent monolith of defensive religious fanaticism. There certainly were embarrassing and even shabby episodes to betray the shallowness, parochialism, divisiveness, and arrogance of some fundamentalists and their leaders. Unfortunately, thoughtful leaders such as the urbane and erudite J. Gresham Machen (1881–1937) have sometimes been overlooked in favor of more flamboyant figures. Also, the painful sincerity of many lay adherents of fundamentalism has often been superficially treated without appreciation of their dilemma in confronting the decline of what they believed to be the cohesive, foundational value structure for both society and church.

During the 1920s the underlying theological cleavage that had been developing within the denominations erupted into open confrontation between conservatives and liberals (or modernists). Until 1910 churchmen in the various communions, whether liberal or conservative, had cooperated in the task of reaching the world for Christ. They wrote for the same journals, prayed for the same causes, and shared similar hopes for the Christianization of mankind. After World War I the workable consensus eroded as the theological debate intensified and a conservative coalition emerged ready to battle for the ascendancy of orthodoxy.

The dividing issues were hardly minor: the authority and inerrancy of the Bible; the virgin birth of Christ; the physical resurrection of Christ; the personal salvation of the believer through Christ's substitutionary atonement; and the second coming of Christ. These were the fundamentals that conservatives defended as the touchstones of historic Christianity.

Among the defenders of orthodoxy, Princeton Seminary professor J. Gresham Machen stands out for the cogency of his arguments in *The Origin of Paul's Religion* (1921), *Christianity and Liberalism* (1923), and *The Virgin Birth of Christ* (1930). Machen claimed that liberalism was not essentially Christian in that it denied the historic creeds which all believers had traditionally affirmed, especially regarding Christ's death to save sinners and his physical resurrection. Thus, Machen and others felt that the modernists should leave the denominations and found new ones devoted to their novel theology with its faith in mankind and science.

Although the best-known popular proponent of liberalism in the 1920s was New York City clergyman Harry Emerson Fosdick, who preached in the famous Riverside Church after 1931, the most cohesive articulation of liberal theology was probably that of Shailer Mathews, dean of the University of Chicago Divinity School, as set forth in *The Faith of Modernism* (1924). He emphasized that Christianity is life, not doctrine, and more a matter of experience and practical morality in following God's will, revealed in the example of Christ, than adherence to doctrinal confessions representative of the faith needs of a past era.

The contending fundamentalist and liberal parties reached the most serious levels of confrontation in the Northern Baptist Convention and the Presbyterian Church in the U.S.A. in 1924 and 1925. Other denominations experienced flurries of activity to restrict the acceptance of liberalism in their ranks. But for various reasons the most intense debate and eventually the most permanent ecclesiastical splits occurred among the Presbyterians and Baptists with their Calvinistic emphasis on strict doctrinal definitions.

Any attempt to follow the course of the contest in most denominations reveals that total polarization did not take place. Usually the balance of political influence resided with a moderate middle party, generally evangelical in viewpoint but not militant enough to join with the more determined fundamentalists in order to root out liberal clergy even at the risk of schism. In the long run, the reluctance of the moderates to vote with their fundamentalist brothers prevented the latter from eliminating the liberal ministers from the denominations.

Eventually, when Baptist and Presbyterian schisms did occur, they were largely precipitated by efforts to form independent mission boards free of liberals. Rather than submit to denominational demands to cease supporting an alternate mission organization, Machen resigned from both Princeton Seminary and the Presbyterian Church in the U.S.A. With his followers he founded Westminster Theological Seminary (Philadelphia) in 1929 and a separate denomination which became known as the Orthodox Presbyterian Church in 1939. Dissident Baptist fundamentalists withdrew from the Northern Baptist Convention to form the General Association of Regular Baptists in 1933; in 1947 another group founded the Conservative Baptist Association.

On the whole, during the 1920s southern denominations did not undergo the same type of wrenching controversy. In the South evangelical Protestantism was thoroughly intertwined with southern cultural conservatism. Compared to their northern counterparts, members of the southern Presbyterian church (Presbyterian Church in the U.S.) and the Southern Baptist Convention found little difficulty in reaffirming orthodox doctrine. Penetration of the region's schools by evolutionary theories of man's origins, however, became a rallying cry for southern fundamentalists. The contest for control of school curriculum reached its zenith in the sensational Scopes trial conducted in Dayton, Tennessee, in 1925.

As in other southern states, the influence of Tennessee fundamentalists was powerful enough to pressure the state legislature to make it unlawful to "teach any theory that denies the story of the divine creation of man as taught in the Bible." In Dayton, a high-school biology teacher, John T. Scopes, continued to teach evolutionary views; he was arrested and brought to trial in 1925. In *Fundamentalism and American Culture,* George Marsden sets the scene:

> In the popular imagination, there were on the one side the small town, the backwoods, half-educated yokels, obscurantism, crackpot hawkers of religion, fundamentalism, the South, and the personification of the agrarian myth himself, William Jennings Bryan. Opposed to these were the city, the clique of New York-Chicago lawyers, intellectuals, journalists, wits, sophisticates, modernists, and the urbane agnostic Clarence Darrow.

The details of this carefully staged trial have become part of American legend, dramatized and distorted in the film *Inherit the Wind.* For many fundamentalists and liberals it was a near apocalyptic, archetypal confrontation and the issues have remained touchstones in the unresolved struggle of fundamentalists to retain an influence on the general culture; or at least to approve the world view and values encountered by their children in public schools.

In the end, Scopes was convicted, then acquitted on a technicality. Bryan lay dead a few days later and fundamentalism became increasingly associated in the popular mind with ignorance, backwardness, and reaction. In short, the term that originally had referred to an orthodox ministerial effort, largely urban, to oppose theological liberalism in the northern denominations came to connote hostility to modern culture and social change.

Unable to achieve orthodox uniformity in the mainline denominations or forestall the drift of American society away from traditional Protestant values toward pluralism and secularization, the militant fundamentalists developed a life, an identity, and ultimately a subculture of their own. Although the vision of a great national campaign coordinated through the World Christian Fundamentals Association (founded in 1919 and led by Baptist William Bell Riley of Minneapolis) was largely dissipated by 1930, fundamentalism as a religious force came to be undergirded by an institutional network of Bible institutes, Bible conferences, itinerant evangelists, periodicals, faith-missions societies, small denominations, radio preachers, publishing houses, and a host of independent congregations. In retrospect, religious fundamentalism has to be seen as a peculiarly American response by numerous evangelicals to the stressful social and intellectual challenges of the times. Unfortunately, in the name of pure Christianity and loyal Americanism, fundamentalists retreated from any significant formative influence in the cultural and intellectual centers of the society. The dispensational theology held by many further encouraged societal withdrawal. Nevertheless, the fundamentalists perpetuated the evangelical dynamic of a Bible-based Christianity and the gospel call for personal commitment to a risen Christ.

The fundamentalist-modernist controversy affecting American Protestantism throughout the 1920s has sometimes been described in overly simplistic terms as a rural-urban conflict between traditional agrarian religionists and progressive urban liberals. However, cities such as Philadelphia, Fort Worth, Minneapolis, Chicago, Denver, and Los Angeles were all centers of fundamentalist strength. But on a more symbolic level, the conflict can perhaps be seen as a clash between two mentalities: the one more comfortable in a preindustrial, homogeneous environment where religious faith is central and traditional authority structures are honored; the other more oriented to the technology and diversity of the modern urban world with its emphasis on individual autonomy, open-ended search for truth, and pluralization of culture.

The Churches and Economic Crisis

The stock-market crash of October 1929, which ended the precarious postwar "normalcy" of the Harding-Coolidge era, shook American society even more deeply than had World War I, and the churches did not escape the worldwide economic upheaval. The decade of upwardly spiraling economy and unlimited opportunity ended; hopes were dashed. Ahead lay the threat of permanent economic class cleavages like those of the Old World. Many Protestants lived above the lowest level of destitution; however, the churches were confronted on all sides by human suffering, confusion, and social anxiety.

There was no revival in the major denominations, such as had often accompanied previous economic deflation. But those evangelistic churches that stressed a better life in heaven and espoused premillennial views of history, particularly the Pentecostal and Holiness communions, often experienced phenomenal growth during the lean years of the thirties. They continued to attract Americans from the middle and especially the lower economic classes, whose numbers were increasing geometrically as hard times set in.

In most churches budgets were slashed, membership dwindled,

Salvation Army Archives and Research Center

The Salvation Army sponsored a variety of programs to meet the needs of people during the depression.

missionary enterprises were curtailed; in some cases ministers were dismissed and sanctuaries closed. It was a bitter, difficult, and disheartening period, and churches struggled along as best they could, as did individuals. In the midst of it, the prohibition experiment, for which many church people had crusaded, came to an end. An editorial in the *Christian Century* stated in 1935 that "the Christian church has come into the depression wholly unprepared to take account of it, and to minister to the deepest human need which it discloses."

The churches did what they could to alleviate the hurts of their parishioners, but without notable success. The suffering was too pervasive and workable solutions eluded earnest churchmen who sought to exercise charity. Manifesting something of the spirit of the social gospel, Franklin Delano Roosevelt's New Deal became the paternal substitute for traditional church charity. The modern world called for big solutions and most of the traditional churches, sapped by secularism and the perplexities of the depression, naturally succumbed to the agenda of the larger society and culture. As historian Winthrop S. Hudson observed: "With its basic theological insights largely emasculated, Protestantism was robbed of any independently grounded vision of life and became more and more the creature of American culture rather than its creator." The times were demanding a renewed emphasis on well-articulated social and ecclesiastical criticism from within the churches.

16

Years of War and Uncertainty

By the 1930s the kernel of theological redefinition began to sprout in America. Its origins, however, go back to the preaching and writings of a sensitive minister serving a small parish on the Swiss border during World War I. As the horrors of war and the disintegration of international order enveloped Europe, Karl Barth (1886–1968) lost confidence in optimistic liberal theology. Its emphasis on human rationality and scientifically induced progress squared with neither reality nor the crucial themes of the New Testament.

The Postliberal Theological Mind

For Barth, liberalism had brushed aside the Pauline insistence on the sovereignty and righteousness of God, the sinfulness of man, and God's initiative in man's salvation through revelation and by grace. Barth articulated these ideas in his *Commentary on the Epistle to the Romans* (1919), which, along with other writings, resoundingly called for a rediscovery of biblical theology as well as renewed appreciation of the Protestant reformers of the sixteenth century. Barth stressed the "infinite qualitative difference" between God and man—a phrase borrowed from Sören Kierkegaard (1813–1855), the Danish religious thinker. Barth rejected "natural theology." If man reaches God by the light of his reason he will find only an idol of his own creation, not the self-revealing God, who is transcendent, wholly other, always Subject and never Object. Zürich's Emil Brunner (1889–1966), who studied in America and in 1938–1939 lectured at Princeton Seminary, was the chief transmitter of Barth's views in the United States, although Brunner himself differed with Barth over natural revelation and other points.

Some American theologians were ready to consider the claims of this fresh theological realism with its exposure of human sinfulness and man's need for divine redeeming grace. They were disillusioned by the harsh depression years and the ominous rumblings of fascism and communism abroad.

The most widely heard American communicator of these convictions was Reinhold Niebuhr (1892–1971). After pastoring a Detroit industrial parish, where he saw firsthand the plight of many workers, Niebuhr joined the faculty of Union Theological Seminary (New York) in 1928, a post he held for thirty-two years. In 1932 Niebuhr published the most devastating theological polemic of its time, *Moral Man and Immoral Society,* which analyzed the prevailing assumptions of liberalism and found them lacking the realism with which to combat the problems of a technological and industrial society. In particular, the book castigated the romantic moralists in education, sociology, and religion. By the end of the decade many influential Protestant liberals had publicly acknowledged that their theological views had been deeply chastened or substantially revised.

These revisions were variously labeled neoorthodoxy, desperation theology, realistic theology, or neosupernaturalism. Those characterizations fail to indicate the great diversity of ideas emerging in the writings of several theologians, among whom was H. Richard Niebuhr, Reinhold's brother. Nevertheless, a distinctive pattern of traits can be identified which marked the evolution of what some have termed the postliberal theological mind.

First, God's sovereignty (theocentrism) was posited over against any attempt to make man central (anthropocentrism) to building theology. This stress on divine transcendence did not denote other-worldliness.

Second, a renewed importance was placed on the Bible as the bearer of divine revelation. Because the neoorthodox readily accepted the conclusions of biblical criticism and generally rejected the Bible as the objective, historical Word of God, many conservatives faulted the movement for its subjective approach to religious truth and authority. On the other hand, biblical studies received new emphasis and impetus, especially after discovery of the Dead Sea Scrolls in 1947.

Third, man's moral predicament was thoroughly recognized, with sin understood to be rooted in human pride and selfishness. Only when encountered by God is man able to commit himself to seeking relative good in a complex and sinful society. In *The Social Sources of Denominationalism* (1929) and *The Kingdom of God in America* (1937) H. Richard Neibuhr pointed out the susceptibility of the churches to being overtaken by the values of the larger society.

A revived interest in Christology was a fourth postliberal trend expressed in a spate of christological treatises during the 1940s and '50s. Highly influential among them was *Existence and the Christ* (1957) by émigré Paul Tillich (1886–1965), who left Nazi Germany in 1933 to teach at New York's Union Seminary. Although they are often considered beyond the limits of neoorthodoxy, and certainly far left of Barth's theology, Tillich's writings, including his three-volume *Systematic Theology* (1951–1963), were pivotal in reinvigorating theological thought in America.

Finally, postliberal thinking explored the nature of the church. With some exceptions, Protestantism as a whole has been largely indifferent toward ecclesiology; likewise liberalism, and, perhaps surprisingly, Roman Catholicism. In the 1920s Catholics began to stress the Pauline metaphor of the church as the Body of Christ rather than the traditional idea of the church as the kingdom of God. Although the notion was initially greeted with disfavor, Pope Pius XII supported it in his 1943 encyclical, *Mystici Corporis Christi,* and opposition subsided. Charles Clayton Morrison sparked new Protestant interest in ecclesiology through his pioneering work on the church, *What Is Christianity?* (1940). Numerous other such books appeared, including Nels Ferré's *Christian Fellowship* (1940). Renewed interest in the church also led to a remarkable liturgical awakening, especially among Roman Catholics, Lutherans, and Episcopalians.

Considered totally, these tendencies indicate substantial revision of the earlier liberal theology. At the same time they do not signify the exclusion of all elements of historic liberalism, but only its demise as a coherent system. Neoorthodoxy's emphasis on divine sovereignty, sin, revelation, and redemption did shift the focus of theological debate back to the central biblical themes of historic Christianity. But it would be years before the implications of the new theology would sift down from seminary professors to preachers in the pulpits to the parishioners in the pews. For most of the last, keeping America removed from growing international tensions was of greater moment than theological reformulation.

Yearning for Peace and Joining in War

Heated debate throughout the 1920s and '30s concerning the repudiation of war as a means to peace quite naturally engaged large numbers of pastors and parishioners, editors and readers, professors and students. American pacifism, wholeheartedly embraced now by many religious leaders, also appealed to political isolationists, leftist youth organizations, and proponents of Gandhi-type nonresistance, as well as detractors of Roosevelt, the anti-British, and pro-fascists. The America First movement drew members from many of these groups.

Adolf Hitler's strident militarism and anti-Semitism, revealed after 1933, coupled with Japan's aggression toward China and Italy's toward Ethiopia, rendered absolute pacifism a more difficult position. But many religious liberals had so overwhelmingly committed themselves to it that they could not retreat. Following Hitler's blitzkrieg against Poland and the outbreak of war in September 1939, the issue came more sharply into focus: participation versus nonparticipation. It is quite clear that the debate continued among both Protestants and Catholics right up until the Japanese bombing of Pearl Harbor, December 7, 1941. Between 1939 and late 1941 various denominational polls indicated that large minorities of clergy, students, and parishioners considered themselves serious pacifists. Most church people, like the population at large, although not declared pacifists, desperately wanted to avoid involvement in another war, and denominational bodies passed strong antiwar resolutions.

American pacifism, stemming from the social gospel and representing a determination to do politically what would best bring about world peace, was not that of the historic pacifistic denominations. The Quakers and Mennonites, basing their total nonresistance on the teachings of Jesus and eschewing political power, for the most part did not involve themselves in the debate. Their status as conscientious objectors was already recognized by the government and at this time draft legislation extended that right to members of any recognized church body, although all young men were required to register. Some predicted that America would not or could not again unite in another war effort. However, the outrage at Japan's sneak attack on Pearl Harbor forged a consolidated America as only such a vicious act of war could. Overnight, pacifism for most outside the traditional pacifistic groups became unpatriotic, unrealistic, and untenable. War became the necessary evil to defeat the more monstrous evil of the Axis powers.

Although some ministers and others refused to register for the draft, and after due process were imprisoned, the conscientious objectors among registrants numbered only about twelve thousand; they were assigned alternate service. Again the churches, although in decline, took up without reluctance their wartime tasks; but a more tempered and mature view of global war's grim business replaced the unrestrained crusading enthusiasm of 1917–1918. Church bodies reversed their antiwar declarations, but none glorified the war or made it a holy cause, although much that was holy was understood to be at stake. Many mainline denominations passed resolutions and laid plans to assist in creating a just postwar world.

A dedicated and professionally trained corps of chaplains from all religious faiths numbered more than eight thousand. Congress appropriated in early 1941 more than twelve million dollars to build six hundred chapels wherever there were American troops; interestingly, this action drew little, if any, protest. The deep human needs magnified by war's fears, separations, and devastation, and the demand for national and personal courage to again defeat "might" and defend "right," contributed to a new tide of religious interest, often called the "postwar revival"; but it began in the foxholes, battleship chapels, military hospitals, homes, and churches well before the end of the war. America's sacrificial defense of the "four freedoms" seemed to enhance the value of each, including the freedom of worship.

Postwar Consensus and Religious Revival

By all the familiar indications America experienced a revival of religious affiliation and activities in the decade and a half following World War II. Membership in religious groups of all types increased twice as fast as the population. A host of new sanctuaries and synagogues were constructed, especially in the expanding suburbs. Religious books topped best-seller lists and purchases of the Revised Standard Version of the Bible (1950) broke all records—two million in its first year alone. Mass evangelism was revitalized, assisted by the numerous new parachurch youth ministries. Religion departments arose within colleges and universities and new seminaries were founded. President Dwight D. Eisenhower extolled the importance of faith and the prayer-breakfast movement was launched to enlist and encourage governmental leaders in the cause of morality and religion. Endorsed by legislation, the phrase *under God* was inserted into the national pledge of allegiance in 1954, and in 1955, "In God We Trust," which had appeared on coins since 1864, became the official national motto. The American Legion organized a "Back to God" campaign.

Various observations have been offered on this upsurge in religious activity, a surprise to many secular journalists and scholars. The war experience itself undoubtedly heightened spiritual concerns, and peace did not alleviate the collective and personal anxieties over the destructive potential of atomic warfare and the developing Cold War with the Soviets. When conflict broke out in Korea in June 1950, summoning Americans back into combat, a third world war seemed imminent. Americans also feared domestic communism. It was during these years that Senator Joseph R. McCarthy, the later discredited denouncer of "reds" and "pinks" in government, reached his zenith.

At the same time, American society was undergoing more flux than was evident to contemporaries. Highly mobile whites were leaving the large cities for homes in the burgeoning bedroom suburbs, while blacks and Hispanics filtered into the old urban neighborhoods. Many professional and managerial types did not put down roots at all but moved every few years as they received promotions in their careers. Easy air travel and the increasingly pervasive influence of television broke down regional barriers and accelerated the pace of change in American life. For many, the postwar period provided personal and economic consolidation after the years of depression and war. And they joined the churches! In 1955 estimates indicated that almost half the population attended some religious service once a week. By 1960 about 70 percent held membership in a religious body. In the same year more than a billion dollars were expended on religious edifices, evidence of prosperity.

Reminiscent of past periods of revival was the new surge of mass evangelism, traditional in its message of personal salvation, but contemporary in its upbeat presentation, use of the media, and its application of the gospel message to the unique anxieties of the atomic age and the confrontation with communism. Leading this movement was a network of youngish evangelistic preachers and musicians circulating among the interdenominational Saturday night Youth for Christ rallies organized after 1943 from coast to coast in major American and Canadian cities, and with close ties to the evangelical churches in each area. Many thousands of youth, and the not-so-young, discovered the liveliness and joy of a new kind of old-time religion on Saturday night; often in contrast to the formalism of their church experience on Sunday morning.

From among the magnetic personalities crisscrossing the continent weekly to fill the evangelists' podiums emerged the one who would become the most widely heard Christian evangelist of all time, William Franklin (Billy) Graham (b. 1918), liberal-arts graduate of Wheaton College (Ill.), ordained Baptist minister, who had been reared in Charlotte, North Carolina. This handsome, tall young man with the dashing smile and disarming southern drawl exuded quiet sincerity and a deeply spiritual desire to be used of God.

Appropriately, a tent-meeting revival campaign launched Graham as a national figure. It was newspaperman William Randolph Hearst who sensed significance in Graham's 1949 Los Angeles evangelistic meetings and sent his reporters to cover them. They found crowds

Billy Graham.

flocking to the big tent night after night for eight weeks, and many, even a few celebrities, making decisions to accept Christ as Savior, to be born again. As this news reached the local headlines and then filtered across America, Christians began to envision similar revivals in *their* cities.

For this purpose, in 1950, Graham and a coterie of like-minded close friends formed the Billy Graham Evangelistic Association. (It is noteworthy that most of those early associates have remained with Graham throughout the years.) In city after city crusades were mounted with ever increasing organizational planning and follow-up, and always were sponsored by a local committee of clergy and business and professional leaders. Graham insisted on the invitation of a majority of Protestant clergy as a prerequisite to a crusade. He, in turn, urged his many converts to grow in their new faith by associating with a church.

Like D. L. Moody before him, Graham elicited enormous response in the three-month Greater London Crusade of 1954, despite British reserve and skepticism. Since then his ministry has been truly global. He has preached repeatedly on every continent in the presence of monarchs, archbishops, presidents, and dignitaries of all kinds, always with the simple gospel call to repentance, saving faith, and hope for the person and the society.

Thirty years' perspective on Graham's ministry suggests several areas of significance for the American churches. While holding to orthodox doctrine, Graham has transcended intolerance and sectarianism in order to unite Christians in the task of evangelism, for which he has been scorned by the ultrafundamentalists. He has also refused an anti-Catholic stance. His personal winsomeness, increasing cosmopolitanism, restrained lifestyle, and the accountability of his business management have enhanced the credibility of evangelicals in general. His utilization of all the media and presentation of testimonies by entertainers and professional athletes have helped break down traditional fundamentalist taboos about cinema, theater, and professional sports. Finally, his sensitivity to the issues surrounding the social application of the gospel has shown growth and increasing insight. In 1967 he testified in Washington to support the War on Poverty, claiming biblical mandate. More recently he has raised moral questions about nuclear armament. He has always spoken out against racism.

Simultaneous with the upsurge of mass evangelism came a national quest for peace of mind. Beginning in 1946 with the publication of Rabbi Joshua Liebman's popular *Peace of Mind,* a primer of religious psychology that pointed toward newness of life through mental discipline, there followed similar themes from Roman Catholic Fulton J. Sheen (*Peace of Soul,* 1949) and Protestant Graham (*Peace with God,* 1953).

But among peace-of-mind advocates, none surpassed Norman Vincent Peale (b. 1898), pastor of Marble Collegiate Church in New York City. Through his syndicated newspaper columns ("Confident Living"), radio and television shows ("The Art of Living"), and magazine *(Guideposts),* he had an audience of perhaps thirty million in the 1950s. His books, beginning with *You Can Win* (1938) and including *The Power of Positive Thinking* (1952), which quickly sold more than two million copies, dispensed his religious psychological

Norman Vincent Peale, advocate of "the power of positive thinking."

self-help counsel to all seekers. His was big-thinking, big-believing, success-oriented Christianity, which matched both the problems and prosperity of the times and capitalized on the new popularity of religion; it especially appealed to professionals and the upwardly mobile middle class. Peale drew criticism from the liberals for his political and social conservativism, from the fundamentalists for watering down the gospel, and from the neoorthodox for his optimism. Despite his detractors, Peale's ministry and writing continue to influence the lives of millions. An ordained minister of the Reformed Church in America, he remains a unique popular phenomenon.

Significantly, the "cult of reassurance" reached its crest just when the demand for conformity and depersonalization of institutional structures in America reached its highest levels. Although their conclusions are probably overgeneralized, several important books portray the postwar shift from traditional individualism to social conformity: David Riesman's *Lonely Crowd* (1950), William H. Whyte's *Organization Man* (1956), and Charles A. Reich's *Greening of America* (1970). The "organization man" sees himself as a unit of the larger society for whom the worst fate is to be isolated. Only by participating with others does he retain a sense of personal value. In Riesman's study he is the "others-directed" individual who seeks respect and affection from a contemporary "jury of peers" who evaluate one's worth and achievement. Reich sees this Everyman attempting to fill a function called for by society and dutifully making personal sacrifices for it.

Numerous historians and sociologists have commented on the shallowness of personal commitment and insight that accompanied much of the postwar religious resurgence. Church membership could mean little more than respectability and belief in the American way of life. President Eisenhower summed it up in 1954: "Our government makes no sense unless it is founded on a deeply felt religious faith—and I don't care what it is." In *Protestant, Catholic, Jew* (1955), Will Herberg suggests that confidence in the American way (democracy, free enterprise, humanitarianism, and optimism) was the real integrating force for many of all faiths. In spite of the plight of minorities and other social problems, the status quo was sanctified. In an era of conflict with "godless communism" it was perhaps natural to merge American interests with God's eternal purposes and identify the churches with the larger society. Some have called this tendency an American civil religion. Church historian Martin E. Marty has asked why so much overlap existed between Christianity and secularism during these years. His answer: "A non-existent God and a completely captive God are very much alike: Under the one or under the other 'all things are permissible.'" The more superficial and ephemeral elements of this religious upswing were swept away in the social turbulence of the 1960s. But there remained many of all ages whose lives were deeply altered by the revival, and who moved beyond their own personal security to carry forward the legacy of true spirituality and piety in the American churches along with zealous commitment to evangelism in a rapidly changing world.

Evangelical Advance

It was during the formative period following World War II that the ideational and institutional base was laid upon which the future gains of conservative Protestantism were built. Of particular significance is the break with stricter 1930s style fundamentalism by those who would adopt the term *neoevangelical.* They were totally orthodox in doctrine but rejected the cultural and theological excesses in fundamentalism—sectarianism, judgmentalism, anti-intellectualism, cultural isolation, and lack of social ethic.

During the 1940s and '50s the neoevangelical thrust was spearheaded by a coterie of prominent preachers, writers, organizations, and institutions. This pacesetting cluster provoked criticism from many fundamentalists and provided an aura of new vitality for evangelical religion. Components in this revitalization were the forming in 1943 of the National Association of Evangelicals (NAE) as a corporate alternative to the Federal Council of Churches (soon to become the National Council of Churches) on the left and the American Council of Christian Churches on the right (organized in 1941 by Carl McIntire, leader of the schismatic Bible Presbyterians); an attempted fresh engagement with society on an intellectual and cultural level—strikingly exemplified by Carl F. H. Henry's *Uneasy Conscience of Fundamentalism* (1947); a broad movement creating fully credentialed educational institutions such as Fuller Theological Seminary (1947), many Christian colleges which upgraded programs, and Bible schools which assumed collegiate status; a dramatic growth in publishing houses and the output of Christian reading material, especially the magazine *Christianity Today* (1956), which gave direction to the new movement. Finally, there emerged new missionary agencies and a host of ministries designed to disciple young people, such as Youth for Christ and Young Life which evangelized teen-agers, and Inter-Varsity Christian Fellowship and Campus Crusade for Christ which served college students. National visibility for evangelical leaders derived from these and other parachurch ministries.

Keen observers of the American religious scene have recognized that neoevangelicalism owes as much or more to the parachurch enterprises as to resurgent denominational life. Leadership, influence, and opinion-setting emanated from the network of seminary and college presidents and professors, editors, authors, and key preachers, many of whom had radio and/or television ministries. An explanation of why the parachurch organizations eclipsed ecclesiastical structures is not difficult. These bodies offer efficiency, centralized decision-making, and can be task rather than parishioner oriented. Unlike congregations and denominations, the parachurch groups can cultivate a far-flung clientele with little obligation for full disclosure or open board meetings. They can mobilize across denominations, utilize lay persons well, and produce specialized services for disparate target groups.

Despite their noteworthy accomplishments, the entrepreneurial spirit of some parachurch agencies has made them vulnerable to personal empire-building and in-group politics. Also, theoretical and practical questions have remained in defining the parachurch bodies' relationship to the church itself. The former are structured much like business corporations, whereas the latter is comprised of voluntary fellowships which may apply biblical values much differently. These definitional tensions continue to blur distinctions in the broader evangelical movement.

The neoevangelicals were not the only component in the resurgence of conservative religion in America. Many small denominations and independent churches grew phenomenally. Among these were the Church of the Nazarene, the Church of God of Cleveland, Tennessee, and the Assemblies of God. Also, in the South, the Church of Christ and the ubiquitous Southern Baptists continued to expand in numbers of both congregations and support institutions. The more sectarian Seventh-Day Adventists gained many new converts as well, although this group is often viewed as a cult by evangelicals.

The Holiness and Pentecostal denominations received special national visibility when President Henry P. Van Dusen of Union Seminary (New York) termed them pivotal to a burgeoning "third force" in American Protestantism in a *Life* magazine article ("The Third Force's Lessons for Others" [June 9, 1958]).

As the 1950s drew to a close it became obvious that America faced an unresolved social-justice agenda. Too presumptively had the ideals of American society been equated with reality. The tensions attending school desegregation after the 1954 Supreme Court decision *(Brown v. Board of Education)* pointed up the ambivalence of many white Christians on the issues of race relations and civil rights. With the initiation of the Montgomery, Alabama, bus boycott in 1956 and the summoning of the National Guard to Little Rock's Central High School in 1957, the question of racial justice could no longer be ignored.

Over the decade the National Council of Churches passed antisegregation and antidiscrimination resolutions. Implementation in local situations proved difficult. Among those evangelicals who easily linked conservative politics and social views with their conservative religion, the growing minority cry for civil rights created unease as the injustices of discrimination in both the North and South demanded notice. Most white American churchgoers were not prepared theologically or personally for a rapid change in race relations. Nor could they have anticipated the dislocation, disarray, and disaffection about to confront the society and various churches in the 1960s. In retrospect, many historians appear accurate when they suggest that the postwar religious revival reflected not the opening of a new era, but the close of an older one.

17

Serving Mankind at Home and Abroad

The United States is by far the most religious of any of the industrialized societies. As Alexis de Tocqueville observed a century and a half ago, the lack of a state church combined with strong religious consciousness provided the basis for voluntary philanthropy rare in other cultures. It is not surprising, therefore, that the relative stability and prosperity of the postwar years undergirded a renewed effort by American churches to respond to human needs around the world, and for many, to do it in closer concert with the greater Body of Christ.

The Flowering of Ecumenism

The ecumenical awakening that occurred after World War II was directly stimulated by encountering the unitive currents flowing in numerous ecclesiastical bodies around the world. The young churches in places such as India, Africa, and China were disturbed by the divisions among the denominations in the West (a phenomenon largely regarded as normal by the "home" churches). Furthermore, these distinctions and rivalries, which had originated centuries before in the ecclesiastical and political histories of Europe and America, were now being perpetuated among them. Many earnest churchmen in the West perceived that such divisions were a stumbling block to the advance of the Christian mission. Christians who accepted or perpetuated such divisions were unconvincing messengers of the Prince of Peace and the spirit of fellowship. Although there had been significant steps toward cooperation earlier in the century, ecumenism flowered in the postwar period. For millions of Christians worldwide, the ecumenical movement became the most encouraging development in twentieth-century Protestantism.

The major ecumenical event was the formation of the World Council of Churches (WCC) at Amsterdam in 1948 as "a fellowship of churches which accept our Lord Jesus Christ as God and Savior." One hundred and forty-seven church bodies from forty-four countries became members; of these twenty-nine were American. The second assembly of the WCC met at Evanston, Illinois, in 1954; this was America's first major ecumenical gathering and a strong force in heightening American interest in ecumenism.

Various strains of cooperative Christianity within the United States converged during this period to create the National Council of the Churches of Christ in the U.S.A. (NCC). After the preliminary planning sessions in 1941, the NCC became official in Cleveland, Ohio, in November 1950. Eight existing Protestant interdenominational agencies merged with twenty-nine church bodies to continue the functions of the newly united agencies. These were the Foreign Missions Conference of North America, Home Mission Council of North America, Federal Council of the Churches of Christ in America, International Council of Religious Education, Missionary Education Movement of the United States and Canada, National Protestant Council on Higher Education, United Council of Church Women, and United Stewardship Council.

As mainline denominational leaders became better acquainted through serving together in ecumenical endeavor, it became apparent that the range of doctrinal differences among them was far narrower than many had assumed. Members of the NCC were pleasantly surprised to find themselves united on such charged subjects as "gospel" and "grace"—doctrines that had been splintering churches since the sixteenth century. But although the *range* of differences appeared narrowed, the *depth* of differences on particular doctrines was substantial: issues such as the nature of the church, the character of the ministry, and the theory and practice of the sacraments. At the third WCC assembly at Lund in 1952, study was directed to Christology in the hope that as Christians were drawn toward the center of their faith, they might move closer to one another. Also emphasized was the importance of the shaping influences of cultural, ethnic, and national factors in perpetuating Christian divisions. The results were only mildly successful and the WCC continues to grapple with these questions.

As time passed it was realized that true ecumenism required discussion among lay persons as well as debate among scholars.

Each quarter of the candle is lit.

A DRAMATIC SYMBOL OF CHURCH UNION
The four parts are moved together.

The four burn as one flame.

A NEW STAR ON AMERICA'S ECCLESIASTICAL FIRMAMENT

Lutheran Church in America is Born

A new star of the first magnitude has appeared on America's ecclesiastical firmament. In an atmosphere of worship, pageantry and business deliberations in the arena of Cobo Hall, Detroit, Mich., a gathering of more than 7,000 persons on June 28 witnessed the consummation of the largest Lutheran church merger in history on this side of the Atlantic. It was the birth of the Lutheran Church in America, which begins its mission with a baptized membership of 3,200,000.

Very fittingly, the founding of the new Church was followed by the celebration of Holy Communion. It is estimated that approximately 5,000 persons knelt before the improvised altars to receive the blessed sacrament. It was probably the largest communion service of Lutherans ever held in America.

The clock showed 9:07 when Dr. Malvin H. Lundeen, chairman of the joint Commission on Lutheran Unity, which for nearly six years had been planning the union, called the constituting convention to order.

Formal statements were made by the presidents of the four merging Churches that the agreement of consolidation had been officially adopted by their respective bodies. The Rev. A. E. Farstrup spoke for the American Evangelical Lutheran Church, Dr. Lundeen for the Augustana Lutheran Church, Dr. Raymond W. Wargelin for the Finnish Evangelical Lutheran Church, and Dr. Franklin Clark Fry for the United Lutheran Church in America.

Then followed a dramatic historical and prophetic feature entitled "That Man May Live." It was a speech oratorio for solo voices and choir, written by Robert E. Huldschiner and directed by the Rev. Robert E. Bornemann. The oratorio sketched the historical background of the four bodies, and a chorus of 25 voices, robed in four colors, recalled the German, Swedish, Danish and Finnish traditions of the merging Churches.

The climactic moment came when four quarters of a massive white candle, each with a separate wick, were lighted by acolytes and then moved together to form a single light to symbolize the union of the four Churches in one body.

As the candle, three feet high and a foot in diameter flickered and then burst into a bright flame on a pedestal inside the improvised chancel, it was encircled with a broad band of gold as a symbol of unity and eternity. The oratorio then closed with the following declaration:

It is not the form that brings us together.
It is not a piece of paper on which we wrote words.
It is not a common song or a common pledge.
It is the One who led us,
The One who seeks man,
The One who became man
To show us the way.

The impressive communion service then followed. The entire floor of the convention arena of Cobo Hall had been transformed into a huge sanctuary for the service, with a large altar on a spacious platform in the center of the floor, and with three auxiliary communion tables extending from the platform into the arena. A giant gold-colored cross was suspended from the ceiling above the altar. Six communion rails and 40 administrants made it possible for the sacrament to be offered to some 175 persons at one time.

Dr. Edward T. Horn III, pastor of Trinity Lutheran Church, Germantown, Pa., served as celebrant; President Farstrup was the lector, and Dr. P. O. Bersell, president emeritus of the Augustana Lutheran Church, was the preacher.

Expressing joy over the consummation of the merger, Dr. Bersell said: "We rejoice that at long last these four Lutheran bodies have come together, because they belong together, they have one Lord and one faith."

Preceding the distribution, the great audience sang Johann Franck's glorious communion hymn, "Deck thyself with joy and gladness," to Johann Crüger's equally glorious chorale. Mrs. Regina Fryxell of Rock Island, Ill., who had an important part in the arrangement of the music of the second setting of the liturgy, was at the organ. The service came to a close with the singing of the soul-moving All Saints' hymn by William Walsham How, "For all the saints who from their labors rest," to R. Vaughan William's gripping tune.

Thus was born the Lutheran Church in America, a part of Christ's militant Church on earth, while grateful believers, with hearts overflowing with praise and devotion, sang a hymn of the Church Triumphant:

From earth's wide bounds, from ocean's farthest coast,
Through gates of pearl streams in the countless host,
Singing to Father, Son, and Holy Ghost:
Alleluia! Alleluia!

The first page of a booklet commemorating the merger of Lutheran groups in America.

Accordingly, "faith and order" discussions were launched at regional and national levels for lay people, including youth. The first of many such meetings convened at Oberlin College, Ohio, in September 1957.

An important aspect of domestic ecumenicity has been that of specific church unions. American church life experienced several significant unions within denominational families before the ecumenical era. For example, Old and New School Presbyterians merged in 1869–1870 to form the Presbyterian Church in the U.S.A., and in 1918, three Lutheran synods merged as the United Lutheran Church. In 1939, the Methodist Episcopal Church, the Methodist Episcopal Church, South, and the Methodist Protestant Church came together to form the Methodist Church.

A number of later mergers have coincided with the ecumenical movement. In 1957, the United Church of Christ enveloped four denominational traditions (Congregational, Christian, Lutheran, and Reformed) and two polities (congregational and presbyterian). In 1958, the United Presbyterian Church joined with the Presbyterian Church in the U.S.A. In 1960, seven Lutheran groups voted to participate in unions with the result that 96 percent of all Lutherans would belong to one of three major bodies: the Lutheran Church-Missouri Synod; the Lutheran Church in America; or the American Lutheran Church. Finally, in 1961, the Unitarian and Universalist churches united in the Unitarian-Universalist Association.

Despite the loftiness of ideals that characterized its leaders, the ecumenical movement, from its inception, has been the target of criticism. Some liberals have faulted it for being too traditional and church union too centralized. Southern Baptists and Missouri Synod Lutherans have spoken against it because their view of the nature of the church does not permit unqualified recognition of other Christian bodies as "true" churches. Other conservatives have found ecumenism theologically too latitudinarian, or politically too activist. The most vigorous criticism, however, has come from the fundamentalists, who have regarded the councils as instruments of "modernism." This sentiment motivated the formation of the American Council of Christian Churches by Carl McIntire in 1941. Roman Catholicism also declined to participate ecumenically. In 1928, Pope Pius XI issued the encyclical *Mortalium animos,* on "Fostering True Religious Unity." The document declared that

> the Apostolic See can by no means take part in these assemblies, nor is it in any way lawful for Catholics to give to such enterprises their encouragement or support. If they did so, they would be giving countenance to a false Christianity quite alien to the one Church of Christ.

A later statement in 1949, however, allowed enough leeway so that Catholics enthusiastic about reunion could participate unofficially in world ecumenical endeavors. The election of a Roman Catholic president of the United States in 1960 (John F. Kennedy) and the installation of the innovative Pope John XXIII in 1958 signaled changing attitudes.

New Trends on the Mission Field

For Christian missions the demise of the western colonial system in Asia and Africa has been the most significant event in the twentieth century. In *Understanding Christian Missions* (1974), missiologist J. Herbert Kane notes three major consequences of this global change. First, the image of Christianity has changed in the minds of Third-World peoples. Missionaries came to those lands along with the colonialists, and so by association the Christian gospel was considered foreign by the natives. Reinforcing this view were the cultural accretions that clung to the missionaries' message. When the colonial powers retreated the missionaries remained, thereby demonstrating that their motives transcended the temporal, political, and material. The Christian faith was revealed as a truly transcultural faith beckoning to "Jew and Greek, slave and free," in the words of Paul.

Second, the retreat of the colonial powers allowed self-definition among the mission churches. They are now free to recognize and affirm their own potentials and indigenous talents in working out what it means to be part of the Body of Christ in a particular culture. A third consequence is the changed role of the missionary from leader and spiritual parent to partner and spiritual servant.

The new national freedoms also led to some more negative consequences for Christian missions. Traditional ethnic religions resurfaced and, in many instances, became aggressively militant. Some missionaries faced expulsion and anticonversion laws were passed to restrict Christian expanse. The ethnic religious offensive also led to dispatching missionaries *to* the West, where secularizing forces were creating fertile soil for Oriental mysticism, transcendental meditation, yoga, and Zen Buddhism.

Missionary interest and activity in the mainline denominations declined sharply toward the end of the 1950s. Between 1958 and 1971 the number of missionaries from America's six largest church bodies dropped from 4,548 to 3,160. More conservative groups and the faith missions, however, held their own during these years; some even increased their foreign outreach. Post-World-War-II statistics clearly suggest the importance of theology in motivating Christian missions.

Evangelical missions, in particular, have dramatically expanded in the past thirty-five years.

Evangelical and other conservative missions have pioneered various innovative methods which are now standard practice. These include a "short term" of one summer to one year to allow experimentation for youth and other aspiring missionaries, or utilization of the services of retired persons or specialists who cannot make a full career commitment to missions. In 1973 alone four thousand Americans served as short-term missionaries. Radio has allowed penetration of areas normally hostile to missionaries. For instance, the Far East Broadcasting Company (established in 1945), based in Manila, uses twenty-two transmitters to broadcast 1,428 program hours each week in sixty-three languages and dialects of Asia and Latin America; it is only one of sixty such stations. Bible correspondence courses have been developed as literacy spreads. The Light of Life Correspondence School, which promotes Bible courses in twenty-four languages of India, has enrolled more than one million students since its inception in the 1940s. The courses are usually free of charge and can be studied at home or in a group.

Other evangelical-inspired programs include the church-growth movement, spearheaded by Donald McGavran, with the credo *Making Converts, Discipling the Nations, Multiplying Churches;* Evangelism-in-Depth (also called saturation evangelism), taking the gospel in verbal form to every family in a given country; and Theological Education by Extension, educational outreach to pastors in remote areas. Several specialized agencies, formerly confined to the United States, have become international: Youth for Christ; the Bible Club Movement; Campus Crusade for Christ; Young Life; and the Navigators. Either directly or indirectly, all are contributing to Christian discipleship throughout the world.

The Roman Catholic Church has been for centuries the leader in missionary outreach and has renewed efforts in this century as immigration has tapered off. With their practice of celibacy and austere lifestyle, Catholic missionaries often outdid their Protestant brethren. Particularly noteworthy is the Catholic Foreign Missionary Society of America, with its headquarters at Maryknoll, New York. Having launched their first missionaries in 1918, they were by 1950 at work in Asia, Africa, Central and South America, and the Pacific islands. Recently the Maryknoll Fathers have become major interpreters and disseminators of Third-World theological thought through their prolific publishing house, Orbis Books. Catholic missions continue to multiply and missionary numbers to increase. Missiologist Stephen C. Neill estimates that by the mid-1970s Roman Catholic missionaries numbered more than sixty thousand worldwide and are more numerous than those of all the non-Roman churches put together.

Changing Roles for the Protestant Clergy

The late 1950s revealed that clerical roles were shifting in many parishes. Although the vast majority of evangelical pastors ministered in traditional ways, others across the denominations began to lose a "sense of vocation," in the words of historian Winthrop S. Hudson. This paralleled Protestantism's diminished influence on the larger culture and the increasing privatization of religion.

Some well-educated ministers entered the newly popular fields of psychology and counseling. Others, discontented with the status quo in their communions, plunged into urban social work, desiring to become agents of change in a society marred by poverty and discrimination. Often more sociological than theological in their analysis of human conditions, these activists formed a vanguard that would be increasingly visible in the debates and demonstrations of the next decade.

18

The Sixties and the Search for Relevance

On an album about growing up in the early 1960s pop recording artist Donald Fagen opens with a song entitled "I.G.Y." (International Geophysical Year, 1958):

> Standing tough under stars and stripes
> We can tell,
> This dream's in sight;
> You've got to admit it,
> At this point in time that it's clear,
> The future looks bright.
> On that train all graphite and glitter,
> Undersea by rail,
> Ninety minutes from New York to Paris—
> Well by '76 we'll be A.O.K.

In retrospect the irony of the lyrics is bitterly clear. But for those embarking on the new decade, the dream seemed real and the times bright. In the words of the youthful President John F. Kennedy, Americans were entering a "New Frontier."

The country did develop momentum just as Kennedy promised, but did not always move in anticipated directions. The Cold War heated up and the nation endured a harrowing series of trials—the fiasco of the Bay of Pigs invasion (April 1961), the construction of the Berlin Wall (summer 1961), and the Cuban missile crisis (October 1962)—before accommodation with the Soviets was reached and the long-awaited test-ban treaty signed. The civil-rights movement crested in confrontations in Selma and Birmingham, Alabama, and elsewhere, culminating in the great 1963 march on Washington, which occasioned the Reverend Martin Luther King, Jr.'s, now immortalized address "I Have a Dream."

Students in particular were affected by these events. In fact, it can be suggested that much of the decade's tumult resulted from simple generational dynamics. In the years between 1945 and 1959, while Americans created an affluent society and expunged the economic traces of the depression years, they bore children by the tens of millions. In real numbers this "baby boom" meant a national population increase from 150 to 180 million people, with an annual rate of increase (19 percent) higher than that of the year of heaviest immigration earlier in the century. By the mid-1960s these babies had grown into a virtual army with unchanneled energy; idealistic, restless, searching, unacquainted with suffering, and accustomed to the spoils of a highly materialistic and television-oriented culture. In a sense, therefore, the generational clash was not surprising and occurred in other western societies as well.

Few areas of American life remained untouched by the ferment of those buoyantly dangerous years. Historians generally agree that the national consensus of the postwar era unraveled in the early sixties. The cool, detached, irenic social criticism of the previous decade gave way to passionate tracts like Michael Harrington's *Other America* (1962), which helped launch President Lyndon B. Johnson's War on Poverty. Betty Friedan's *Feminine Mystique* (1963) explored the attitudes and structures of American culture which kept women "in their place," removed from full equality with men. With others she helped launch the National Organization for Women in 1966, which worked to raise the consciousness of women and society on feminist issues; and accordingly drew criticism from traditionalists both in and out of the churches. A new realism and depth of social commentary shaped films and novels, signaling erosion of the old restraints and views of social reality portrayed in the public arts. Novels such as Joseph Heller's *Catch 22* (1961) and Ken Kesey's *One Flew Over the Cuckoo's Nest* (1962) and movies such as *Dr. Strangelove* (1963) and *The Graduate* (1967) became immediately influential, furthering the popularizing of relativism and existentialism while at the same time exposing social crime.

As the sixties progressed, cultural rifts widened, and the nation encountered dissension and upheaval of a magnitude comparable only to that of 1861. Racial tensions, political assassinations, radical theological currents, widespread disenchantment among youth, embroilment in a foreign war, incessant cries for social and economic equality—these forces simultaneously created a precarious social climate in which traditional answers, such as those thought to be offered by institutionalized religion, appeared to many both anemic and irrelevant. It was a time of testing for American churches.

Radical Theology in the Age of Aquarius

As the predictable and patriotic uniformity of the 1950s was displaced by dissent and diversity in the 1960s, radical intellectual currents burst from beneath the surface with new vitality. Sociologist C. Wright Mills issued the clarion call in 1960 when he wrote: "The age of complacency is ending. Let the old women complain wisely about the 'end of ideology.' We are beginning to move again." Liberal American theologians picked up the cue and rationalistic theological trends born earlier in the century now expanded in new and more controversial directions. Although not subject to wide public discussion, these tendencies nevertheless exerted a strong influence on the shape of future theological discourse and eventually found their way, through schools and periodicals, to lay people.

Paralleling the usual religious sources such as Scripture, ecclesiastical forms, and theological traditions were several secular sources which nourished the radical theology of the 1960s. Foundational was the persistence of the scientific mood, which assumed facts to be determined exclusively by empirical scientific inquiry, be it natural, historical, or social. This orientation intensified as competitive military and space technology pointed optimistically to science as an ever-sufficient supplier of answers to human dilemmas.

A second factor was the notion that all human experience is historical or developmental and thus relative to time and place. Religious ideas therefore become culturebound reflections of man's evolving experience rather than purveyors of timeless truth or divine revelation.

The "this-worldly" focus of modern culture also nurtured radical theology. Stemming from the Renaissance, and merging with various strands of American utilitarianism and pragmatism, this emphasis shifted religious concerns from matters of salvation to the meaning or usefulness of religion for this life, be it for self-fulfillment, ethical norms, or peace of mind. Concomitant was spiraling interest in psychology, sociology, and anthropology which, cradled in the scientific method, riveted scholars' attention to earthly matters and natural explanations of human behavior.

A fourth stimulus to radical theology, and one often overlooked by its critics, was the subtle shift in ethical concern from personal holiness to love of one's neighbor. Social community became more important than castigating personal vices, except as these directly affected other people. Situational ethics, usually defined as "loving actions," replaced adherence to moral absolutes as the basis for human moral choices.

Interestingly, a prime catalyst in the new theological radicalism flowed from the writings of a man executed by the Nazi regime for his part in a conspiracy to assassinate Adolf Hitler. Dietrich Bonhoeffer's *Letters and Papers from Prison* (1953) summoned Christians to rethink the demands of their faith in a "world come of age." Bonhoeffer set the tone for radical theology when he wrote:

> Our relationship with God is not a 'religious' relation to a Supreme Being, absolute in power and goodness . . . but our relation to God is in 'being there for others' in participation in the being of Jesus.

God, said Bonhoeffer, is encountered in the horizontal relations common to our worldly existence.

One of the first Americans to respond to Bonhoeffer's concerns was H. Richard Niebuhr with his provocative essay, *Radical Monotheism and Western Culture* (1960), which grappled with questions of religious experience in the modern secular world. Gabriel Vahanian elevated to theological chic a phrase of Friedrich Wilhelm Nietzsche in *The Death of God: The Culture of Our Post-Christian Era* (1961). Then three controversial best sellers appeared in rapid succession: Bishop John Robinson's *Honest to God* (1963) in Great Britain; Pierre Berton's *Comfortable Pew* (1965) in Canada; and Harvey Cox's *Secular City* (1965) in the United States. All three claimed to be making Christianity acceptable to modern man and providing a bold challenge to contemporary churches.

Equally, if not more, provocative was the appearance of several additional books which either proclaimed the "death of God," or insisted on an entirely "secular" interpretation of the gospel. In *Radical Theology and the Death of God* (1966), William Hamilton and Thomas J. J. Altizer argued "that there was once a God to whom adoration, praise and trust were appropriate, possible and even necessary, but . . . now there is no such God." They were not themselves denying God's existence, however. As Hamilton explained: "We are not talking about the absence of the experience of God, but of the experience of the absence of God." The only possible response to this conspicuous absence of the divine, they contended, was a radical embracing of the profane, a complete rejection of "other-worldliness," and a hopeful waiting for God's return.

In a less spectacular vein, Paul Van Buren offered *The Secular Meaning of the Gospel* (1963), which drew upon linguistic analysis to argue that traditional language used to describe God and his ways ("God-talk") is empirically meaningless. He contended that the gospel would become significant for contemporary man only when it is understood in a thoroughly secular fashion, by translating biblical terms into the empirical and ethical terms of a scientific, technological society. From still another quarter, John B. Cobb asserted that theology must predicate an evolving rather than a static God. Only by adopting the orientations of evolution and process philosophy can theology speak meaningfully to the changing modern world.

Maturation and Confusion in Roman Catholicism

The relationship of Roman Catholicism to American society has always been ambivalent. Since their migration to Maryland in the 1630s Catholics have been a minority in an overwhelmingly Protestant America. The legal separation of church and state added to internal difficulties in adjusting to the post-Reformation world. Anti-Catholic hostility in the nineteenth century and the formidable task of assimilating millions of immigrants aggravated the situation. But for most of those years Roman Catholicism proved remarkably pliant in shifting historical circumstances. Perhaps the greatest test came in the 1960s.

Roman Catholic numbers peaked in the United States in 1959, held steady until 1965, and then sharply declined. The decline was somewhat obscured, however, by three major events: the elevation of the feisty John XXIII to the papacy in 1958; the election of the first Roman Catholic to the presidency of the United States in 1960 (Kennedy); and the heady excitement of the second Vatican council, 1962–1965. Of these the third was most radical for Catholic tradition as a whole. There had not been such a Vatican council since 1869–1870, and before that a period of three hundred years had elapsed since the Council of Trent. Although hesitation gripped the participants throughout the planning and actual deliberations, major changes were effected.

The council, like Pope John, was a blend of tradition and forward-looking attitudes, and this mix appears throughout the council's documents. While they address themselves to the twentieth century and bear marks of new theological departures, they remain at the same time in the mainstream of Catholic orthodoxy and, in fact, reaffirm many of the positions of Vatican I and Trent.

Notwithstanding, Vatican II touched every feature of church life in fresh and occasionally dramatic ways. Among developments emanating from Vatican II were more interfaith contact and collaboration (many non-Catholics attended the council); more participation by laity, especially women, in the church's mission; a new attentiveness to social and economic trends as indicators of needed directions for ministry; sweeping liturgical changes; more sharing of responsibility among different levels of hierarchy and with lay councils; and a considerable change in theology without change of "official" doctrine. A number of the American hierarchy, especially Joseph Cardinal Ritter of Saint Louis and Albert Cardinal Meyer of Chicago, were prominent for their leadership in reform at the council.

But the response of most American bishops was cautious, probably due to habitual lack of experimentation, and more importantly, the pressure of other problems. None denied, however, that the church was in deep trouble. Catholic magazines and newsletters lamented the plight of parochial schools. Declining numbers of seminarians and female novices combined with an exodus from the priesthood to force the hiring of more lay teachers, creating heavier financial burdens. Too, the migrations to the suburbs left many inner-city parishes stranded with small congregations unable to properly maintain church property.

While most bishops hesitated at the threshold of change, eager young priests, with the support of youthful parishioners, launched enthusiastically into uncharted waters in their quest for relevance. The results were mainly in the form of unauthorized liturgical experiments which might wait years for official approval. Among numerous changes were that English replaced Latin; the priest said Mass facing the congregation; hymns, often Protestant, were sung accompanied by guitars and percussion during services; experimental communities and "people's altars" added variety; compulsory abstinence from meat on Fridays was terminated.

Reactions converged from both the left and the right. The conservative response first targeted the vernacular Mass, and was led in part by the Catholic Traditionalist Movement of Father Gommar A. DePauw. Other rightist groups, such as Catholics United for the Faith, organized to combat abortion and the influence of secularism in parochial schools. Those on the left sought more extensive changes in areas such as birth control, obligatory celibacy of priests, and papal infallibility.

A 1967 study of the life and ministry of priests reported a sharp decline in devotional practices among clergy and a new proneness to question church authority on such "decided" issues as abortion, divorce, and contraception. The Vatican II decrees on ecumenism gave priests and nuns flexibility to collaborate with those of other religious persuasions, and resulted in active participation in the civil-rights movement and demonstrations protesting the Vietnam War. Fathers Daniel and Philip Berrigan and other priests risked their reputations in acts of civil disobedience. Nuns too stood in the front lines at Selma and Birmingham, Alabama; exchanged habits for street clothes; called for greater recognition of their personhood; and in 1972 expressed their desire for full ministerial equality with men.

Overall, American Catholics did not openly revolt during the sixties. Many, especially the young, simply ignored church teaching. Others continued in their traditional beliefs and practices despite unprecedented changes going on around them. The conservative wing identified itself with leaders like Fulton J. Sheen and Francis Cardinal Spellman; liberals turned to Pope John and his reformist council decrees. John's successor, Paul VI (reigned 1963–1978), found the situation so unsettling that he sought to undo some of the more "extreme" measures of Vatican II. Subsequent confusion and debate widened the already dangerous rift. These controversies and their consequences were inseparable from the tumult fulminating in the larger society.

New Wineskins: The Churches and Ecclesiastical Experimentation

The new directions in theological discourse and liturgical practice for both Protestants and Catholics were reflective of a general quest for social and institutional relevance. Ecclesiastical leaders worked to demonstrate that "the church as institution" and "the church as community of the Spirit" were not mutually exclusive concepts and that both contributed to healthy parish life.

Multiple factors exacerbated the churches' dilemma, especially toward the close of the decade when protest became most acute. Even when confronted with pervasive secularization, many church leaders recognized only slowly that Christianity no longer commanded an automatic hearing and homage. The long-term, if sometimes uneasy, alliance between reason and moral-religious faith had seemingly run its course. Particularly for youth, intellectuals, and shapers of the media, pluralism had come to mean that there was no single, final truth in issues of religion, art, morals, and politics. Pluralism stood for subjectivism, relativism, and privatism in these matters. The secularizing trend was further reflected in a series of Supreme Court decisions that sought to remove overt religious observances from the public schools.

The conflictual drama was played out in local churches across America. Progressive young Protestant ministers clashed with wary vestrymen in struggles over church segregation in the South. Inner-city pastors met frustration in their attempts to acquaint affluent, suburban Christians with the blight of hard-core poverty. Experimental ministries struggled to gain attention and support. Priests and Catholic laity desiring immediate implementation of Vatican II decrees were pitted against bishops who feared rapid shifts from traditional patterns. Most church adherents affirmed that the churches *should* embody dedication to the social good; agreement as to the means of achievement remained elusive.

Nonetheless, the 1960s witnessed a resurgence, however controversial and disjointed, of that socially active style of faith which has been a recurrent force in American Christianity. Spawned by the Second Awakening in the early 1800s, and broadened later in the century in the social-gospel movement, it now resurfaced. Like their predecessors, the new generation of Christian activists quested after the kingdom of God on earth, but with a more realistic sense of the intransigence of evil and the functions of power. They could be found organizing welfare unions, tenants' councils, rent strikes, and school boycotts. Some joined civil-rights marches, led open-housing marches, faced arrest and court appearances. Strong action was, however, the exception rather than the rule for most clergy and laity. A substantial gap existed between many church professionals and their parishioners. Political and religious conservatives challenged much of the social activism as well as the implications of the radical theologies.

A unique and youthful popular movement for religious reformation was the Jesus People. Intense, simplistic, fluid, often communal, the Jesus People drew mainly from fundamentalist and Pentecostal teaching, but with a wide range of ideology and style. The movement dispersed rapidly throughout the country from its birth in the San Francisco-Berkeley area of California. Some groups departed radically from theological orthodoxy and demanded complete and disciplined separation from the world, including one's family. Others sprang from the efforts of ambient evangelists like Arthur Blessitt and Duane Pederson, both unconnected to any organized religious institution. Still others formed their own "house churches" or campus-oriented ministry such as the Christian World Liberation Front in Berkeley.

Although some Jesus People did relate to evangelical organizations such as Inter-Varsity Christian Fellowship and Campus Crusade for Christ, the movement on the whole was sharply critical of the familiar, institutional churches. It was a zealous, if sometimes misguided, protest against traditional religious structures, which in the minds of the Jesus People had compromised with the dominant social and economic values of postwar America. It was another attempt to return to basic New Testament Christianity, unencumbered by ecclesiastical machinery and open to the Holy Spirit.

The Legacy of the Sixties

The revolutionary ferment of the sixties produced in the seventies a changed America. Public pressure hastened the inglorious close of the Vietnam War in 1975, perhaps undermining governmental authority in future foreign wars and further eroding American self-confidence and optimism, already weakened by the memory of unsettling assassinations, the Watergate scandal, and embarrassing frustrations in foreign policy.

Sweeping civil-rights legislation delivered blacks new status and voting power and inspired other minorities, but not without riots and unrest. Women of all ages pursued further education, turning to the marketplace, and often the divorce court, as they aspired to claim the equality secured by legislation and court decision. They emerged as a potent political force but also were accused of abandoning and weakening home and family life. A tidal wave of pop psychology and sexology focused attention on the autonomous self and its fulfillment as the sine qua non of life, rejecting traditional religion as an oppressive, redundant moral authority—the tyrant parent to be jettisoned by the liberated adult. The sexual revolution continues unabated, reaching even young teen-agers.

It was this erosion of authority of all kinds, but especially moral authority, that most troubled and chagrined the earnestly religious, both Christian and Jew. Disrespect, drug and alcohol abuse, divorce, increased crime, overt sexuality were but the daily manifestations of a void at the core of American life. Many Christians were also troubled by the restrictive posture of the Supreme Court regarding religion in the schools. Although its recentness inhibits full analysis, the decade of the 1960s may mark a watershed in American history and values, and perhaps a fundamental transition in western culture itself. The term *post-Christian* seems to quite accurately describe its legacy.

Once more disillusionment and a feeling of helplessness against the confusing drift of events threatened individual and institution alike. The War on Poverty had won only a bridgehead against poverty, urban blight, malnutrition, and inferior schools. For the first time galloping inflation was accompanied by worldwide recession and high unemployment. Those religious leaders who had embraced the reform causes of the sixties and had closely identified with a remade secular order saw much of their supporting dynamic fade as students returned to career preparation and the public retreated to private satisfactions. Some relevance-hungry theologians, in the spirit of the radical theologies, offered "religionless Christianity" and even "Christian atheism"! Neither proved to be more than a passing fancy, and held little appeal for the laity. It was not that religion, representing the focus of life's commitments, was disappearing from American society; it was rather relocating in movements other than churchly institutions, the only standards of choice being individual tastes and felt needs. Eastern religions, gurus, meditation, and exotic cults enjoyed new appeal and even Satanism and witchcraft claimed religious recognition.

It is against this backdrop that a resurgence of evangelical and fundamentalistic Protestantism took America by surprise in the 1970s, infusing popular vitality into the term *born again.* The "anything goes" public attitude also granted respect to those who were "turned on" by this kind of Christianity, and startling statistics revealed that there were many more of the born again in America than anyone had supposed. While the more liberal mainline denominations suffered decline in church memberships, many conservative, evangelical groups experienced phenomenal growth. This renascence of evangelical faith held wide implications for American religion and politics in the later seventies and eighties, a fact attested to by the expressed evangelical sympathies of all three major presidential candidates in the election of 1980 (Jimmy Carter, Ronald Reagan, and John Anderson).

19

The Black Churches in the Twentieth Century

The progress of black Americans toward racial and economic equality has been erratic. From their forced arrival on America's shores in the early seventeenth century they have faced oppressive forces perpetuating qualitative distinctions between the "civilized white" and the "primitive black."

The Thirteenth Amendment of 1865 did not greatly alter the social status of blacks. Most of the four million ex-slaves were cast into an alien and hostile society where they experienced the full effects of racial prejudice and human contradiction. Those in the South who owned no land were forced into sharecropping, which differed little in effect from medieval serfdom. Jim Crow laws insured limits on black mobility and political participation. Because the North depended hardly at all on black labor, and their fewer numbers in the North made blacks less threatening to white hegemony, legal restrictions there were less severe.

The most important institution for the post-Civil-War black was the church. Independent black churches had been established early by freedmen to avoid the imposed segregation in white churches and to fulfill a desire for their own religious expression and community. The years 1865–1900 witnessed the fusion of these visible black churches

Billy Graham Center Museum

A black congregation at worship.

with the invisible institution of black Christianity that had taken root among the slaves. The resulting growth in numbers produced a structured religious community that was also the chief social organization of the black masses. From their churches emanated mutual-aid societies, schools, new forms of music and dance, and, perhaps most important, opportunities for development of black leadership.

The Continuing Migration Northward and Cityward

The combination of Jim Crow laws, lack of economic opportunity in the rural South, and new limits on foreign immigration imposed by the federal government encouraged a mass exodus of southern blacks to the urban centers of the North during and following World War I. Previously, about nine-tenths of all blacks lived in the South with four-fifths of these in rural areas. They continued to move to southern cities as well as those in the North and West so that by 1960 nearly two-thirds of American blacks were urban dwellers. The resulting crisis in black life resembled that created by sudden emancipation in the previous century.

The masses of blacks who participated in the social dislocation of these decades traded the seeming certainties of racial segregation, poverty, and inferior status for the uncertainties and unique hostilities city life offers poor newcomers. Added to the economic, familial, and social stresses was the absence of the familiar black church and the refuge it represented. The story of the black church in the twentieth century is one of adaptation to the shifting conditions of black life as it became more urbanized, and later of activism to change those conditions.

Black Church Life in Flux

Urban life, especially in the North, had its rewards as well as its harsher realities for migrant blacks. Traditional social inferiority did give way to rising status as black and white children attended the same schools; some blacks in time achieved the roles of policemen and firemen, positions of trust and authority; blacks voted alongside whites. Such experiences allowed blacks to acquire a new concept of themselves that centuries of subjugation had kept them from discovering.

Perhaps the most significant factor in blacks' new urban experience was the opportunity for education and the rapid upward mobility

Salvation Army Archives and Research Center

A Salvation Army open-air meeting in Atlanta, 1948.

education could bring at the time. Consequently, occupational differentiation accelerated among the black populations of northern cities. For example, preachers accounted for about half of the black professional class in the South; in northern cities (where nearly nine-tenths of northern blacks lived) only one black professional in ten was a preacher. As new socio-economic classes came into existence among blacks the black church had to adapt to the needs of different classes.

A minority of blacks, freedmen of long standing who had risen to the middle class, were acclimated to mainstream American life and assimilated into "white" churches. About two-thirds of these were Baptists; another third was Methodist, with a sprinkling of Episcopalians, Presbyterians, and Catholics. More numerous were blacks of middle-class and lower-middle-class economic and social values who kept to the traditional black churches. These included the African Methodist Episcopal Church (1816), the African Methodist Episcopal Zion Church (1821), the Christian Methodist Episcopal Church (1870), and the National Baptist Convention, U.S.A. Inc. (1886); all of these groups represent a relinquishing of that "otherworldly" character which marked indigenous black expressions of Christian faith in America. Their close association with the middle-class white population and their educational achievement nurtured a more "this-worldly" posture toward social and economic life, illustrating the dynamics seen in early Methodism and other religious bodies that originated among marginal classes and then merged into the mainstream.

Not included in these groups of black Christians are hundreds of thousands of others who migrated to northern cities. Poor, perhaps illiterate, these migrants often felt alienated from their middle-class brethren. Their need for familiar "down-home" religion helped give birth to the phenomenon of the storefront church. As the name implies, services are conducted in rented or abandoned inner-city stores or occasionally in houses. They often owe their existence to a "Jack-leg" preacher, that is, a semiliterate holy man who gathers about him blacks seeking a religious leader and teacher. In a 1933 survey of black churches in twelve cities, 777 out of 2,104 church buildings were storefronts.

The storefront churches breed intimacy and affirm identity. They have become preserves of black folk tradition where, through spiritual song and recitation, the burdensome history can be recounted. Sermons are simple and worship involves the body and emotions as hearers respond with "Amen!" and "That's right!" Singing is often accompanied with shouting, holy dancing, and other forms of free spiritual expression and participation.

Many blacks, like American Indians, were not completely comfortable with American Christianity, the "white man's religion"; unlike the Indians, they lacked any coherent memory of their traditional religions to which they might turn as an alternative. This void invited the rise of new non- (or anti-) Christian movements which claimed to provide a basis for racial identity and pride. In light of later developments in black consciousness, two urban religious movements merit special comment.

The first was the Universal Negro Improvement Association (UNIA) founded by Marcus Garvey in New York City. Garvey (1887–1940) was a widely traveled Jamaican who, like Father Divine (see chap. 12), eventually arrived in New York and settled upon it as the most appropriate place to foster a wide-scale black movement. His program called for a literal rather than a mythological return to the African homeland, and he self-consciously borrowed the Jewish interpretation of a people in diaspora awaiting a return to their rightful origins.

Before he was imprisoned in 1925 for mail fraud and deported in 1927, Garvey's organization operated two steamship lines and created a nurses' corps, a manufacturing corporation, and an unarmed African Legion. It also published a respectable newspaper and several lesser publications. While the masses were encouraged and even inspired by Garvey's message, whites scoffed and some black leaders carped at the UNIA as an opéra bouffe. But to the masses of alienated blacks, even those who carped, the undertones of Garvey's message of a new day for black people were pertinent. It was Garvey who coined the phrase *black is beautiful,* and by doing so thrilled a race that had not dared to believe it.

A more durable ideology, which drew for inspiration on several earlier expressions of black nationalism, arose in Detroit in the 1930s when a silk peddler of obscure origins, who called himself W. D. Fard, began to make himself known. Fard himself was eclipsed by his self-proclaimed messenger, Elijah Muhammad (alias Elijah Poole [1897–1975], the son of a Baptist minister), who went on to build the Nation of Islam, or "Black Muslims," on Fard's foundation. Like other extraecclesiastical black religious movements, the Nation of Islam appealed to alienated and unemployed urban blacks and stressed the nurture of pride. The Muslims developed a successful network of cooperative business institutions and required their followers to repudiate their former lives, confining their associations solely within the context of the religion. The most vivid introduction to the Black Muslims is the *Autobiography of Malcolm X* (1965), the life story of the movement's fiery spokesman who eventually met his death at the hands of men who probably once had been his fellow devotees.

When the first signs of recession appeared in the mid-1920s, blacks were among the first to lose their jobs. By October 1933, about 33 percent of the American black population was on relief, a figure three to four times greater than that for whites. As in white Protestantism, the fastest growing churches among blacks in these years were those smaller ones of independent and Pentecostal-Holiness background. But suffering was epidemic despite religious comfort. Because of their small or nonexistent reserve of capital, blacks were soon in positions of dire economic want. Even in starvation there was discrimination, for in few places was relief administered on a basis of equality. As distress and pessimism gripped American blacks, many began to see that their personal democracy would be insured only through aggressive political influence.

With the emergence of Franklin Delano Roosevelt's recovery programs, the large majority of blacks switched their political allegiance from the Republican Party of Abraham Lincoln to the Democratic Party. The New Deal president captured the imaginations of oppressed blacks and as black specialists and advisers found their way into various New Deal governmental departments they began to press for economic and political equality. The prejudicial forces they challenged were graphically revealed in the early years of World War II when military boards discriminated against black voluntarism and the armed services maintained segregation. More immediate was the hostility of whites at home, many of them Southerners influenced by the Ku Klux Klan and similar groups dedicated to white supremacy even in wartime.

The liberation impulse released by World War II was felt around the world. American blacks could not help but be affected by these liberating currents. Black women formerly condemned to domestic service found new independence in war work. Returning black servicemen felt they had demonstrated not only courage in combat but also competence in handling the machines of a technological society. They were unwilling to accept the traditional roles assigned blacks in American society.

The changing black mood and new white attitudes converged to produce dramatic advances in the postwar years. President Harry S. Truman abolished segregation in the armed forces, ordered an end to discrimination in federal employment, and initiated a committee to prevent job discrimination in private industries. In 1957, Congress passed the first civil-rights law since 1875, providing federal protection for black voting rights and creating the Civil Rights Commission. The Supreme Court's historic decision in *Brown v. Board of Education* (1954) overturned the "separate but equal" doctrine asserted in 1896.

The Court now held that "separate educational facilities are inherently unequal," and by implication it ordered racial integration of all public schools.

Although national opinion was receptive to such changes, dominant elements in southern white society were hostile. White Citizens' Councils, pledged to uphold segregation, spread throughout the region. Some whites resorted to violence. Eight states vowed to ignore the *Brown* decision and private schools began to proliferate. White resistance to integration, combined with heightened expectations among blacks, produced an upsurge of militancy.

The black churches had been less than dynamic in their participation in interracial activities, but within their walls ferment had been quietly brewing. Some of the younger ministers, trained in integrated northern institutions, spoke in measured tones about the churches' responsibility in seeking freedom from social oppression. Some of the younger, educated lay persons, especially in cities, were groping for some instrument of organization to lead a drive against segregation. Older church members who had been passive, but not unmoved, did not obstruct the rising new forces.

A new phase of the struggle began in 1956 when blacks in Montgomery, Alabama, put an end to segregated seating in the city's public transportation by a mass bus boycott. The key figure in this successful campaign was the young pastor of the Dexter Avenue Baptist Church, Martin Luther King, Jr. (1929–1968). Born in Atlanta, King was educated at Morehouse College, Crozer Theological Seminary, and Boston University, from which he received the Ph.D. degree in 1955. Following the Montgomery achievement, King in 1957 became the first president of the Southern Christian Leadership Conference (SCLC), founded to extend the drive for integration throughout the South. In a 1960 article in the *Christian Century*, he described his view of the Christian gospel and its contemporary demands:

> The gospel at its best deals with the whole man, not only his soul but his body, not only his spiritual well-being, but his material well-being. Any religion that professes to be concerned about the souls of men and is not concerned about the slums that damn them, the economic conditions that strangle them, and the social conditions that cripple them is a spiritually moribund religion awaiting burial.

King's approach was that of nonviolent resistance, learned from the life and teachings of the Indian leader, Mahatma Gandhi. In this same article he wrote:

> The whole Gandhian concept of *satyagraha (satya* is truth which equals love, and *graha* is force; *satyagraha* thus means truth or love-force) was profoundly significant to me. As I delved deeper into the philosophy of Gandhi my skepticism concerning the power of love gradually diminished, and I came to see for the first time that the Christian doctrine of love operating through the Gandhian method of nonviolence was one of the most potent weapons available to oppressed people in their struggle for freedom.

Like his Indian mentor, King's passion was to translate religious fervor into political action. Other black clergymen and particularly college students rallied to his support, as did leaders of many northern white churches.

Their commitment grew stronger in proportion to the violence that met the movement. Civil-rights workers, white and black alike, were clubbed, beaten, and even killed. The violence received so much exposure in the media, especially on television, that there was widespread revulsion against it. Millions of white Americans who otherwise might have remained indifferent to the civil-rights crusade became sympathetic. The wide support for the movement was dramatized in August 1963, when more than two hundred thousand black and white Americans marched in Washington, D.C., in a gigantic demonstration calling for "complete equality in citizenship." The following year Congress passed a sweeping civil-rights law, committing the federal government to positive action on behalf of minorities. Through the struggles of black migrations and the civil-rights movement the black church was transformed from refuge to social/cultural/religious force, profoundly affecting the religious thought and behavior of blacks and many whites as well.

Black Power and Christ's Power

The very success of the civil-rights movement caused some militant young activists, epitomized by Stokely Carmichael, to doubt its methods and goals. In their view, the laws and court decisions won on the behalf of blacks did not really defeat racism. Further, the struggle for civil rights was largely irrelevant to the problems of the poor in the ghettos. And, the militants felt, the philosophy of nonviolence was degrading to blacks. They expounded a revived form of black nationalism, based on racial pride and exaltation of the African heritage. Under the slogan *black power,* they called for a new movement comprised only of blacks. Emphases now shifted from nonviolent resistance to more aggressive strategies.

Although King and his followers rejected such an orientation, the militant message struck a chord in the nation's ghettos, which were becoming more explosive. Riots in such cities as Los Angeles, Detroit, and Newark resulted in violent deaths and destruction of entire sections of the inner cities. In April 1968, the assassination of King, at age thirty-nine, provoked riots in more than one hundred cities and allowed more room for the ascendancy of militant groups such as the Black Panthers and the Black Muslims, often led by younger spokesmen. King's untimely death left a leadership void that was never filled.

Most of these vigorous militants for black equality had grown up in the black evangelical and fundamentalist churches. This socialization was put aside and replaced by an existential, pragmatic, or secular view that was often anti-Christian in outlook. The militants viewed the conservative, fundamentalist churches as a major brake on the movement's progress. The strength of the black churches to preserve solidarity in the black cause was questioned. The two largest black Baptist denominations, along with the black Methodists, were accused of inaction. Such sentiments challenged black Christians to rethink their faith in this new epoch of heightened consciousness and emerging identity.

Black theology, reflective of other radical theologies devoted to the liberation of the oppressed, was expressed in various ways by such thinkers as Albert Cleage, Major J. Jones, J. Deotis Roberts, and James H. Cone. Among the most significant approaches were Cone's *Black Theology and Black Power* (1969) and *A Black Theology of Liberation* (1970). In the former he supplies his rationale for linking the gospel of Christ and the black-power movement:

> It is not my thesis that all Black Power advocates are Christians or even wish to be so. Nor is it my purpose to twist their language or to make an alien interpretation of it. My concern is, rather, to show that the goal and message of Black Power is consistent with the gospel of Jesus Christ. Indeed, I have even suggested that if Christ is present among the oppressed, as he promised, he must be working through the activity of Black Power. This alone is my thesis.

As the activism of the 1960s slowed, black militant groups likewise gravitated toward more moderate positions. Positive social action, however, continued, particularly among churchmen. The Reverend Jesse Jackson organized People United to Save Humanity (PUSH) in 1971, with a comprehensive program to upgrade the quality of life in black communities. Black ministers from the major black Protestant denominations came together in various organizations to find ways to combat white racism and enhance black leadership, while the National Office for Black Catholics monitored the same trends in its church. Although their roles shifted in the 1960s and their nuances are generally not understood by white churchgoers, the black churches continue to be a center of black community structure as well as the communicators of hope to millions of adherents. Nor should it be overlooked that the predominantly black National Baptist Convention, U.S.A., is the nation's fourth largest denomination, with a membership of approximately 5.5 million.

20

Recent Trends and Interpretations

The bicentennial celebration of the American Revolution in 1976 gave occasion in many churches for memorializing America's spiritual heritage. The privileges of religious liberty were highlighted along with the roles of churchly leaders in establishing the Republic. On the whole, no orgy of state worship or idolization broke forth. Numerous Christians, however, were prompted to re-examine the linkages between religion, morality, and the public order—in short, to rediscover the importance of religious thought and practice for understanding the nature of contemporary society and for planning and facing the future.

A Gallup poll, conducted during the last week of August 1976, surprisingly identified a rising religious consciousness in the United States. For the first time in nearly two decades the sampling recorded growth in worship attendance. During a typical week of that bicentennial year, approximately 42 percent of Americans attended a church or synagogue. Six out of ten affirmed religion as "very important" in their personal lives, and seven of ten claimed church membership. More specifically, one-third of those interviewed attested to a born-again experience, a conversion wherein the respondent made a commitment to Jesus Christ. Almost half (48 percent) of the Protestants surveyed offered such a testimony, as well as 18 percent of Catholics. Based on these statistics, and perhaps in consideration of President Jimmy

Carter's avowed Southern Baptist faith, both *Newsweek* magazine and George Gallup, Jr., dubbed 1976 "The Year of the Evangelical."

Gallup's delineation of "evangelical" was straightforward and unconcerned with nuances: minimally, an evangelical has experienced a personal conversion to Christ; holds to a literal, authoritative interpretation of the Bible; and seeks to witness to others about his faith. Although the media seemed to discover the phrase *born again* during the 1976 presidential campaign, those familiar with American religious history recognize the decisive call to conversion and commitment as a vibrant current swirling through three hundred years of church life in the New World. However, since early in the twentieth century, except in revivalistic groups such as the Southern Baptists, the current has been gradually shunted out of mainstream denominational channels. Now, both in and out of traditional ecclesiastical structures, many thousands claimed renewed meaning and fresh spiritual vision from a confrontation with the risen Lord.

From the viewpoint of a pollster, Gallup suggested various reasons for the upsurge in religious awareness. Among these were President Carter's candid discussion of his faith; a disillusionment with material attainment and the tarnishing of the "American dream"; the shift toward inward reality in an age of technology and mass organization; the creative communication of biblical ideas by many clergy, especially to youth; and a typical cyclic upswing after a period of decline. Based on his and other findings, Gallup reiterated the observation, long held by casual observers, that Americans continue to be the most religiously active citizenry among the industrialized nations of the world. On the other hand, Gallup found it difficult to juxtapose this high level of religious consciousness over against the crime, violence, substance addiction, social turmoil, racial prejudice, eroding morals, and flourishing secularism prevalent in America. Perhaps this condition is partially explained by differentiating between religious feeling or sentiment and carefully thought out beliefs and values that lead to actions. Religious feeling or sentiment is pervasive but, as sociologist Peter Berger lamented in 1975, "the spirit has gone out of American religious institutions" to reshape rather than be shaped by society's agendas.

The Pluralism of Evangelicalism

Drawing on the resources of the cresting born-again population, senior theologian Carl F. H. Henry, along with other thoughtful leaders, hoped to fashion a broad evangelical coalition that would develop perspectives and positions that could directly influence contemporary American society and thought, especially in the areas of social/political policy and cultural/intellectual foundations. The vehicle for mounting this coalition would be a "truly great interdenominational university," from which scholarly and creative analyses, grounded in a Christian world view, would inform the churches and society of biblically based options for action. Such a coalition, with or without a university, was not to be. Instead of seizing the opportunity for new levels of cooperation, the various leaders, institutions, and groups that affirmed basic evangelical beliefs could display only slight consensus regarding cultural and political implications of the gospel, beyond promoting private and public morality and charity.

Explaining the fragmentation of the evangelical movement is at once both simple and complex. Contrary to the appearance of uniformity the outside observer might ascribe to those who call themselves evangelical, substantial differences exist within the movement, if indeed such diversity can accurately be termed a movement; "mosaic" is probably a more suitable description.

A variety of theological perspectives and traditions have conditioned the soil from which American evangelicalism springs: the Calvinistic heritage with its rational and precise doctrinal formulation and biblically developed world view; the Wesleyan Arminian impulse with its stress on free will, Holiness, and vitality; the Anabaptist legacy of separation of church and state, sometimes focused in pacifistic community living in radical contrast to the larger society. Less pronounced, but also identifiable, are influences from pietistic Lutheranism and scholarly Episcopalian circles. Further complicating any simplistic analysis is the breakdown of these broad traditions into contemporary denominational (or "nondenominational") communions, cutting across educational and economic levels, and each with its own historic, ethnic, racial, or regional theological rationale.

At the same time, certain evangelical convictions have been shaped by forceful transdenominational waves that have swept across geographical and ecclesiastical boundaries. Prominent among these is revivalism with its emphasis on the individual and a simple gospel message, of which the television evangelists represent the latest version; also the separatistic piety and strict categories of twentieth-century fundamentalism, the contemporary fragments of which make up something of an exclusivistic subculture within the broader evangelical stream.

A third transdenominational force is the charismatic phenomenon, whether of historic Pentecostalism or that which is spread throughout a wide denominational spectrum. Not entirely coterminous with typical evangelical identities, and facing strong resistance in some quarters, the movement highlights "speaking in tongues" as a prayer language flowing from an intimate experience of God's presence. The gifts of healing and prophecy are also valued. The charismatic practice of spiritual gifts began to flow beyond the Pentecostal denominations with the formation of the Full Gospel Businessmen's Fellowship in Los Angeles in 1951, and attained national recognition a decade later when it penetrated mainline denominations. Episcopalian, Lutheran, Methodist, Presbyterian, and Roman Catholic parishes have been the most receptive, along with some Reformed and Baptist congregations. With their poignant style of caring, fellowship, and worship, while concurrently honoring the various denominational traditions, the charismatics provide a special variant of Christian spirituality with pervasive transdenominational networks.

Added to the foregoing characteristics of evangelicalism is a whole galaxy of parachurch organizations and agencies—evangelistic associations, student and professional fellowships, home- and foreign-mission societies, day schools, Bible institutes, colleges, seminaries, publishing houses, bookstores, movie producers, summer camps and conferences, radio and television networks and programs, specialized helping ministries—all representing evangelical vision and a supporting constituency. The range of good works performed and numbers of lives touched by this cascade of Christian effort is astounding. At the same time the rivalry for financial donations and need for broad appeal can lead to undue emphasis on personality and reluctance to cooperate on goals beyond evangelism and benevolence.

Evangelicalism's subgroups perhaps defy full categorization. Historian Timothy L. Smith suggests twelve streams, which include millions of conservatives in mainline denominations; theologian Robert Webber finds at least fourteen variants. Richard Quebedeaux, employing gossipy style in *The Young Evangelicals* (1974) and *The Worldly Evangelicals* (1978), divides evangelicals into four tendencies, largely defined by relationships to secular culture, political and social values, science, and by degree of cooperation with nonevangelicals.

Most representative of the evangelical mainstream are the Southern Baptist Convention in the border and southern states and the National Association of Evangelicals (NAE), headquartered in Wheaton, Illinois, in the North. Although some Southern Baptists do not consider themselves "evangelicals," the nearly-fourteen-million-member communion reflects evangelical priorities, albeit adapted to southern cultural distinctions. With its missionary arm, various boards, publications, educational institutions and networks, which reach into the West and North, the convention heavily defines church life and attitudes in its region of strength. With a membership of 13,782,644, the Southern Baptists, in 1981, stood as the second largest church body in the United States (after the Roman Catholics with more than fifty-one million).

Since its founding in 1943, the NAE has served as a framework for cooperation and fellowship of 3.5 million parishioners drawn from thirty-six thousand congregations in forty-three denominations, including some Pentecostal and pacifistic groups. Because parachurch organizations as well as denominations or individual congregations can be members, the NAE acts as a clearing-house and coordinator for many small denominations and agencies in areas such as missions, evangelism, and world relief, and lobbies government on religion and schools, the media, the chaplaincy, and other pertinent issues. The NAE headquarters in Wheaton joins with Wheaton College, the Billy Graham Center, and several dozen other parachurch organizations and publishers to make that community a center of moderate evangelical influence, one with worldwide linkages.

By the mid-1970s it became evident that the meaning and application of the evangelical heritage in church, society, and biblical scholarship was undergoing vigorous debate. Numerous anthologies and monographs sought to explain evangelicals to outsiders and to themselves. Representative are Donald W. Dayton's *Discovering an Evangelical Heritage* (1976), *The Evangelicals,* edited by David F. Wells and John D. Woodbridge (1975), and Harold Lindsell's *Battle for the Bible* (1976). The last, along with a spate of other works, intensified an already heated discussion regarding the nature of biblical inspiration and inerrancy.

Books such as Carl F. H. Henry's *Evangelicals in Search of Identity* (1976) and Robert K. Johnston's *Evangelicals at an Impasse* (1979) called for carefully developed theological answers to vital questions facing thoughtful Christians and the church at large. A current sampling of these issues includes proper hermeneutics for understanding and applying an authoritative Bible to all of life; the role of women in church, family, and society; homosexuality; a biblical concept of social justice and Christian political involvement; Christian lifestyles; nuclear disarmament; and abortion. Such influential journals as *Christianity Today, The Reformed Journal, Eternity, Sojourners,* and *Christian Scholar's Review* have featured articles and book reviews examining these and other pertinent questions. During the 1970s and early 1980s the scope, complexity, and diversity of evangelical writing on churchly and public topics have been substantial. The level of argument has been elevated by a diverse, highly educated coterie of professors, journalists, pastors, and politicians grappling with the meaning of Christian discipleship, private and public, in an affluent society and an interdependent world.

Some interpreters have found scriptural warrant to link conservative religion with conservative politics and laissez-faire economics. Others have developed biblically based reformist and even radical stances in contrast to the social and political values typical of middle-American evangelicals. Some of those challenging the status quo formed the Evangelicals for Social Action, which issued *The Chicago Declaration* (1974), calling for greater social application of the gospel and political efforts to promote civil and economic justice for the powerless at home and abroad.

Denominational Growth and Adjustment

In addition to the upsurge among evangelical Protestants during the 1970s, advance was registered in other religious bodies conservative in outlook. Among these are the Eastern Orthodox churches, the Church of Jesus Christ of Latter-day Saints (Mormons), the Seventh-Day Adventists, and the Jehovah's Witnesses. The rapid increase of parishioners in the conservative wing of Lutheranism (often considered part of evangelicalism), represented by the Wisconsin Evangelical Lutheran Church and The Lutheran Church-Missouri Synod, was partially disrupted by a split in the latter communion over the nature of scriptural inerrancy, a debate that led to a division in Concordia Seminary, Saint Louis, and the founding of the one-hundred-thousand member Association of Evangelical Lutheran Churches in 1976.

Pope John Paul II.

Theological conservatism in Roman Catholicism was reaffirmed with the election of the Polish Karol Wojytla to the papacy in 1978. A heroic figure in many minds, Pope John Paul II is creative, erudite, quick-witted, and unpredictable in reaching out to the world's hundreds of millions of Catholics. His globe-straddling tours to tend his scattered flock have taken him to disparate peoples and cultures, including the United States in 1979, where he received extraordinary welcome. It soon became evident that in addition to meeting human need wherever found, this pope would also seek to restore order to Roman Catholicism and reassert traditional doctrines and disciplines, particularly in regard to priestly celibacy and ordaining women. In the United States, Catholic membership statistics registered growth in the early 1980s. Of particular significance are the burgeoning Hispanic parishes in the Southwest.

In contrast, the more liberal and pluralistic mainline denominations all experienced a decline in membership during the 1970s. For some denominations membership statistics also reveal a heavy representation of older persons and women. Given the spectrum of issues and forces that buffeted the traditional denominations, perhaps the remarkable fact is that so many members remained loyal to their congregations. As one denominational leader remarked, "Only the committed remained; it was a winnowing process."

The ordination of women proved especially disturbing to the Presbyterians and Episcopalians, unlike the Methodists, Baptists, Congregationalists, and Unitarians. Differences over female clergy contributed to the formation of such new denominations as the Presbyterian Church in America and the Anglican Orthodox Church. Even more disquieting is the question of ordaining practicing homosexuals. Although the local officials of some communions have ordained homosexuals, most denominations have declined to endorse committee reports fully recommending such. The National Council of Churches has also held back from accepting into affiliation the Fellowship of Metropolitan Community Churches, a communion of more than one hundred congregations of gays.

Probably most troublesome for the laity has been the commitment by national denominational leaders to domestic and international social and political goals not shared by large segments of the grass-roots congregations. Such issues include advocating payment of "reparations funds" to blacks to redress past discrimination (a response to James Forman's "Black Manifesto"); monitoring multinational corporations; and supplying food and medical aid to African guerrilla liberation forces through the World Council of Churches.

Within the denominations various caucuses have arisen since 1960 to effect policy, clarify mission, or lobby for a viewpoint. These include ethnic and minority advocacy groups as well as caucuses comprised of evangelicals. Prominent among the latter are the Presbyterian Lay Committee and Presbyterians United for Biblical Concerns; also the Good News Movement among Methodists and the Fellowship of Witness within the Episcopal church. Charismatic fellowships also exist within most denominations.

Denominational mergers attest to the continuing quest for Protestant unity. Most dramatic was the healing of a breach in Presbyterianism dating from the Civil War. In 1982 both respective national assemblies of the (Southern) Presbyterian Church in the U.S. and the (Northern) Presbyterian Church in the U.S.A. voted to merge, dependent on confirmation in the local presbyteries. Confirmed in 1983, the resulting Presbyterian Church U.S.A. became the fifth largest ecclesiastical body in the country, after Roman Catholics, Southern Baptists, United Methodists, and black Baptists. Based on consultations and commitments, a tripartite union of Lutheran denominations is projected for 1988, bringing into one communion the Lutheran Church in America, the American Lutheran Church, and the American Evangelical Lutherans.

On the international scene the World Council of Churches has continued to assemble every seven years, gathering in New Delhi (1961), Uppsala (1968), Nairobi (1975), and Vancouver, Canada (1983). As Third-World membership has grown and liberation consciousness increased, the posture of the body has turned more leftward socially, economically, and politically. In Nairobi support was voted for "nonmilitary guerilla programs," a reflection of the liberation-theology sentiments of many council members and a cause of criticism from some American mainline publicists. The Vancouver gathering strongly opposed the production of nuclear arms. The most significant international gathering of conservative evangelicals took place in Lausanne in 1974, where both evangelism and alleviation of human need and exploitation were affirmed as essential in the ministry of the church. Above all, no matter what their ecclesiastical orientation, religious leaders in the West are becoming increasingly conscious of the numerical shift to Third-World churches. The majority of Christians in the world no longer reside in Europe and North America, a demographic development certain to attain greater importance in the future.

The Gospel, the Media, and Politics

> I believe that God has raised up this powerful technology of radio and television expressly to reach every man, woman, boy and girl on earth with the even more powerful message of the gospel.

Ben Armstrong's affirmation in *The Electric Church* (1979) highlights the core motivation of every radio and television evangelist since religious radio broadcasting started in 1921 at station KDKA in Pittsburgh. By the 1930s religious radio was part of the assumed listening habits of Americans. Television programing followed in the 1950s. During the 1960s religious broadcasting reached an advanced stage with the multiplication of radio stations devoted largely to evangelically oriented programs; these comprised 20 percent of all radio stations in the United States by the 1980s. Because of the enormous costs, technical complexity, and competition for limited air waves, only 4 percent of television stations were acquired for Christian ministry. But by extensive use of purchased commercial time, television evangelism also emerged as a highly potent force in the religious milieu.

The visibility and large clientele of "televangelism" or the "electric church" are enhanced by several factors, some social and some technical. As a medium television offers an illusion of intimacy. Viewers can readily imagine personal relationships with the masterful performers. Especially for the elderly person or shut-in who lacks other meaningful connections, a continuing contact with a television personality can lead to extraordinary feelings of trust and friendship on the part of the viewer. Computerized mailing lists with personalized, targeted audiences finesse viewers into a loyal contributing constituency. Also, the success of the television ministries, although often exaggerated, suggests that a responsive chord has been struck among significant segments of the public. As the authors observe in *Prime Time Preachers* (1981), the American populace is generally more religiously oriented than government and media elites recognize; millions of dollars are regularly donated to support the electronic prophets' call to individual peace with God and moral rehabilitation for society.

The numerical strength of the electronic church and its impact on local congregational life have proved debatable. Critics charge that it fosters "armchair religion" which encourages privatism, demands only financial contributions, and draws off human and monetary resources from the local parish witness. Also, as with other mass-media communications, the message has to be upbeat, simplified, condensed, and geared toward quick solutions. Because of the huge amounts of money involved, some observers have sought more financial disclosure, especially because many of the religious media stars use their television program as a centerpiece to fund other endeavors. Most controversial has been the involvement of televangelists Jerry Falwell, James Robison, Jimmy Swaggart, and others with conservative, "right-wing" political causes. Given their goal of turning America back to God, and the fact that so many political issues involve deep moral questions, it should not be surprising that attempts would be made to organize the devout who had previously been relatively inactive politically. Computerization of mailing lists provided the mechanism to mobilize large numbers, including Catholics and other non-fundamentalists, at the grass-roots level.

The Christian New Right, as the political coalition has come to be termed, has aimed its appeal at those seeking to preserve traditional family values against the perceived threats posed by "gay rights," the Equal Rights Amendment, and the Supreme Court decisions on abortion. Also at issue is values formation in the public schools; the teaching about sex and evolutionary theory while prohibiting prayer and ignoring creationism is viewed as undermining to faith and morals. There is fear of government interference, especially by the activist role of the courts in striking down antipornography and antiabortion laws; and by bureaucratic monitoring of religious schools. Finally, the United States is seen as declining internationally and facing military eclipse by the forces of communism.

The reason for the national malaise, according to publicists for the Christian New Right, is "secular humanism," the relativistic, humanistic, materialistic ideology of a liberal elite of several hundred thousand who have gained control of the media, education, government bureaucracies, and the courts. As a counter force, the mobilization of the Moral Majority by Falwell in 1979 and appearance of presidential candidate Ronald Reagan before thousands of fundamentalist ministers at the Dallas, Texas, national affairs briefing in 1980 signaled the emergence of the newly organized opposition. Although other conservative groups and single-issue lobbies joined the cause, it was the Moral Majority and Falwell who became household words.

In retrospect, much of the reaction to the Christian New Right by the secular press was overblown, and even inconsistent, given the precedent of political involvement by liberal clergymen. Accusations of fascist or totalitarian intentions were not appropriate. Furthermore, 1980 voting statistics, as well as analyses of television audiences, suggest that the religious and political clout of the televangelists was less than they or their adversaries claimed. More moderate evaluators, some of them evangelicals, faulted the Christian New Right for blaming others for society's ills; for idealizing the American past and merging God's priorities with those of the nation; for emphasizing individual morality but remaining silent on social injustices. Nevertheless, no matter how limited or extensive the influence of the Christian New Right, its rise has revealed the existence of a vast pool of highly

Jerry Falwell, speaking about moral issues (particularly abortion), at the U.S. Supreme Court building.

religious Americans who hold strong value differences with the directions society and public policy have taken. These citizens, although not necessarily in full agreement with Moral Majority ideology, hold the potential for a burgeoning social movement, heretofore unrecognized by politicians and social scientists. Jeremy Rifkin in *The Emerging Order* (1979) even suggests that this "is now the single most important cultural force in American life." Only the future will indicate the accuracy of Rifkin's speculation.

Facing the Future

By the mid-1980s it was evident that America was a nation in transition, gripped by a "sweeping irreversible cultural revolution . . . transforming the rules that once guided American life," according to pollster Daniel Yankelovich. Adding to the complexity is the contradiction between hoped-for solutions to human dilemmas and the mixed results of their applications.

Affluence and consumer goods unknown in previous human history have led to materialism, pollution, depletion of resources, and a satiation of choices that draw off attention from the spiritual and moral spheres. Science and technology, despite unbelievable medical and electronic advances, have precipitated new uncertainties through the threat of nuclear war. Mass communications, rapid mobility, and centralized political administrations have contributed to the demise of mediating institutions—the home, the parish and synagogue, schools, neighborhoods—where for previous generations meaning, values, and personhood were shaped. The recent self-fulfillment spree has ushered in isolation and death of community rather than human ennoblement. The erosion of an overarching framework of ethics and values has reduced domestic politics to a conflict of competing interests and opposing moralities. Futurologists fear that the prevalent social fragmentation may devolve into either anarchic individualism or government-imposed conformity and order, assisted by some brand of statism.

In the midst of this pluralism stands the Christian community, the churches which in all their humanness and division are called to be *the church,* the salt of the earth and a shining light. If the churches are to provide moral and ethical insights and spread the light of compassion and hope to a society in flux they would do well to avoid two extremes. On the one hand, moralistic triumphalism, promoting a limited or self-serving agenda, must be eschewed because it squanders credibility among the sensitive and thoughtful. Conversely, culturally accommodating blandness and lack of discriminating conviction denude the gospel of its transforming quality, making it high on good intentions but low on authentic New Testament faith and discipleship.

Biblical disciples do not stand alone. Inspired by fellowship in the household of believers, they find the strength to suffer and serve, worship and celebrate. Whether Puritan in Massachusetts Bay Colony, Moravian in Pennsylvania forest, Methodist on western frontier, Roman Catholic in Baltimore, or contemporary Baptist on the Gulf Coast, vitality flows from the Word proclaimed in the communities of faith. It is an ideal that calls every Christian to leap barriers of time, tribe, institution, and nation and join that company of the committed whose citizenship resides in two municipalities, the city of man and the City of God.

Bibliographic Essay and Chapter Bibliographies

Following are selected bibliographies for each of the twenty chapters of this book. An attempt has been made to include recent literature on each major subject as well as older works that have become classics in their respective areas.

Readers wishing to consult other surveys of American religious history should begin with Sydney E. Ahlstrom's *Religious History of the American People* (New Haven: Yale University Press, 1972). It is a lucidly written, encyclopedic treatment of the subject, and encompasses American faiths additional to Christianity (such as Judaism). Clifton E. Olmstead's *History of Religion in the United States* (Englewood Cliffs, N.J.: Prentice-Hall, 1960) is an older survey but admirably disentangles the complex denominational story of the American churches. Robert T. Handy's *History of the Churches in the United States and Canada* (New York: Oxford University Press, 1976) is less comprehensive than Ahlstrom's but marked by succinct insights into the role of the churches in North American history.

Martin E. Marty's *Righteous Empire: The Protestant Experience in America* (New York: Dial, 1970) emphasizes the Puritan-Protestant influence in America, as does Winthrop S. Hudson's *American Protestantism* (Chicago: University of Chicago Press, 1961). James J. Hennesey's *American Catholics: A History of the Roman Catholic Community in the United States* (New York: Oxford University Press, 1982) usefully relates the American Catholic experience. Those seeking a more popular treatment with outstanding illustrations can consult Eerdmans' *Handbook to Christianity in America* (Grand Rapids: Eerdmans, 1983), edited by Mark A. Noll and others. The most helpful and penetrating study of American religious thought is still *The Shaping of American Religion,* edited by James Ward Smith and A. Leland Jamison (Princeton: Princeton University Press, 1961). The first two volumes of this four-volume set contain thematic essays; the other two are bibliographical. For a detailed look at particular religious bodies in North America the reader should see Arthur C. Piepkorn's *Profiles in Belief: The Religious Bodies of the United States and Canada,* four volumes (New York: Harper and Row, 1977–79).

Those interested in primary source material on American religion may consult *American Christianity: An Historical Interpretation with Representative Documents,* edited by H. Shelton Smith and others, two volumes (New York: Charles Scribner's Sons, 1960–63). In addition to an excellent choice of primary documents, this set also offers insightful contextual essays for each major period of American religious history.

A similar recent project, begun under the editorship of Edwin S. Gaustad, is entitled *A Documentary History of Religion in America* (Grand Rapids: Eerdmans). The first volume of this series appeared in 1982 and others are forthcoming.

Other helpful books that have influenced the writing of this one include William A. Clebsch's *From Sacred to Profane America: The Role of Religion in American History* (New York: Harper and Row, 1968); Sidney E. Mead's *Lively Experiment: The Shaping of Christianity in America* (New York: Harper and Row, 1963); Winthrop S. Hudson's *Great Tradition of the American Churches* (New York: Harper and Brothers, 1953) and *Religion in America,* 3d edition (New York: Charles Scribner's Sons, 1981); also Peter W. Williams's *Popular Religion in America: Symbolic Change and the Modernization Process in Historical Perspective* (Englewood Cliffs, N.J.: Prentice-Hall, 1980) and Edwin S. Gaustad's *Religious History of America* (New York: Harper and Row, 1966).

Chapter 1—The Reforming Impulse

Bainton, Roland H. *Here I Stand: A Life of Martin Luther.* Nashville: Abingdon, 1950.

Burns, Edward M. *The Counter Reformation.* Princeton: Princeton University Press, 1964.

Cohn, Norman. *The Pursuit of the Millennium: Revolutionary Messianism in Medieval and Reformation Europe and Its Bearing on Modern Totalitarian Movements.* New York: Harper Torchbooks, 1961.

Gilmore, Myron. *The World of Humanism, 1453–1517.* New York: Harper Torchbooks, 1952.

Green, Robert W., ed. *Protestantism, Capitalism, and Social Science: The Weber Thesis Controversy.* Lexington, Mass.: Heath, 1973.

McNeill, John T. *The History and Character of Calvinism.* New York: Oxford University Press, 1954.

Walzer, Michael. *The Revolution of the Saints: A Study in the Origins of Radical Politics.* Cambridge: Harvard University Press, 1965.

Williams, George H. *The Radical Reformation.* Philadelphia: Westminister, 1962.

Chapter 2—English Reformation and Puritan Beginnings

Barbour, Hugh. *The Quakers in Puritan England.* New Haven: Yale University Press, 1964.

George, Charles, and Katherine George. *The Protestant Mind of the English Reformation, 1570–1640.* Princeton: Princeton University Press, 1961.

Haller, William. *The Rise of Puritanism.* New York: Columbia University Press, 1938.

Hill, Christopher. *The World Turned Upside Down: Radical Ideas During the English Revolution.* Hammondsworth, Middlesex: Penguin, 1975.

Little, David. *Religion, Order, and Law: A Study in Pre-Revolutionary England.* New York: Harper and Brothers, 1969.

Morton, A. L. *The World of the Ranters: Religious Radicalism in the English Revolution.* London: Lawrence and Wishart, 1970.

Notestein, Wallace. *The English People on the Eve of Colonialization: 1603–1630.* New York: Harper and Brothers, 1954.

Parker, Thomas M. *The English Reformation to 1558.* New York: Oxford University Press, 1950.

Wright, Louis B. *Religion and Empire: The Alliance Between Piety and Commerce in English Expansion, 1558–1625.* Chapel Hill: University of North Carolina Press, 1943.

Chapter 3—The Protestant Empire Founded

Bacon, Margaret Hope. *The Quiet Rebels: The Story of the Quakers in America.* New York: Basic, 1969.

Bowden, Henry Warner. *American Indians and Christian Missions: Studies in Cultural Conflict.* Chicago: University of Chicago Press, 1981.

Boyer, Paul, and Stephen Nissenbaum. *Salem Possessed: The Social Origins of Witchcraft.* Cambridge: Harvard University Press, 1974.

Bushman, Richard L. *From Puritan to Yankee: Character and the Social Order in Connecticut, 1690–1765.* Cambridge: Harvard University Press, 1967.

Davidson, Elizabeth H. *The Establishment of the English Church in the Continental American Colonies.* Durham, N.C.: Duke University Press, 1936.

Demos, John Putnam. *Entertaining Satan: Witchcraft and the Culture of Early New England.* New York: Oxford University Press, 1982.

Ellis, John Tracy. *Catholics in Colonial America.* Baltimore: Helicon, 1965.

Foster, Stephen. *Their Solitary Way: The Puritan Social Ethic in the First Century of Settlement in New England.* New Haven: Yale University Press, 1971.

Miller, Perry. *Errand into the Wilderness.* Cambridge: Harvard University Press, 1956.

———. *Roger Williams: His Contribution to the American Tradition.* Indianapolis: Bobbs-Merrill, 1953.

Morgan, Edmund S. *The Puritan Family: Religion and Domestic Relations in Seventeenth-Century New England.* New York: Harper Torchbooks, 1966; Westport, Conn.: Greenwood, 1980.

Vaughan, Alden T., and Francis J. Bremer. *Puritan New England: Essays on Religion, Society, and Culture.* New York: St. Martin, 1977.

Wentz, Abdel R. *A Basic History of Lutheranism in America.* Philadelphia: Muhlenberg, 1955.

Chapter 4—Awakening

Gaustad, Edwin S. *The Great Awakening in New England.* Chicago: Quadrangle, 1968; New York: Times Press, 1972.

Goen, Clarence C. *Revivalism and Separatism in New England: Strict Congregationalists and Separate Baptists in the Great Awakening.* New Haven: Yale University Press, 1962.

Heimert, Alan E. *Religion and the American Mind from the Great Awakening to the Revolution.* Cambridge: Harvard University Press, 1966.

Henry, Stuart C. *George Whitefield: Wayfaring Witness.* New York: Abingdon, 1957.

Lovejoy, David S. *Religious Enthusiasm and the Great Awakening.* Englewood Cliffs, N.J.: Prentice-Hall, 1969.

Maxson, Charles Hartshorn. *The Great Awakening in the Middle Colonies*. Chicago: University of Chicago Press, 1920.

Miller, Perry. *Jonathan Edwards*. Cleveland: Meridian, 1949; Amherst: University of Massachusetts Press, 1981.

Tanis, James R. *Dutch Calvinistic Pietism in the Middle Colonies: A Study in the Life of Theodorus Jacobus Frelinghuysen*. The Hague: Martinus Nijhof, 1967.

Chapter 5—The Church and Revolution

Aldridge, Owen. *Benjamin Franklin and Nature's God*. Durham, N.C.: Duke University Press, 1967.

Bailyn, Bernard. *The Ideological Origins of the American Revolution*. Cambridge: Harvard University Press, 1967.

Baldwin, Alice M. *The New England Clergy and the American Revolution*. Durham, N.C.: Duke University Press, 1928.

Haroutunian, Joseph. *Piety versus Moralism: The Passing of the New England Theology*. 1932. Reprint. New York: Harper Torchbooks, 1970.

Hatch, Nathan O. *The Sacred Cause of Liberty: Republican Thought and the Millennium in Revolutionary New England*. New Haven: Yale University Press, 1977.

Koch, Gustav A. *Republican Religion: The American Revolution and the Cult of Reason*. New York: Henry Holt, 1933.

Marsden, George. "The American Revolution." In *Christian Perspectives on History*. Grand Rapids: The National Union of Christian Schools, 1973.

May, Henry F. *The Enlightenment in America*. New York: Oxford University Press, 1976.

Noll, Mark A. *Christians in the American Revolution*. Grand Rapids: Eerdmans, 1978.

Smith, Page. *Religious Origins of the American Revolution*. Chico, Calif.: Scholars Press, 1976.

Chapter 6—New Churches for a New Society

Cherry, Conrad. *God's New Israel: Religious Interpretations of American Destiny*. New York: Prentice-Hall, 1971.

Friedrich, Carl J. *Transcendent Justice: The Religious Dimensions of Constitutionalism*. Durham, N.C.: Duke University Press, 1964.

Miller, Perry. *The Life of the Mind in America: From the Revolution to the Civil War*. New York: Harcourt, Brace and World, 1965; New York: Harper and Row, 1970.

Nagel, Paul C. *One Nation Indivisible: The Union in American Thought, 1776–1861*. New York: Oxford University Press, 1964; Westport, Conn.: Greenwood, 1980.

———. *This Sacred Trust: American Nationality, 1798–1898*. New York: Oxford University Press, 1971; Westport, Conn.: Greenwood, 1980.

Smith, Elwyn A., ed. *The Religion of the Republic: Is There an American Religion?* Philadelphia: Fortress, 1970.

Stokes, Anson Phelps. *Church and State in the United States*. New York: Harper and Brothers, 1950; Westport, Conn.: Greenwood, 1975.

Chapter 7—The Second Awakening: Eastern and Western

Cross, Whitney R. *The Burned-Over District: The Social and Intellectual History of Enthusiastic Religion in Western New York, 1800–1850.* Ithaca, N.Y.: Cornell University Press, 1950; New York: Octagon, 1981.

Johnson, Charles A. *The Frontier Camp Meeting: Religion's Harvest Time.* Dallas: Southern Methodist University Press, 1955.

Marsden, George. *The Evangelical Mind and the New School Presbyterian Experience: A Case Study of Thought and Theology in Nineteenth Century America.* New Haven: Yale University Press, 1970.

Miyakawa, T. Scott. *Protestants and Pioneers: Individualism and Conformity on the American Frontier.* Chicago: University of Chicago Press, 1964.

Posey, Walter B. *Frontier Mission: A History of Religion West of the Southern Appalachians to 1861.* Lexington: University Press of Kentucky, 1966.

Sweet, William W. *Religion in the Development of American Culture, 1765 to 1840.* New York: Charles Scribner's Sons, 1952; Magnolia, Mass.: Peter Smith, 1963.

Weisberger, Bernard A. *They Gathered at the River: The Story of the Great Revivalists and Their Impact upon Religion in America.* Boston: Little, Brown, 1958; New York: Octagon, 1979.

Chapter 8—The Christian Social Vision

Barnes, Gilbert H. *The Anti-Slavery Impulse, 1830–1844.* New York: Appleton-Century, 1933.

Bodo, John R. *The Protestant Clergy and Public Issues, 1812–1845.* Princeton: Princeton University Press, 1954; Philadelphia: Porcupine, 1980.

Cole, Charles C., Jr. *The Social Ideas of Northern Evangelists, 1826–1860.* New York: Octagon, 1966. Originally published as *The Secular Ideas of the Northern Evangelists.* New York: Columbia University Press, 1954.

Douglas, Ann. *The Feminization of American Culture.* New York: Alfred Knopf, 1977.

Elsbree, O. W. *The Rise of the Missionary Spirit in America, 1790–1815.* Williamsport, Penn.: Williamsport Printing, 1928; Philadelphia: Porcupine, 1980.

Foster, Charles I. *An Errand of Mercy: The Evangelical United Front, 1790–1837.* Chapel Hill: University of North Carolina Press, 1954.

Loveland, Anne C. *Southern Evangelicals and the Social Order, 1800–1860.* Baton Rouge: Louisiana State University Press, 1980.

McLoughlin, William C. *Revivals, Awakening, and Reform.* Chicago: University of Chicago Press, 1978.

Smith, Timothy L. *Revivalism and Social Reform: American Protestantism in Mid-Nineteenth Century America.* Baltimore: Johns Hopkins University Press, 1980. Originally published as *Revivalism and Social Reform in Mid-Nineteenth Century America.* Nashville: Abingdon, 1957.

Tyler, Alice F. *Freedom's Ferment: Phases of American Social History to 1860.* Freeport, N.Y.: Books for Libraries, 1970. Originally published as *Freedom's Ferment: Phases of American Social History from the Colonial Period to the Outbreak of the Civil War.* Minneapolis: University of Minnesota Press, 1944.

Chapter 9—New Departures in American Religious Thought and Practice

Andrews, Edward D. *The People Called Shakers: A Search for the Perfect Society.* New York: Oxford University Press, 1953; Magnolia, Mass.: Peter Smith, 1964.

Bestor, Arthur E., Jr. *Backwoods Utopias: The Sectarian Origins and Owenite Phases of Communitarian Socialism in America, 1663–1829.* Philadelphia: University of Pennsylvania Press, 1950.

Brodie, Fawn. *No Man Knows My History: The Life of Joseph Smith, the Mormon Prophet.* New York: Alfred Knopf, 1945.

Brown, Richard D. *Modernization: The Transformation of American Life, 1600–1865.* New York: Hill and Wang, 1976.

Ellis, John Tracy. *American Catholicism.* Chicago: University of Chicago Press, 1969.

Holloway, Mark. *Heaven on Earth: Utopian Communities in America, 1680–1880.* Revised edition. New York: Dover, 1966.

Hutchison, William R. *The Transcendentalist Ministers: Church Reform in the New England Renaissance.* New Haven: Yale University Press, 1959; Boston: Beacon, 1965.

Marty, Martin E. *The Infidel: Free Thought and American Religion.* Cleveland: Meridian, 1961; Magnolia, Mass.: Peter Smith, 1967.

Mead, Sydney E. *Nathaniel William Taylor, 1786–1858: A Connecticut Liberal.* Chicago: University of Chicago Press, 1942; Hamden, Conn.: Archon, 1967.

West, Ray B. *Kingdom of the Saints: The Story of Brigham Young and the Mormons.* New York: Viking, 1957.

Chapter 10—War and Expiation

Cash, W. J. *The Mind of the South.* New York: Vintage, 1941.

Clebsch, William A. "Christian Interpretations of the Civil War." *Church History* 30 (June 1961): 212–22.

Davis, David B. *The Problem of Slavery in Western Culture.* Ithaca, N.Y.: Cornell University Press, 1966.

Filler, Louis. *The Crusade Against Slavery, 1830–1860.* New York: Harper and Row, 1960.

Frazier, E. Franklin. *The Negro Church in America.* New York: Schocken, 1964.

Fredrickson, George M. *The Inner Civil War: Northern Intellectuals and the Crisis of the Union.* New York: Harper and Row, 1965.

Gossett, Thomas R. *Race: The History of an Idea in America.* Dallas: Southern Methodist University Press, 1963.

Matthews, Donald G. *Religion in the Old South.* Chicago: University of Chicago Press, 1979.

Nelsen, Hart M., et al. *The Black Church in America.* New York: Basic, 1971.

Pressly, Thomas J. *Americans Interpret Their Civil War.* New York: Collier, 1962; New York: Free Press, 1965.

Reimers, David M. *White Protestantism and the Negro.* New York: Oxford University Press, 1965.

Washington, Joseph R. *Black Religion: The Negro and Christianity in the United States.* Boston: Beacon, 1964.

Wolf, William J. *Lincoln's Religion.* New York: Pilgrim, 1970. Originally published as *The Almost Chosen People: A Study of the Religion of Abraham Lincoln.* Garden City, N.Y.: Doubleday, 1959.

Chapter 11—Evangelism and Holiness

Anderson, Robert Mapes. *Vision of the Disinherited: The Making of American Pentecostalism.* New York: Oxford University Press, 1979.

Barabas, Steven. *So Great Salvation: The History and Message of the Keswick Convention.* London, 1952.

Burnett, C. C. *In the Last Days: A History of the Assemblies of God.* Springfield, Mo.: Gospel Publishing House, 1962.

Clark, Elmer T. *The Small Sects in America.* New York: Abingdon, 1949; Glouchester, Mass.: Peter Smith, 1964.

Findlay, James F. *Moody, American Evangelist, 1837–1899.* Chicago: University of Chicago Press, 1969.

Geiger, Kenneth, comp. *The Word and the Doctrine: Studies in Contemporary Wesleyan-Arminian Theology.* Kansas City, Mo.: Beacon Hill, 1965.

McLoughlin, William G. *Modern Revivalism: Charles Grandison Finney to Billy Graham.* New York: Ronald Press, 1959.

Rose, Delbert R. *A Theology of Christian Experience: Interpreting the Historic Wesleyan Message.* Minneapolis: Bethany Fellowship, 1965.

Smith, Timothy L. *Called Unto Holiness.* Kansas City, Mo.: Nazarene Publishing House, 1962.

Stevenson, Herbert F., ed. *Keswick's Authentic Voice.* Grand Rapids: Zondervan, 1959.

Synan, Vinson. *The Holiness-Pentecostal Movement in the United States.* Grand Rapids: Eerdmans, 1971.

Wood, William. *Culture and Personality Aspects of the Pentecostal Holiness Religion.* The Hague: Mouton, 1965.

Chapter 12—The Churches and the New Intellectual Climate

Carter, Paul A. *The Spiritual Crisis of the Gilded Age.* DeKalb: Northern Illinois University Press, 1971.

Clark, Michael D. *Worldly Theologians: The Persistence of Religion in Nineteenth Century American Thought.* Landham, Md.: University Press of America, 1982.

Commager, Henry Steele. *The American Mind: An Interpretation of American Thought and Character Since the 1880's.* New Haven: Yale University Press, 1950.

Foster, Frank Hugh. *The Modern Movement in American Theology: Sketches in the History of American Protestant Thought from the Civil War to the World War.* New York: Revell, 1939.

Gaustad, Edwin S. *Dissent in American Religion.* Chicago: University of Chicago Press, 1973.

Hofstadter, Richard. *Social Darwinism in American Thought.* Boston: Beacon, 1944.

Lasch, Christopher. *The New Radicalism in America, 1889–1963: The Intellectual as a Social Type.* New York: Vintage, 1965.

Persons, Stow, ed. *Evolutionary Thought in America.* New Haven: Yale University Press, 1950.

Radest, Howard B. *Toward Common Ground: The Story of the Ethical Societies in the United States.* New York: Ungar, 1969.

Weber, Timothy P. *Living in the Shadow of the Second Coming: Premillenialism 1875–1982.* Enlarged edition. Grand Rapids: Zondervan, 1983.

Weisenberger, Francis P. *Ordeal of Faith: The Crisis of Church-Going America, 1865–1900.* New York: Philosophical Library, 1959.

White, Edward A. *Science and Religion in American Thought: The Impact of Naturalism.* Stanford, Calif.: Stanford University Press, 1952.

Chapter 13—The Churches and the "Incorporation" of America

Abell, Aaron I. *The Urban Impact on American Protestantism, 1865–1900.* Cambridge: Harvard University Press, 1943.

Carter, Paul A. *The Decline and Revival of the Social Gospel: Social and Political Liberalism in American Protestant Churches, 1920–1940.* Ithaca, N.Y.: Cornell University Press, 1954; Hamden, Conn.: Archon, 1971.

Cross, Robert D., ed. *The Church and the City, 1865–1910.* Indianapolis: Bobbs-Merrill, 1967.

Dombrowski, James. *The Early Days of Christian Socialism in America.* New York: Columbia University Press, 1936; New York: Octagon, 1966.

Ewen, Stuart. *Captains of Consciousness: Advertising and the Social Roots of Consumer Culture.* New York: McGraw-Hill, 1976.

Handy, Robert T., ed. *The Social Gospel in America, 1870–1920.* New York: Oxford University Press, 1966.

Higham, John. *Strangers in the Land: Patterns of American Nativism, 1860–1925.* New Brunswick, N.J.: Rutgers University Press, 1955; Westport, Conn.: Greenwood, 1981.

Linkh, Richard M. *American Catholicism and European Immigration, 1900–1924.* Staten Island, N.Y.: Center for Migration Studies, 1975.

May, Henry F. *Protestant Churches and Industrial America.* New York: Harper and Brothers, 1949.

Miller, Randall M., and Thomas D. Marzik, eds. *Immigrants and Religion in Urban America.* Philadelphia: Temple University Press, 1977.

Piehl, Mel. *Breaking Bread: The Catholic Worker and the Origin of Catholic Radicalism in America.* Philadelphia: Temple University Press, 1982.

Thomas, John L. *Alternative America: Henry George, Edward Bellamy, Henry Demarset Lloyd and the Adversary Tradition.* Cambridge: Harvard University Press, Belknap Press, 1983.

Whalen, William J. *Minority Religions in America.* Revised edition. Staten Island, N.Y.: Alba House, 1981.

Chapter 14—A New American Empire and the "White Man's Burden"

Abrams, Ritt. *Preachers Present Arms*. Wellesley, Mass.: Roundtable Press, 1933.

Bell, George K. A. *The Kingship of Christ: The Story of the World Council of Churches*. Baltimore: Penguin, 1954; Westport, Conn.: Greenwood, 1979.

Cavert, Samuel McCrea. *The American Churches in the Ecumenical Movement, 1900–1968*. New York: Association, 1968.

Handy, Robert T. *We Witness Together: A History of Cooperative Home Missions*. New York: Friendship, 1956.

Hopkins, C. Howard. *John R. Mott, 1865–1955: A Biography*. Grand Rapids: Eerdmans, 1979.

Latourette, Kenneth Scott. *The Great Century in the Americas, Australasia, and Africa, A.D. 1800–A.D. 1914*. Vol. 5, *A History of the Expansion of Christianity*. New York: Harper and Brothers, 1943.

__________. *The Great Century in Northern Africa and Asia, A.D. 1800–A.D. 1914*. Vol. 6, *A History of the Expansion of Christianity*. New York: Harper and Brothers, 1944.

MacFarland, Charles S. *Christian Unity in the Making: The First Twenty-Five Years of the Federal Council of the Churches of Christ in America, 1905–1930*. New York: Federal Council of Churches of Christ in America, 1948.

Mackenzie, Kenneth M. *The Robe and the Sword: The Methodist Church and the Rise of American Imperialism*. Washington, D.C.: Public Affairs Press, 1961.

Rouse, Ruth, and Stephen C. Neill, eds. *A History of the Ecumenical Movement, 1517–1948*. Philadelphia: Westminister, 1954.

Varg, Paul A. *Missionaries, Chinese, and Diplomats: The American Protestant Missionary Movement in China, 1890–1952*. Princeton, N.J.: Princeton University Press, 1958; New York: Octagon, 1977.

Chapter 15—The Churches in War, Prosperity, and Depression

Carter, Paul A. *The Decline and Revival of the Social Gospel: Social and Political Liberalism in American Protestant Churches, 1920–1940*. Ithaca, N.Y.: Cornell University Press, 1956; Hamden, Conn.: Archon, 1971.

Cauthen, Kenneth. *The Impact of American Religious Liberalism*. New York: Harper and Row, 1962.

Cross, Robert D. *The Modernist Movement in the Roman Church: Its Origins and Outcome*. Cambridge: Cambridge University Press, 1934.

Dewey, John. *A Common Faith*. New Haven: Yale University Press, 1934.

Furniss, Norman K. *The Fundamentalist Controversy, 1918–1931*. New Haven: Yale University Press, 1954; Hamden, Conn.: Archon, 1963.

Handy, Robert T. *The American Religious Depression, 1925–1935*. Philadelphia: Fortress, 1968.

Machen, J. Gresham. *Christianity and Liberalism*. New York: Macmillan, 1923; Grand Rapids: Eerdmans, 1956.

Marsden, George. *Fundamentalism and American Culture: The Shaping of Twentieth-Century Evangelicalism, 1870–1925.* New York: Oxford University Press, 1980.

Miller, Robert M. *American Protestantism and Social Issues, 1919–1939.* Chapel Hill: University of North Carolina Press, 1958.

Chapter 16—Years of War and Uncertainty

Berger, Peter L. *The Noise of Solemn Assemblies: Christian Commitment and the Religious Establishment in America.* Garden City, N.Y.: Doubleday, 1961.

Eckardt, A. Roy. *The Surge of Piety in America: An Appraisal.* New York: Association, 1958.

Galbraith, John Kenneth. *The Affluent Society.* Boston: Houghton Mifflin, 1958.

Goodman, Paul. *Growing Up Absurd.* New York: Albert Knopf, 1956; New York: Random House, 1960.

Hammar, George. *Christian Realism in American Theology: A Study of Reinhold Niebuhr, W. M. Horton, and H. P. Van Dusen.* Uppsala: Appelberg, 1940.

Herberg, Will. *Protestant, Catholic, Jew: An Essay in American Religious Sociology.* Garden City, N.Y.: Doubleday, 1955.

Moberg, David. *The Great Reversal: Evangelism versus Social Concern.* Philadelphia: Lippincott, 1972.

Nash, Ronald H. *The New Evangelicalism.* Grand Rapids: Zondervan, 1963.

Pollack, John. *Billy Graham—Evangelist to the World: An Authorized Biography of the Decisive Years.* New York: Harper and Row, 1979.

Riesman, David, et al. *The Lonely Crowd: A Study of the Changing American Character.* New Haven: Yale University Press, 1950.

Schneider, Herbert Wallace. *Religion in 20th Century America.* Cambridge: Harvard University Press, 1967.

Chapter 17—Serving Mankind at Home and Abroad

Barrett, David B., ed. *World Christian Encyclopedia: A Comparative Study of Churches and Religions in the Modern World, AD 1900–2000.* Nairobi and New York: Oxford University Press, 1982.

Brown, Robert M., and Gustave Weigel, S. J. *An American Dialogue: A Protestant Looks at Catholicism and a Catholic Looks at Protestantism.* Garden City, N.Y.: Doubleday, 1961.

Fey, Harold E., ed. *A History of the Ecumenical Movement, 1948–1968.* Philadelphia: Westminister, 1970.

Forman, Charles W., ed. *Christianity in the Non-Western World.* Englewood Cliffs, N.J.: Prentice-Hall, 1967: Freeport, N.Y.: Books for Libraries, 1970.

Howard, David M. *Student Power in World Evangelism.* Downers Grove, Ill.: Inter-Varsity, 1970.

Kane, J. Herbert. *A Global View of Christian Missions.* Grand Rapids: Baker, 1971.

Lenski, Gerhard. *The Religious Factor: A Sociological Study of Religion's Impact on Politics, Economics, and Family Life.* Garden City, N.Y.: Doubleday, 1961; Westport, Conn.: Greenwood, 1977.

Marty, Martin. E. *The New Shape of American Religion.* New York: Harper and Row, 1959; Westport, Conn.: Greenwood, 1978.

Murch, James D. *Cooperation Without Compromise: A History of the National Association of Evangelicals.* Grand Rapids: Eerdmans, 1956.

Neill, Stephen C. *Colonialism and Christian Missions.* New York: McGraw-Hill, 1966.

Chapter 18—The Sixties and the Search for Relevance

Altizer, Thomas J. J., and William Hamilton. *Radical Theology and the Death of God.* Indianapolis: Bobbs-Merrill, 1966; Hammondsworth, Middlesex: Penguin, 1968.

Carroll, Jackson W., Douglas W. Johnson, and Martin E. Marty. *Religion in America: 1950 to the Present.* New York: Harper and Row, 1979.

Clark, Elizabeth, and Herbert W. Richardson, eds. *Women and Religion: Readings in the Western Tradition from Aeschylus to Mary Daly.* New York: Harper and Row, 1976.

Cox, Harvey. *The Secular City: Secularization and Urbanization in Theological Perspective.* New York: Macmillan, 1965.

__________. *Turning East: The Promise and Peril of the New Orientalism.* New York: Simon and Schuster, 1977.

Daedalus. "Religion in America." Winter 1967. Entire issue.

Gettleman, Marvin E., and David Mermelstein. *The Great Society Reader: The Failure of American Liberalism.* New York: Vintage, 1967.

Guiness, Os. *The Dust of Death: A Critique of the Counter-Culture.* Downers Grove, Ill.: Inter-Varsity, 1973.

Harrington, Michael. *The Other America.* Baltimore: Penguin, 1962.

Novak, Michael. *A Theology for Radical Politics.* New York: Herder and Herder, 1969.

Poterfield, Amanda. *Feminine Spirituality in America: From Sarah Edwards to Martha Graham.* Philadelphia: Temple University Press, 1980.

Roszak, Theodore. *The Making of a Counter-Culture.* Garden City, N.Y.: Doubleday, 1969.

Vahanian, Gabriel. *The Death of God: The Culture of Our Post-Christian Era.* New York: George Braziller, 1961.

Wakin, Edward, and Joseph F. Scheuer. *The De-Romanization of the American Catholic Church.* New York: Macmillan, 1966.

Chapter 19—The Black Churches in the Twentieth Century

Burkett, Randall K. *Garveyism as a Religious Movement: The Institutionalization of a Black Civil Religion.* Metuchen, N.J.: Scarecrow, 1978.

Cone, James H. *Black Theology and Black Power.* New York: Seabury, 1969.

__________. *A Black Theology of Liberation.* Philadelphia: Lippincott, 1970.

Cronon, E. David. *Black Moses: The Story of Marcus Garvey and the Universal Negro Improvement Association.* Madison: University of Wisconsin Press, 1955.

Essien-Udom, E. U. *Black Nationalism: The Search for an Identity in America.* Chicago: University of Chicago Press, 1962; New York: Dell, 1964.

Glenn, Norval D., and Erin Gotard. "The Religion of Blacks in the United States: Some Recent Trends and Current Characteristics." *American Journal of Sociology* 83 (September 1977): 443–51.

Haynes, Titus. *Fundamentalism in Black Inner City Storefront Churches.* New York: Vantage, 1980.

King, Martin Luther, Jr. *Stride Toward Freedom.* New York: Harper and Brothers, 1958.

Lincoln, C. Eric. *The Black Muslims in America.* Boston: Beacon, 1961.

Little, Malcolm. *The Autobiography of Malcolm X.* New York: Grove, 1965.

Thomas, Latta R. *Biblical Faith and the Black American.* Valley Forge, Penn.: Judson, 1976.

Zinn, Howard. *SNCC: The New Abolitionists.* Boston: Beacon, 1964.

Chapter 20—Recent Trends and Interpretations

Acquaviva, S. S. *The Decline of the Sacred in Industrial Society.* Translated by Patricia Lipscomb. New York: Harper and Row, 1979.

Armstrong, Ben. *The Electric Church.* Nashville: Thomas Nelson, 1979.

Bloesch, Donald G. *The Future of Evangelical Christianity.* Garden City, N.Y.: Doubleday, 1983.

Ellwood, Robert S., Jr. *Alternative Altars: Unconventional and Eastern Spirituality in America.* Chicago: University of Chicago Press, 1979.

Fackre, Gabriel. *The Religious Right and Christian Faith.* Grand Rapids: Eerdmans, 1982.

Fowler, Robert Booth. *A New Engagement: Evangelical Political Thought, 1966–1976.* Grand Rapids: Eerdmans, 1982.

Gallup, George, Jr., and David Poling. *The Search for America's Faith.* Nashville: Abingdon, 1980.

Gilkey, Langdon. *Catholicism Confronts Modernity: A Protestant View.* New York: Seabury, 1975.

Glock, Charles Y., and Robert N. Bellah, eds. *The New Religious Consciousness.* Berkeley: University of California Press, 1976.

Guiness, Os. *The Gravedigging File: Papers on the Subversion of the Modern Church.* Downers Grove, Ill.: Inter-Varsity, 1983.

Hadden, Jeffrey K., and Charles E. Swann. *Prime-Time Preachers: The Rising Power of Televangelism.* Reading, Mass.: Addison-Wesley, 1981.

Hale, J. Russell. *The Unchurched: Who They Are and Why They Stay Away.* San Francisco: Harper and Row, 1980.

Harrell, David Edwin, Jr. *All Things Are Possible: The Healing and Charismatic Revivals in Modern America.* Bloomington: Indiana University Press, 1975.

Hunter, James Davison. *American Evangelicalism: Conservative Religion and the Quandry of Modernity.* New Brunswick, N.J.: Rutgers University Press, 1983.

Johnston, Jon. *Will Evangelicalism Survive Its Own Popularity?* Grand Rapids: Zondervan, 1980.

Kelley, Dean M. *Why Conservative Churches Are Growing: A Study in the Sociology of Religion.* New York: Harper and Row, 1972.

Marty, Martin E. *A Nation of Behavers.* Chicago: University of Chicago Press, 1976.

Mead, Frank S. *Handbook of Denominations.* 7th edition. Nashville: Abingdon, 1980.

Quebedeaux, Richard. *The Worldly Evangelicals.* San Francisco: Harper and Row, 1978.

__________. *The Young Evangelicals: Revolution in Orthodoxy.* New York: Harper and Row, 1974.

Robbins, Thomas, and Dick Anthony, eds. *In Gods We Trust: New Patterns of Religious Pluralism in America.* New Brunswick, N.J.: Transaction, 1980.

Van Allen, Rodger, ed. *American Religious Values and the Future of America.* Philadelphia: Fortress, 1978.

Index of Subjects